TRUTH in nonfiction

TRUTH in nonfiction

* * essays * * * * * * * * * * * *

edited by DAVID LAZAR

University of Iowa Press, Iowa City

For Tom
I n Friendship
David

University of Iowa Press, Iowa City 52242

Copyright © 2008 by the University of Iowa Press

www.uiowapress.org

Printed in the United States of America

The University of Iowa Press is a member of Green Press
Initiative and is committed to preserving natural resources.

Printed on acid-free paper

Library of Congress Cataloging-in-Publication Data

Truth in nonfiction: Essays/edited by David Lazar.

    p.   cm.

  Includes bibliographical references and index.

  ISBN-13: 978-1-58729-654-3 (pbk.)

  ISBN-10: 1-58729-654-3 (pbk.)

1. Autobiography.   2. Biography as a literary form.   3. Truth

in literature.   I. Lazar, David, 1957–

CT25.T785 2008   2007043803

809'.93592 — dc22

08   09   10   11   12   P   5   4   3   2   1

Contents

Acknowledgments

✳ ✳

I'd like to thank my editors at Iowa: Holly Carver, Charlotte Wright, and Joseph Parsons, who did such a delightful job of shepherding this project, making the editorial process so . . . epistolary. Kris Bjork was a superb copyeditor. From Columbia College Chicago, thanks go to two of my students, Kristen Radtke and Steven Yaccino, for their transcriptions; Amy Pelak and Paula Parsons, coordinators of services; Dok Kang, our technologist; Professor Jeffrey Schiff; and the chair of the English Department, Kenneth Daley, who was generous to a fault in his support. Please don't take that literally, Ken. I'm especially indebted to Whitney Huber Lazar, for her many contributions and conversations, and Kim Dana Kupperman for her crack editing skills, and general two cents. To the contributors to this volume, thank you for your commitment to the spirit of the project.

Finally, I would like to thank a golden group of students whose questions and answers have enriched me over the years. They're teachers themselves, so they'll understand that when I dedicate this book to them, I'm also dedicating it to the many other students who have enriched my life, and continue to do so: Michael Danko, Michelle Disler, Jennifer Dunning, Kelley Evans, Shannen Lakanen, Patrick Madden, Desirae Matherly, Rachael Pridgeon. "Truth springs from argument amongst friends" (Hume).

An Introduction to Truth

> (I hope you will forgive me if I use the word "truth." The moment I say "truth"
> I expect people to ask: "What is truth?" "Does truth exist?" Let us imagine
> that it exists. The word exists, therefore the feeling exists.)
> —HÉLÈNE CIXOUS, "The School of the Dead,"
> *Three Steps on the Ladder of Writing*

✳ ✳

My title, of course, is in jest.

What is the truth, asked Francis Bacon, and stayed to give an answer, unlike his Jesting Pilate, who had other business.

Growing up Jewish, I didn't have much of a sense of who Pilate was until I started listening to *Jesus Christ Superstar*. And that was a really Jesting Pilate. So, when I first read Bacon, I connected his Jesting Pilate to the cartoonish Broadway swagger that had been my strongest historical truth. That Jesting Pilate had stayed for an answer, I seem to remember. Bacon would eventually bear witness, then, to my fancy, as "a mixture of a lie doth ever add pleasure." Bacon's Pilate, a figure of his own imagination, becomes a cited figure in sermons, homilies. Where does the truth lie?

In "To the Reader," Montaigne's introduction to the *Essays*, he writes, "It is myself that I *portray* [emphasis added]." You've got to have some artifice, that spoonful of sugar, to create yourself on the page, and to make the medicine of fact go down. It's the tension between Wayne Koestenbaum's Ms. Fancy and Mrs. Fact. (How wedded are we to the truth?) Pilate, no matter how despicable, may have sung and danced. The historical record is, I believe, silent in this regard. Nonfiction blends fact and artifice in an attempt to arrive at truth, or truths. This frequently includes great leaps of the imagination. And like it or not, *Jesus Christ Superstar* is a work of musical nonfiction.

I always want to read Bacon as though he is jesting, perhaps because he has more of Pilate and Montaigne in him, I always feel, than he wants to admit, or at first seems obvious: "One of the fathers, in great severity, called poesy *vinum daemonum*, because it filleth the imagination; and yet, it is but with the shadow of a lie."

Bernard Williams, in his eminently useful book *Truth and Truthfulness* (not truthiness), reminds us of the shifting meanings, the difficult etymology of truth. Do we speak of truth as opposed to lying, or as a necessary conjunction?

Is truth accuracy, sincerity, a form of authenticity? And as for authenticity, either that's a can of worms, or it isn't, depending of course, on whether you're stuck inside of Western Philosophy with the Memphis blues again.

How do we verify? Do we care to? (Do we dare to eat the apple of knowledge and say it's true? Or is it a peach?) Do we choose to? Is truth a subcategory of faith? How do you respond when someone says, "This is really true"? Why did they choose to say it then? It maketh me nervous.

For writers of nonfiction, truths have lies or falsehoods as their usual binaries, though they can have quite different implications. Much of the public discussion has focused on the former, in sometimes reductive, sometimes useful terms. Lies, the deception of the reader through the creation of false experience, have been the rallying cry that has caused readers and most critics to gather their pitchforks and torches in search of the monsters of deception whose experience they have taken as "real." But there are other kinds of falsehoods that seem to me as or more important: marks of self-deception in writers of nonfiction, forms of psychological manipulation, the drawing of conclusions, and epiphanies that seem labored, unworthy, unbelievable, false. However, these same falsehoods can be useful if the writer of essays or memoir can catch herself or himself in the act, displaying the insight and ability to self-correct that is among the rare pleasures of different forms of memory writing.

Invention, compression, the use of the imagination. Several of the writers in this volume speak to these practices as necessities of autobiographical nonfiction — especially since there are readers who would herd them into the camp of the liars. In her essay on Montaigne in *The Common Reader*, Virginia Woolf says, "One writes for a very few people, who understand." Vivian Gornick leads the call for a more educated readership of memoirs, who understand the role of invention. Others would demur at what they see as liberal license.

And, also, in the subject of which I treat, our manners and notions, testimonies and instances, how fabulous soever, provided they are possible, serve as well as the true; whether they have really happened or no, at Rome or Paris, to John or Peter 'tis still within the verge of human capacity, which serves me to good use I see, and make my advantage of it, as well in shadow as in substance; and among the various readings thereof in history, I cull out the most rare and memorable to fit my own turn. There are authors whose only end and design it is, to give an account of things that have happened; mine, if I could arrive unto it, should be to deliver of what may happen. There is a just liberty allowed in the schools, of supposing similitudes, when they have none at hand. I do not, however, make any use of that privilege, and as to that matter, in superstitious religion, surpass all historical authority. In the examples which I here bring in, of what I have heard, read, done, or said, I have forbidden myself to dare to alter even the most light and indifferent circumstances: my conscience does not falsify one tittle; what my ignorance may do, I cannot say. And this it is that makes me sometimes doubt in my own mind, whether a divine, or a philosopher, and such men of exact and tender prudence and conscience, are fit to write history: for how can they stake their reputation upon a popular faith? How be responsible for the opinions of men they do not know? And with what assurance deliver their conjectures for current pay? Of actions performed before their own eyes, wherein several persons were actors, they would be unwilling to give evidence upon oath before a judge; and there is no man, so familiarly known to them, for whose intentions they would become absolute caution. For my part, I think it less hazardous to write of things past, than present, by how much the writer is only to give an account of things every one knows he must of necessity borrow upon trust." (Montaigne, "Of the Force of the Imagination.")

Montaigne does both.

How do we verify? How do you respond when someone says, or writes, "the truth of the matter"?

Williams suggests that in contemporary philosophy, truth is a dubious commodity, whereas truthfulness has some plausibility. Has a belief in truth telling dimmed in other kinds of writing, in nonfiction? Bacon writes, "it will be acknowledged even by those that practice it not, that clear and round dealing is the honor of man's nature, and that mixture of falsehood is like alloy in coin of gold and silver, which may make the metal work the better, but it embaseth it." Is our metal in danger? Has our epistemological metallurgy found new alloys? "The question," says Montaigne, "is not who will hit the ring, but who will make the best runs at it." Perhaps part of the reason for the rise of the lyric essay is that truth in nonfiction is requiring us to tell it, as Emily Dickinson would suggest, slant.

"We are born to inquire after truth; it belongs to a greater power to possess it. It is not, as Democritus said, hid in the bottom of the deeps, but rather elevated to an infinite height in the divine knowledge" (Montaigne, "Of the

TRUTH in nonfiction

A Weedy Garden

PAUL LISICKY

❊ ❊

1

Mark and I are walking up Eighth Avenue through our neighborhood in Chelsea, talking about memoir, thinking about breakfast. I'm in a bit of an up-mood after having gotten an e-mail from an older man, a fan of *Famous Builder*, who wrote to say, among others things, that he was moved by the warmth extended between myself and my family.

"Maybe you should tell him what you left out," Mark says, stepping into the crosswalk at Eighteenth. He looks toward the taller buildings of Midtown, with a mischievous grin.

"What do you mean?"

And he starts ticking off a list of issues that could be fodder for a month's worth of Oprah.

I take in a breath. I think to myself, well, if you'd had Mark's childhood, if you'd been abandoned on the Pacific Coast Highway, hundreds of miles from home, you'd think the same thing. There's a line from an early poem of his that I think about in times like these: "I was made, not born." Which pretty much sums up his feelings on family.

But I never meant my memoir to be exactly *about* my family. Sure, it uses the stuff of my childhood to think about identity and self-invention, but it's not the whole story.

Not that I say that to him now. *He* knows that.

And of what happened and of what didn't in the list alluded to above? Well, that's for me to keep.

2

These days, it's almost easy to forget that young American writers who came of age during the 1980s had two choices when it came to the study of creative writing. You could be a poet, or you could be a fiction writer, and anything that fell between the cracks simply wasn't named—forget Frank Conroy, Montaigne, Augustine. I'm not sure I could have even told the story of an "I," even if a memoir workshop were a part of the curriculum. I'd spent the better part of my teenage years investing most of my energy on the project

1

of my own self-erasure, preferable at the time to being called a faggot, which seemed far more terrifying than being murdered. I'm not joking. Not that I was ever called such a thing; I was far too successful in making sure I could walk through the day without leaving any mark.

Such self-annihilation unleashes its opposing force, of course: the need to say *I exist*, through a medium that suggests permanency. To my late-teenage mind, there was either the creative life or death, and as melodramatic as that sounds today, I chose the former. And here's where the problem begins. When I take a poetry workshop at my Jesuit liberal arts college, I'm very quickly up against the fact that an "I" invariably leads me to talk about love and desire, and I can't do that. The story of desire is the story of a boy and a girl. The expression of same-sex love is, what? Unspoken, off-limits, enforced in the way that the deepest cultural prohibitions are always enforced: without directness. And this force inside me, this force I've been working so hard to trap and kennel — doesn't it also make me live? How can I make do with writing polite poems about faith and grass and water? Even if I had the bravery and nerve to depict the experience of following the bearded boy past the chapel: who would want to hear it? Wouldn't gayness itself take over the entire piece, becoming its single subject? It wouldn't leave room for the parts of me that don't fit conveniently underneath that label: the self that writes liturgical songs, but is embarrassed about writing liturgical songs for fear that it makes me seem chaste and priestly. The self that collects racing car decals and Matchbox cars. The self that wants to design and build new cities but is entirely put off by the more practical aspects of the field. The self that is dedicated to animals and great open patches of marsh. If I can't make use of the whole of me, then aren't I participating in a more complex form of self-erasure?

So it shouldn't come as a surprise that, despite my love of musicality and description, and my deep-down resistance to linearity — can I even *tell* a story with a chronological plot? — I end up in the fiction camp. Fiction: where one becomes a self by escaping oneself. Or, better yet, where one can be many selves at once.

3

This notion of the Unified Self: I argue against it daily when looking at ads, or glancing through the "just for you" lists that come up on Amazon or iTunes. So many external forces telling us who we are, what we should be. Not that they always come from outside us. Tonight I pick up the free gay paper from the health food store down the street and come upon this in a review of upcoming books: "When it comes to the life of the mind, we 'mos aren't always the most literary of the lot. We're more likely to curl up in front of the roaring fire with the latest *People* magazine than with *Daniel Deronda*." No, I say aloud. No, too, to the current expectation that to be gay on the page is to be ironic and glib: some version of David or Augusten. *No.* I think about the relief I felt when coming upon the writing of Butler and Kosofsky Sedgwick in the early 1990s, the sense of possibility those texts offered us, the promise of multiplicity and reach. What could be more debilitating than to shovel oneself into some narrow trench, as if the point of life were sameness, consistency? As if there could only be one sad, linear truth we could ever know.

4

"Later, I'd come down with another sore throat, but at that moment, I could have been anything: the spaniel tearing through the hollies, the water sparkling in his deep blue bowl." (*Famous Builder*, 2002)

5

Another way to think about truth: the memoirs of Dirk Bogarde. In one volume the speaker's mother loves her son with the tenderness of a saint, while in another she's pricklier than a witch in a folk tale. It would be wrong, I think, to read the series of books as evidence of chronological development, or progress, assigning more authority to the final book in the series. Instead, place these narratives inside a room of your imagination and feel the room heating up with moisture and sweat. The mumbling, first quiet, then getting louder: *I'm* right. No, *I'm* right.

6

At some point, after ten years of writing novels, the project of fiction stops tugging at me—at least for a time. The cause-and-effect linearity, the immersion in the sensory—all of it feels less like revelation, less like a vehicle for a consciousness. I miss a sense of inquiry, the work of making meaning of an image. Occasionally, I'm even unsettled by the control I can lose over the long haul of a narrative, the ways in which a character can morph like a werewolf, stalking the landscape of a book, making it his country. I don't like it. I'm looking for a template to follow, a lamppost, a guide. It's also becoming clear to me that my fiction is a lot more heightened and concerned with extremity than I actually know myself to be. Where is the side of me that's eager to make people laugh, to lift and distract them from their boredom and

But the truth comes down to this: Michael's book is different than mine, and his has yet to be written.

8

"You are the buildings protecting us. You are the boy slamming the sidewalk with his skateboard wheels, the woman with the plaid bag slung over her shoulder, the cold salted pretzels served up night after night by the vendors." (*Famous Builder*, 2002)

9

Once we hold memoirists to the standards of journalism and privilege agreed-upon truths to emotional interpretation, the whole genre falls apart—it loses its reason for being. I'm not at all speaking for best-selling memoirists who pass off wholly invented episodes as experience. That's an entirely different matter. But let's save our righteous indignation for the conscious manipulators of facts in our times. (Do you hear that, Oprah?) And we know exactly who they are.

10

Your Truth, My Truth. So many Truths pressing against us that if we absolutely consider what's at stake, our own Truth inevitably swells and swells, fatter and fatter, until we're almost sick with what we contain. No, says the Unified Self. No, says the Tenets of the Undergraduate Poetry Workshop. No, says the Right and the Wrong, the Spoken and the Unspoken, the In and the Out, the *I exist* and the *you're not here*. So large with life that we can't help but blow from the pressure of holding so much in, exploding onto the page in fragments.

Which feels just about right to me.

Truth in Personal Narrative

VIVIAN GORNICK

✳ ✳ ✳ ✳ ✳ ✳ ✳ ✳ ✳ ✳ ✳ ✳ ✳ ✳ ✳ ✳ ✳ ✳ ✳ ✳

Once, in Texas, at an association of engineers, I gave a reading from my memoir *Fierce Attachments*. No sooner had I finished speaking, than a woman in the audience raised her hand to ask a question: "If I come to New York, can I take a walk with your Mama?" When the laughter died down I told her that, actually, she wouldn't want to take a walk with my mother, it was the woman in the book she wanted to walk with. They were not exactly the same.

Shortly afterwards, I attended a dinner party in New York where, an hour into the evening, one of the guests (a stranger to me) blurted out in a voice filled with disappointment, "Why, you're nothing like the woman who wrote *Fierce Attachments*!" At the end of the evening she cocked her head at me, and said, "Well, you're *something* like her." I understood perfectly. She had come expecting to have dinner with the narrator of the book, not with me; again, not exactly the same.

On both occasions, what was desired was the presence of two people who existed only between the pages of a book. In our actual persons, neither Mama nor I could give satisfaction. We ourselves were just a rough draft of the written characters. Moreover, these characters could not live independent of the story which had called them into life, as they existed for the sole purpose of serving that story. In the flesh, neither Mama nor I were serving anything but the unaesthetic spill of everyday thought and feeling that routinely floods us all, only a select part of which, in this case, invoked the principals in a tale of psychological embroilment that had as its protagonist, neither me nor my mother, but rather our "fierce attachment." Let me explain:

At the heart of my memoir lay a revelation that had taken me two years of writing to isolate: I could not leave my mother because I had become my mother. This complicated insight was my bit of wisdom, the history I wanted badly to trace out. The context in which the book is set — our life in the Bronx in the 1950s, alternating with walks taken in Manhattan in the 1980s — was the situation; the story was the insight. What mattered most to me was not the literalness of the situation, but the emotional truth of the story. If the book has any strength at all, it is because I remained scrupulously faithful to the story, not the situation.

A personal narrative is a tale taken from life—that is, from actual not imagined occurrences—and is related by a first person narrator who is undeniably the writer. Beyond these bare requirements, it has the same responsibility as the novel or the short story: to shape a piece of experience out of the raw materials of one's own life so that it moves from a tale of private interest to one that has meaning for the disinterested reader. What actually happened is only raw material; what matters is what the memoirist makes of what happened; or, put differently, what matters is the way the memoirist reflects on what happened. As V. S. Pritchett said of the genre: "It's all in the art, you get no credit for living."

Some of the greatest memoirs written, if held to the standard of literal accuracy that is required in other kinds of nonfiction writing would never pass the test. When Thomas De Quincey wrote *Confessions of an English Opium-Eater*, he led his readers to believe that his addiction was behind him; not true; he was taking opium when he wrote the book, and continued to take it for the next thirty years. To this day, there are readers who cry "Liar!" at one of the most profound descriptions ever given of the heaven and hell of drug-taking; a description that De Quincey had every right to present as personal testament, not as a tale of fabrication. Edmund Gosse's *Father and Son*, a coming of age memoir published in 1907, when Gosse was fifty-seven years old, recounts conversations that purportedly took place when he was eight years old. The book, upon publication, was instantly recognized as a masterpiece, but people who had known the Gosses protested that Edmund made those conversations up; which, of course, he had; without them the story of his relationship with his father could not have gained power. George Orwell's brilliant short memoir of his experience of boarding school, *Such, Such Were the Joys*, was denounced by people who had been his classmates. Filled with "inaccuracies," they insisted, as if their memories of the school were more legitimate than Orwell's: the way people who are siblings argue over their various impressions of what "really" happened when they were growing up.

On and on it goes, until finally one realizes that there is a vast misunderstanding abroad about how to read a memoir. To state the case briefly: memoirs belong to the category of literature, not of journalism. It is a misunderstanding to read a memoir as though the writer owes the reader the same record of literal accuracy that is owed in newspaper reporting or historical narrative. What is owed the reader of a memoir is the ability to persuade that the narrator is trying, as honestly as possible, to get to the bottom of the tale at hand. And that, as D. H. Lawrence might have put it, takes some diving.

The key word in any discussion of the genre is "reflection." It is the depth of reflection that makes or breaks the work. And again, what is being reflected on is the experience — emotional by definition — embedded in a relationship, a circumstance, a set of events. This experience is the "truth" that the writer is after. Now here comes the tricky part. For the reader to feel and understand what the narrator feels and understands — the whole point of the writing, yes? — these reflections must be set in a context that is itself clarifying. Of necessity then, the context is composed — composed, mind you, not invented — out of a mass of fragmentary memories whose wholeness must be supplied. Here is where the memoir resembles any piece of literary writing; and here is where we run into all the trouble this kind of writing gives to readers who do not clearly grasp the requirements of composition as they differ from factual transmission.

Some years ago, I spoke at an eastern college before a group of writing program students and their teachers. It was my intention, during this talk, to define the genre as I understand it, as I practice it, and as I teach it. I spoke for an hour out of a book on the subject that I had written (*The Situation and the Story: The Art of Personal Narrative*), and then I read from *Fierce Attachments*. I was at pains during this talk to make a definite distinction between what the writer of personal narrative does, and what the writer of biography, newspaper writing, or literary journalism does. I spoke at length of how hard the memoirist must work to first figure out what the experience is; then pull from one's ordinary, everyday self the coherent narrator (or persona) best able to tell the story; and finally, and perhaps most importantly, develop the organizing principle around which the memoir will take shape; because without shape you have diary entries, analytic transcripts, police blotter descriptions: you do not have a memoir.

At a question and answer period after my talk at the college, I was bombarded with questions that had more to do with the literal actuality of the events behind my story than with any of the writing questions that I had assumed the talk and reading would generate. In the course of responding to these questions, I casually said that on a few occasions in the book I had made a composite out of the elements of two or more incidents — none of which had been fabricated — for the purpose of moving the narrative forward. (I might also have added that I had played fast and loose with time, for the very same reasons, relating incidents that were chronologically out of order, for the sake of narrative development.) I had said these things times without number, at other talks and readings, and in nearly every class I ever taught. It never occurred to me that such practices would not be seen as entirely within the province of the memoirist. To my amazement, these words were taken as a "confession," and a student in the audience rushed off to send the scandalous news to an online magazine; whereupon a radio book critic was subsequently allowed to denounce me as "the latest culprit . . . in a series of similar revelations," comparing me with those other great "liars," Binyamin Wilkomirski, Doris Kearns Goodwin, and Jayson Blair.

Now, look at this: I, a memoirist who had composed (composed, mind you, not invented) a narrative drawn entirely from the materials of my own experience, was being compared with a psychopath who had invented a Holocaust memoir out of whole cloth; a historian who was accused of incorporating other people's work into her own without attribution; a dishonest newspaper reporter who had made up many of the stories he submitted to the *New York Times*.

It seemed to me then, as it does now, that these inappropriate analogies are proof, if proof be needed, that memoir writing is a genre still in need of an informed readership.

Bride in Beige

MARK DOTY

❋ ❋

1

My sister was married in Memphis, in 1960, in a beige two-piece suit she chose herself, with beige lace covering the jacket and a matching pillbox hat. She was seventeen. I was in first grade. I remember her showing me a picture of her outfit before the day, wanting me to understand its elegance and world-liness. I think at the time I did — though it was a very different thing to look back at that glamorous choice forty-some years later, when I was writing a memoir concerned with the process of esthetic education. How long had it been since I thought of the wedding outfit! There it was, in memory, as if it had been folded carefully in some drawer in the mind, still that stiff rustle to its pearly underlining, luster unchanged by time — which is the ironic way of memory. Things you remember often change and date, any more immediate perception replaced by the stories we tell about them. But that which we don't know we remember — well, those things seem untouched.

Why, in the Tennessee of 1960, would a young woman choose not to wear a white dress? What was being announced? Did she, I wonder, make that choice herself? Did my parents, knowing she was a few months pregnant, forbid virginal white, or was my sister being proudly modern, a young woman ahead of her time?

These questions became part of my text. Questions are a central part of *Firebird*, the book I was writing, because plenty of the past is unclear to me. Well, the images themselves are crystalline (intricate layer of lace, buttons artfully covered in satin, all of it like buttercream frosting). It's how to understand them that isn't clear. Recollection offers its wealth of stuff, but what to do with it all, what meaning to make of it? Memory's an active, dynamic force, not just a recording one; over the course of a life, as perspective shifts, we keep moving into different relationships to the past, reconsidering, so that *what happened* turns out to be nothing stable, but a scribbled-over field of revisions, rife with questions, half its contents hidden.

When I gave my manuscript to the copyeditor (not uncharacteristically a precise, attentive reader, with a strong sense that there were facts to be determined), I included my questions in that scene. In the margin, the vigilant editor wrote, *Why don't you just ask her?*

At the same time, we believe that poems are *after* truth, seeking a kind of emotional veracity; they want to get at essential stuff and will use whatever means necessary to do so.

Similarly, the poet's memoir is after truth, while nonfiction based in a journalism or even traditional fictional practice tends to be after accuracy. This is why people are sometimes startled that I've written four memoirs — can I possibly have that much life to talk about? Or why some readers think that in order to write a memoir you need to have an interesting, dramatic life.

Poets understand, of course, that you look into experience to see what you can find there, that there is always more to see, and that you may actually be *better off* without a compelling story. Because what you're writing is not about "what happened," it's about the experience of happening.

5

Which is not to suggest that memoir's a liar's holiday, free from ethical obligation. When we represent other people, when we claim that such representations are attempts to get at the truth of experience, there's no escaping from responsibility. But it's a childish version of ethics simply to declare that it's wrong to make things up, and it seems like far too easy a position to claim that what makes a memoir ethical is that it's factually accurate.

I want to suggest that beyond the personal ethics of memoir — how fair or unfair we are to other people in our lives — and beyond the matter of accuracy, there's a higher ethical standard, which has to do with the ethics of art: that what is made is commensurate with the real.

I don't know that any art can be that, finally; the real is always larger than we can apprehend, alive with dimensions, shifting, a great confluence of causes and effects. But it's an imperative that we try to make something thrumming with the seen and the unseen, with the whispers of ghosts and the pressures of the hour, the comings and goings of the living and the dead.

And here's where making things up comes in: there is only a degree to which the narration of history can do the work of achieving something as dimensional as reality is. Everyone's had the experience of being excited about some perception or experience, only to recount it later and discover that our recital of the tale has none of the charm and charge of the moment. Narration has a tendency to flatten out the depths of things, as if the recounting of events in time made everything merely a matter of a chain of consequences, diminishing each experience to a cause of something else. I saw a field of daffodils, we say, and I felt lifted. And our listener says, And then?

Perhaps this is why the lyric was invented, to take us outside of the chain of causality and thus deeper into the moment, when that host of daffodils can gleam with a pure, purposeless life.

6

"Making things up" is very imprecise. I mean by that phrase a host of things: eliding some moments, juxtaposing others because they resonate together or comment upon one another, stretching time out in certain instances, trying to look more deeply into a moment, as if the recollecting imagination were a camera observing what is remembered, and that camera eye were capable of tunneling in for a close-up, opening the closed doors or hidden drawers, reaching into the inner life of the dream. After all, the scene that unfolds in the mind's eye is an active form of dreaming, and for the dreamer, what is the limit of possibility?

7

In Memphis, in those same years, my father used to take me to a children's museum called the Pink Palace. The best exhibit was a tree that had somehow moved indoors. It was huge, at least to me, and dwelt behind a wall pierced with dozens of tiny doors. I could open the doors at ground level myself, and look into whatever scene lay around the roots of the tree: mushrooms, ferns, a stuffed fox. My father would have to lift me up to look into the other windows, and that is one of my best memories of him, the tenderness implicit in holding your son up into the air so he could *see*.

Bird's nests, squirrels, an owl — there was plenty to look at, but in truth what I loved about the tree wasn't what was revealed, but the experience of revelation. Open the door. Shut it again and the secret is restored to mystery; open again and the veil is lifted. No matter how many times you look, even if all the small doors were thrown open at once, you still couldn't see the whole! As if all that were offered to us were portholes, this frame or that, and none provided a grasp of the thing entire. And therefore it was necessary to move from one to the next, to keep trying to assemble a description in the mind.

And now, I'll place behind that wall of doors the beige suit, which I've lifted up from the tissue wrappings of memory, and placed there on display, the matching hat hung above it. What do the windows yield? *Why don't you just ask her*, repeats the copyeditor, but in truth she doesn't have the answers either. The wedding suit's a confluence of forces, a storm of meanings. No ordinary dress for her, but something cloven — two pieces — composed, already educated in the way things happen. Did she save to buy it, did my parents pay? The ambition of its wearer to become a woman of the world. Emblem of defiance. Lesson in style: here's the emblem of shame, the snowfield of purity denied her, but who wanted that? Gaze of a boy capable of being entranced by glamour. Cropping into the frame, all the things I'm not telling—my sister's intoxicating boyfriend, his shiny motorcycle, the black woman who comes to clean for the people next door, her children waiting outside while she works, the music on my sister's record player, our childhoods swirling to a strange close, rock 'n' roll the music of moving up and out into the world, my sister's little daughter swelling inside her like a blonde bean. The message (who gives it?) to keep your ardor for the world withheld, though it doesn't ever work, and ardor wells up for the boyfriend, for records, for dancing in the mirror, for the blacks in their sealed-off realm. . . . And now I want to write the book again, out of ardor for the tactile caramel of the wedding suit, a tailored form of desire.

The Forest of Memory

KATHRYN HARRISON

✳ ✳

As a girl contemplating the mysteries and attractions of independence, of growing up and moving away from home to attend college and then graduate school—moving toward what I believed would be my real, or real*er* life—I never imagined myself entering the world of adults as an *only child*. Wasn't this a state of being that ended, necessarily, with childhood? After all, no one spoke of "only adults." As far as I could tell, unattached adults included the not-yet-married who were looking for love, single mothers or fathers who'd perhaps given up on love, divorcées on the rebound, people confirmed in spinsterhood or bachelordom, and those who had married and were subsequently widowed. My mother, once an only child, had solved the problem of motherhood by leaving me with her parents and now was no longer *only*, but *single*. In the wake of my father's departure she had a handful of affairs and, by the time I was ten, had embarked on what would become her last, with a man who left (but did not divorce) his devoutly Catholic wife to live with my mother, whom he nursed through her cancer, remaining at her side until the end of her short life. Long before I had the ability to articulate the observation, I understood that the aloneness of adults was measured in terms of romantic coupling. The term for it—the state of being single—sounded enough like *singular* to seem desirable to me. Certainly it was a much more attractive word than *only*, with its connotations of meagerness, of deprivation, its annoying habit of rhyming with *lonely*.

I was born in 1961 and raised among families in which single parents were very much an exception to the nuclear rule; all of my peers seemed to have at least one brother or sister. The worst of being an only child, I felt, was the pity it elicited from adults who assumed that I lacked what they considered a genuine childhood. Evidently such an undertaking was impossible in the absence of siblings. But a family of seven lived next door to my grandparents, and whenever I liked I could sample their noise and chaos and petulant squabbling and then escape when I'd had my fill of what struck me as a more uncomfortably Darwinian existence than my own.

By virtue of being middle-aged I am no longer an only child. At least I don't call myself one, not any more than I began to identify myself as an orphan after my grandmother's death left me, at the age of thirty, the single living member of my original family. Unencumbered by primary relations, neither do I have even one aunt, uncle, or cousin, because my mother had no siblings and my father was gone by the time I turned one. But, if I don't admit to being an only child, I do admit to having become, unarguably, the sole keeper of my history.

Who else would care to preserve my bronzed baby shoes, my christening dress, or my grade school report cards? Who else to inherit my mother's baby teeth, my grandfather's reading glasses, my grandmother's purse (and in it her wallet filled with old credit cards, many for businesses that no longer exist)? My great-grandfather's Masonic ring. A silver baby rattle, blackened by tarnish—whose? A tiny Torah scroll wound inside a sterling, filigreed ark, and (in the same lockbox, hidden in one envelope sealed inside another) an antique gold pendant in the form of a swastika, that ancient cosmic symbol that before 1935 had yet to become an object of terror and loathing. A crystal goblet commemorating the coronation of Edward VIII on May 12, 1937. Three canes that once belonged to my grandfather (one unscrews to reveal a hidden dagger, the weapon of a gentleman who walked alone, at night, in dangerous cities). A pair of very beautiful hardwood shoe trees (also his). And hundreds of photographs, many of people I no longer recognize, if I ever did, others taken decades before I was born. I could go on, and on, boring even myself, because the entire inventory of my family's material history, as an anthropologist would call such a collection, belongs to me. It is mine to do with what I will, to make sense of, perhaps, assembling the pieces into a coherent whole, a kind of narrative group portrait complete with background and foreground. Or to make into fiction, to invent a history that is possible, but untrue.

That swastika, to take the most dramatic, and puzzling, example: where, and from whom, did my Jewish grandmother acquire such an object? Why did she keep it? Her only sibling, an older sister who lived in Paris, barely survived the German Occupation. Wrapped up as the gold swastika is, hidden for the shameful thing it has become, upon such a piece of evidence I could begin to fabricate a sinister relative, a diseased branch on my family tree. Like all the contents of those boxes stacked in my basement, the swastika is solid, immutable. No, this is not true: a fire could melt it down, consign it to the same fate as that of gold fillings pried from the teeth of those who weren't, like my great-aunt, saved by a Christian friend, but if not immutable then unchanged in all the years that it has been hidden in the lockbox.

But what of my memories, decades old and unavoidably inaccurate? No matter my devotion to preserving them, I have no lockbox. Instead, a mind.

Not a brain, but whatever it is that animates my brain: a highly permeable assemblage of loves and fears and plans, strengths and frailties, desire and dread and the intent — dimly conscious at best — to manage all these in service of that slippery entity, *me*. Myself, as distinct from the rest of humanity. I try honorably to remember things as they really were, but the context in which I revisit a scene from my past — walking through a park, listening as my daughter practices piano, alone or in company — whatever my preoccupation, it necessarily contaminates the original. If biology, chemistry, and psychiatry can agree on anything, it is that memories are not received but created. What's more, they're subject to automatic, unavoidable revision. Honor is useless here.

Just last evening, my husband alluded to a mishap he believed he had witnessed. In 1994, our daughter, then four, and our son, two, stepped into an elevator while I was folding his stroller. I looked up, the doors closed, my children ascended without me. As we were visiting a big apartment building, with a whole bank of elevators, an hour of panicked weeping elapsed before a woman who found them in the laundry room reunited the three of us in the lobby.

"You weren't there," I said, disagreeing with my husband.

"Yes, I was."

"No, if you'd been with us, if there had been two parents in that situation, it never would have happened."

"But I was sure I was there." He looked at me, confused.

"It's just that we've spoken of what happened enough times that you think you were with us, but you weren't." He nodded slowly, not quite convinced. "We could call Lori," I said. "She'll remember that it was just me and the kids." Lori was the friend whom I'd taken our children to see, and who enlisted her doorman and neighbors to help find and return them.

My husband shrugged and went back to what he'd been reading. "That's okay," he said, choosing to believe me because I had the means to correct his misperception.

But what of my memories? There is nothing that unfolded in the house of my childhood that anyone can confirm, or deny. Countless transactions, most without consequence, but some fraught with significance — primal, formative, determinate — lack any witness other than myself. In the abstract, my being free of siblings, of parents, of anyone who might object to my dissembling, or even take note of an untruth, might provide me a tempting invitation to reinvent history. But only in the abstract, only in theory. When I test the idea, contemplating how completely possible it is to rewrite my early years, it frightens me. What I feel isn't freedom but a freefall, and what could check the speed of my descent? Humans agree that what we call reality depends on its being observed by at least one person. When a tree falls in my forest of memories and no one else hears it, has it happened? Is there a sound of one hand clapping? To be less philosophical, imagine yourself at a cocktail party, moving from one clot of guests to the next, one conversation to another. Are not these inadvertent opportunities to eavesdrop on the self as it slides from one context into another, shedding some pretenses, picking up others, revealing what, minutes before, it had hidden, sufficiently disturbing? If identity is fluid under these pedestrian circumstances, how reliable is the self whose past exists only inside her own head? How, without parents or siblings, can I really know what or who I was?

Among my memories, that part of my history represented by nothing more material than traces of neurochemicals in my cerebral cortex, Christmas morning, 1966 has achieved the status of the gold swastika. It is the most puzzling and disturbing of all I possess. I woke up early, so early that it was still dark outside. But winter mornings were dark, and I was always up before my grandparents or my mother. I got out of bed; I didn't check the time. Either I couldn't yet read a clock, or I was too intent on the stocking that hung from one of my bed's tall posts. My grandparents' house included a hearth that was greeting-card perfect for hanging a Christmas stocking; the mantel was carved from a massive oak beam and outfitted with hooks from which dangled pokers and pincers and bellows, even a bed warmer and a chestnut roaster, but I was not encouraged to leave my empty stocking in their company. I wonder if this wasn't because a single stocking looked too forlorn there by itself, too *only*.

I stood on the end of my bed to lift the bulging thing from over the post's finial, unobstructed by the bed's canopy, which had been removed because it gathered dust and made me wheeze. How satisfying was the stocking's weight and the way tissue paper wrappings crinkled from within it. This stocking was one I inherited from my mother and had her name, Carole, embroidered across its top. Below was an appliquéd tree of green wool felt, decorated with pea-sized ornaments made of colored glass and candles fashioned from minuscule strips of white patent leather, each about the size of half a toothpick, an orange bead for a flame. As if it were still hers, I carried the stocking to my mother's room to unpack its contents with her. With regard to the issue of Santa Claus's identity, I teetered on a cusp between what I wished and what I feared. That it might have been my mother who assembled so perfect an array of tiny gifts, that she could have known me so well—enough to penetrate my desires and satisfy them—was a more seductive and cherished idea than that of a jolly old man who squeezed down chimneys. In service to the latter conceit, my grandfather effected the standard transformations, reducing the cookies and cocoa left on the mantel to crumbs and dregs, a thank you note written in an unfamiliar hand. And he performed a supplementary trick, dipping his shoes into the cold ashes and leaving a trail of footprints from there to my bedroom and back, a trail so convincing that I was afraid it was true, what I'd been told. Santa Claus, corpulent and sweating, had been far more perverse than I could have expected from my department store visit to his red velour lap, criminal enough to break into our home and creep about while we slept.

But, as I wanted the stocking to be my mother's work, I intended to watch her as I undid it, in order to gauge her investment in my pleasure. I remember—I can see—my mother's bed, which, as revealed by the moonlight, had not been slept in, and I stood for some minutes holding the stocking and trying to imagine a benign reason for her absence. Was there such a thing? Had I a brother or sister, I would have gone at once to his or her room that we might confer over this unexpected—alarming—turn of events. But I was alone, and so I walked by myself through the hall to the shadowy living room, anxious speculations about my mother's whereabouts rendering me immune to the sinister power of a portrait whose subject, I'd convinced myself, climbed out of her frame to do mischief unobserved. When I'd determined my mother was nowhere in the house, I went to my grandmother's bedside and touched her shoulder. A light sleeper, she woke instantly and sat forward rather than up from her pillows, piled high to keep her that much more upright and to offset the breathlessness caused by her rheumatic heart.

"What?" she said. "What is it?" When I told her she swung her feet over the side of the bed and stamped one in anger. "If that doesn't—" she began, but didn't finish. Instead she snapped on the light and woke my grandfather. "Gone!" she announced to his startled countenance. "How do you like that! She's gone! Snuck off in the middle of the night!"

Immediately I understood that alerting my grandmother to my mother's disappearance had been exactly the wrong response. My mother wasn't lost—she'd escaped. And I had betrayed her, I, who was always searching to discover the means of ingratiating myself, of proving my worth to my re- mote and distracted young mother, of insinuating myself between her and the lovely reflection in her mirror, between her and the novel in her lap, the telephone receiver in her hand. Meaning well, I had done something awful and irrevocable.

The fight my mother had with my grandmother later that morning, when she accused my mother of being a—what word would she have used? Not slut. Certainly not whore. Well, whatever my grandmother did or didn't say, their fight was what my mother would end up calling "the last last straw, the absolute, final end." Tart? Maybe, except tart wasn't a word my grandmother used in anger. She thought tart was funny. Ditto trollop. Cheap, I guess. She might have called my mother cheap for sneaking out to spend the night with a boyfriend. Cheap, like other comparatively mild slurs, was a word my grandmother could pronounce as a dire insult. But just as possibly, she might have used no words, she might have just screamed: that was a standard, and unanswerable, strategy. My grandmother's inarticulate animal howls that seemed to presage madness, or violence, or both, often won her an argument, either because of their inherent power to terrorize or because they testified to her ruthlessness, her stop-at-nothing determination to win.

A month or two later, my mother moved out, for good. Unwittingly, I had been the catalyst for my own abandonment.

The painter René Magritte remembered the suicide of his mother, Regina, as happening in this way. In 1912, Magritte, the youngest in the family, was fourteen. He shared a bedroom with his mother, and one night awoke to find her gone. He roused the rest of the household, and they searched but could find her nowhere inside. But beyond the front door, traces of her steps led to a nearby bridge over the river Sambre, into which the woman had thrown herself. In the middle of the night, René stood on the bank and watched as his mother's corpse was pulled from the water, her face covered by her nightdress, her body naked, and luminously white in the moonlight.

Asked what they remembered of the death of Mme. Magritte, the artist's childhood friends recalled that, though they themselves had all cried in fear and grief, René betrayed no emotion in the weeks following his mother's death and from that point forward never spoke of her. As a famous painter, Magritte gave many interviews; in all of these he mentioned his mother's suicide no more than two times. Asked (rather idiotically) if the event had marked him, he said only that it had been a shock. His 1954 outline for an autobiography included a single, abbreviated reference, in the third rather than the first person: "In 1912, his mother, Regina, does not want to live anymore. She throws herself in Sambre."

Veils and curtains recur in Magritte's paintings, as do faces hidden behind hands or by objects or replaced outright by a death's-head or an orb made of light. It's easy to guess why such images might retain so strong a hold on the artist's imagination.

The thing is, though Magritte did wake to discover that his mother's bed was empty, he never saw her body recovered from the Sambre. As a number of onlookers testified, the boy wasn't there on the riverbank.

Psychology, a science Magritte dismissed as false, an attempt to explain what cannot be explained, to render irreducible mystery to pedestrian cause and effect, calls such memories as the artist's screen memories, which typically date back to childhood and which a child creates to protect himself from a truth he finds even more traumatic than what he invents to hide it. But what could be worse than the scene Magritte believed he witnessed? The face of his dead mother unveiled? Her body, for which he must have harbored—as all children do—a desire to possess, covered by a winding sheet and taken from him forever? A desire enflamed at the time of her death, when, caught up in the turmoil of adolescence, he still shared her bedroom, saw her in a night-dress that revealed perhaps a little more than it ought?

"It may indeed be questioned whether we have any memories at all *from* our childhood," Freud writes in his 1899 paper on the topic. "Memories *relating* to childhood may be all that we possess."

It is only as I consider my early years with the express purpose of divining how I feel, or felt, about having been an only child that I understand—suddenly and with no little anxiety—why this story of Magritte and his mother's suicide has compelled and disturbed me for so many years. Ever since I learned of it, accidentally, while pursuing the larger topic of memory and how reliably (factually) true it might or might not be, I've revisited the scene over and over, picturing the artist as he pictured himself, seeing a boy, a boy the same age as my son is now—how clearly, then, can I imagine his form, the slope of his shoulders, the balled fists at his sides—as he stands on the banks of a river to watch as the corpse of his mother is pulled from the water. Of course the body frightens the boy in its faceless nakedness, its flesh I see as if rendered by the surrealist himself, gray and shadowed, like the shuttered house in his 1954 painting, "The Empire of Light," in which a simple nighttime landscape is made sinister by its having a brightly daylit sky overhead.

Magritte and I knew only the same few facts: one night we awoke; we found our mothers' beds empty; we alerted our families; a tragedy ensued. That the artist's story, far more dire than my own, included a set of ghostly footprints leading to a terrible truth would appeal, naturally, to a child who followed the ashy tracks of an intruder in her home, one who threatened to steal an idea she valued above all her possessions: that, contrary to appearances, her mother had been paying her careful attention all along. But if Magritte unconsciously fabricated a narrative to explain his terror, might the Christmas memory in question, over which I've puzzled for forty years — holding it dear as one does guard the instrument of a dangerous wound (the way, for example, a soldier might preserve a piece of shrapnel dug out of his chest) — might that morning never have happened? Or might it have happened very differently from the way I believe it did?

The pieces of the story are, all of them, as emblematic of my early unhappiness as are, say, a dove and olive branch ready examples of religious iconography. My mother's bed that she hadn't slept in was the bed I visited each day after she moved out, standing before the lie it spoke, its sheets changed weekly as if to suggest, like the rest of her room, that her return was imminent. The Christmas stocking, whose content I fetishized and displayed each year, never playing with the toys or eating the candies but arranging them in a tableau on my dresser, a little altar to my fearful worship of my mother: what better evocation of the celebrated position of my single parent, who removed herself from the realm of the everyday mother to become a kind of holiday apparition? The night itself, when Christmas Eve becomes Christmas Day, is the one upon which a child's worthiness — her naughtiness or niceness — is judged and found either sufficient or wanting and well represents the everlastingly long night of my soul, obsessed as I was to become with the idea of my goodness and what it might afford me, if not the return of my mother then some other reward, someone else's admiration. The bedpost with its missing canopy recalls asthma, a looming threat of suffocation (and the grandmother, too, propped up on her pillows to avoid feeling smothered). And, finally, the most troubling aspect of the memory, that it was my actions that caused my mother to leave me, is almost too neatly textbook to be true. Don't all children hold themselves responsible for their abandonment?

Do I remember this night so vividly, with a heightened, almost hallucinatory attention to detail, because it evoked my childhood so perfectly, or did I unconsciously collect and/or fabricate symbols of my past to assemble them into a story in order that I might contain them within the mnemonic device of a narrative so as not to lose these critical aspects of myself?

Within the embrace of psychotherapy, in whose arms I've spent an hour each week for fifteen years, "the feelings are the facts." Which is all very well, assuming the availability of reality checks. Of, say, a brother or sister who might call me on the claim of straight As — "There must have been a frigging B in there somewhere," he'd say. "P. E.," I'd answer, "and that doesn't count." But maybe it would count to my brother, the one I don't have. He might be a professional ball player, a perfect uncle for my son, who dreams of a glorious future as a New York Yankee. Or what about my sister, who might say, in her intimate knowledge of my flaws, "Piss off. You're always hiding inside your head, behind your good grades, whatever." But I wouldn't waste their voices on my grades — for topics like that I have my boxes in the basement.

I didn't mind being an only child, when I was a child. I understood the bargain it implied, that if I'd had siblings I would have lost my monopoly over my grandparents' affection, halve or even more drastically reduce my mother's infrequent attention. Like most children in such a position, I knew the stresses of the family in which I'd landed: a pair of guardians who were, respectively, seventy-one and sixty-two at my birth, old if not frail; a child-mother who never grew up; endless conflicts arising from our dwindling financial resources. Another child in the family would have applied that much more pressure to what was already as frayed as the carpets and drapes, the sprung sofa upholstered in an impractical pink chintz. Another child would have endangered me.

But, as an adult, having long ago reached the age at which I'd expected to have left my only childhood far behind, I mind it very much. I want a witness, or better, two, three, to what I remember, a person or persons to whom I could turn and ask, "Remember that Christmas, the one when Mom. . . ."

¿La Verdad?

Notes on the Writing of *Silent Dancing*, a Partial Remembrance of a Puerto Rican Childhood (a Memoir in Prose and Poetry)

JUDITH ORTIZ COFER

> Many bright colours; many distinct sounds; some human beings, caricatures; comic; several violent moments of being, always including a circle of the scene which they cut out: and all surrounded by a vast space—that is a rough visual description of childhood. This is how I shape it. . . .
> —VIRGINIA WOOLF, "A Sketch of the Past"

✳ ✳ ✳ ✳ ✳ ✳ ✳ ✳ ✳ ✳ ✳ ✳ ✳ ✳ ✳ ✳ ✳ ✳ ✳ ✳

I began to work on *Silent Dancing* soon after my first novel, *The Line of the Sun*, was published in 1989. I was not sure what to call what I was shaping into a book. At the time, the somewhat awkward term, creative nonfiction, had not yet been popularized to describe the strange morphing of fictional technique and nonfiction writing. At one point, I mentioned to a friend that I was working on a memoir; in a dubious tone, she said to me: "Why don't you wait till you are famous to write a memoir?" I realized that memoir was not the right label for what I wanted to accomplish in these narratives, as it has come to be attached to celebrity or notoriety, neither of which I possess in enough quantity to justify a book about my exploits. I wrote the preface to *Silent Dancing* in an attempt to give shape to my vision. I turned to Virginia Woolf and to my grandmother for guidance, the strongest voices I had known in my formative years. Everyone is afraid of Virginia Woolf and I never knew anyone who would tangle with my *abuela*, especially after she had made one of her pontifical declarations. I chose my allies carefully.

At that time I had no models for the book I had envisioned, which was a blending of poetry and prose. In the essays I hoped to dramatize key events I had witnessed or participated in through the use of fictional techniques. I was not interested in telling my life's story, which was, still is, I hope, very much in progress. I wanted my *moments of being* to be created out of the melding of experiences that I had first filtered through my early poems. It was my aim to have these narratives joined at the hip to the poems, sometimes, but not always, directly addressing one another. It was my intention that the poems amplify meaning by refraction, not as a handy mirror, there merely to serve the essays.

I hoped the book could be experienced personally, entered into as one does a novel, expecting to live an alternate life. I wanted the stories to have the direct psychic impact on the reader that conventional autobiography and nonfiction seemed to lack, since their aim was often telling a life, not sharing it. I knew that the events of my life, although not extraordinary, might seem foreign and my characters unfamiliar to some readers, yet I hoped that they, the readers, would be willing to suspend disbelief, would want to do so, because the story itself was interesting, perhaps even relevant to some aspect of their lives, and not necessarily because they wanted or needed to know about Judith Ortiz Cofer's life. I trusted the poems to establish an emotional link between reader and text, a common ground. The role of the poet is to locate within the language of the raw human experience what Czeslaw Milosz called "the only homeland."

Poems are always true. You can feel their truth; it resonates within you like the sound of pure crystal. And when you hear good poems, the question, *did this really happen?*, which we often hear from inexperienced readers, is of no consequence because it does not matter. The truth of poetry is like quantum physics. One should accept it even if one does not quite grasp it. *Es la pura verdad.*

> "Look into Thy Heart and Write."
> —Sir Philip Sidney

Nag. Nag. Nag. I believe Sir Philip may have been admonishing himself when he spoke these words. As a writer I am a self-nag. The questions I have, that I need answered, are nagging questions that try to be answered in poems, stories, essays, and novels. In writing *Silent Dancing*, one of the questions I asked myself was: how does nonfiction arrive at the truth that lies beyond the fact? What proportion of facts is necessary to make a story a work of creative nonfiction as opposed to fictionalized autobiography? Is Tim O'Brien's novel in stories, *The Things They Carried*, less true than his memoir *If I Die in a Combat Zone*? Which book teaches you the truth of the Viet Nam experience and its effects on a generation of young men, such as the author himself—who in a story calls the narrator Tim O'Brien? Is it simply a matter of sticking to the facts? In my work of fiction, *The Line of the Sun*, I drew heavily on autobiographical material, yet gave myself complete license to explore potential and alternate lives for my characters that were often based on real living people. Of course I had the usual disclaimer in the front of the book — any similarity between the characters and events in this novel is purely coincidental, etc. . . .

Here is another disclaimer. And this is a fact. In writing fiction, I feel free to invent the emotional landscape of my characters in order to advance the plot; I will do almost anything to advance the plot — but I am a scrupulous researcher of historical facts and events. I try to be accurate in my reporting of things that actually happened and in descriptions of places that exist in the real world, although names and other less important details may be changed to protect both the innocent and the guilty. Factual accuracy is an important part of the contract my books offer to my readers. It does not mean I do not make mistakes. But they are honest mistakes. Accuracy in reporting confirmable information is a rule I follow in all my writing. The truth of art is different from the fact of history. Both may claim to be *la verdad*, but to appropriate or revise factual truth, unless you have established the appropriate contract with your reader, is a sort of moving violation. Excluded from this injunction are, of course, science fiction, fantasy, speculative writing — these genres operate under a separate set of assumptions which are normally a given between reader and text.

GUNS, LA FAMILIA, LIES, AND MEMORY

I once read about a criminal law professor who asked a class to write down their accounts of an incident they had just witnessed in his classroom in which a student had drawn a gun on a classmate during an argument. This classical experiment first took place in 1901. It has been reenacted thousands of times over the past century with astonishingly similar results. No one remembers the truth with perfect accuracy. Yet we often expect eyewitness accounts to serve as the basis for our judgments in events including daily occurrences — car wrecks, minor and major accidents, and personal confrontations — and, of course, in court proceedings leading to legal and criminal indictments.

In writing my novel, I used objective and subjective sources to give my scenes credibility. I researched the geography, weather, and history of my locations. I called my mother and other relatives in New Jersey and Puerto Rico. Then I chose the most interesting versions of family stories and fictionalized them. But in writing *Silent Dancing*, I wanted to stay within view of the actual events; after all, it was to be based on my life. In gathering factual background information for the essays I found my facts in books and documents as usual. The credibility problem, I soon discovered, began with the accounts my personal informants were giving me: *Abuela, Abuelo, Mami, Tío, Tía*—my relatives were approximately as reliable in their descriptions of events we had all shared as had been the eyewitnesses in the classic experiment of the gunshot. If I asked them to tell the story in a group, the dominant talkers usually took charge of the "facts," constantly correcting the speaker; others might be nodding in polite agreement, or the Doubting Thomases would be shielding their contemptuous gazes from the nosy one (*yo*) who had come into their midst to challenge them about the past. When I interviewed them individually, the stories varied dramatically, even wildly, one from the other.

Are my relatives liars? Are they more inventive than other people's relatives? Were they revising the past for my benefit? I do not think so. I have read various studies on the nature of memory, and I am convinced that the past is something most of us revise automatically, and without malice or evil intent or even any conscious awareness of doing so. We are constantly changing our personal narrative so that it matches our idea of who we are and in what role we see ourselves—but our version of *la pura verdad* is, of course, not necessarily what others may have experienced, even if they were participants in our moment of being. And so, in retrospect, we are never in quite the same place as others; even when we are physically together, our minds are processing the same information through our own very private filters. Our memories are shaped individually and independently. The angle, the focus, the lighting, make all the difference in how the memory will be preserved and our individual perception is what makes us completely unique, at least to ourselves. Our story must be original, and we will make sure that it is, by revising it as we live and learn.

Once I understood that memory is relative, and that my relatives were practicing their particular theory of relativity, I made my decision to go with Virginia Woolf's definition of what constitutes the truth in writing from memory—personal impressions, the tracks you follow back to your moments of being. I chose to write *Silent Dancing* out of *my* deepest emotional connections to *my* unique version of past events. This is where the poems became even more crucial to the undertaking.

WHAT TOOK ME TO LA VERDAD

The poems in *Silent Dancing* were written years before the essays and were my first attempts at investigating the truth of my life as a witness to it; I wanted to understand the dichotomy at the center of my particular human experience and perhaps along the way learn how it affected those of us caught up in it. And more than that, I wanted to make art out of my discoveries, which means that I had to find the universal in the particular: how could I make my individual life experience as a Puerto Rican girl growing up on the island and on the mainland part of a homeland I could share through language? My humble discovery: that we are all strangers in a strange land at some point in our lives — at some time in our lives we have all felt alienated, confused, unable to make ourselves understood. In my essay, "The Looking-Glass Shame," I propose that we all go through our foreigner phase; at least in adolescence, we become the minority. If we have common ground, then my work is more than a sociological introduction into the secret lives of Puerto Ricans. It is a story of transformation through language. Anyway, that is how *I* shape it.

Whose Truth?

PHYLLIS ROSE

Going public with your own life — and who knows who else's

❋ ❋ ❋ ❋ ❋ ❋ ❋ ❋ ❋ ❋ ❋ ❋ ❋ ❋ ❋ ❋ ❋ ❋ ❋

I published a memoir once. As memoirs go, it was not shocking. No one had abused me in my childhood. No one in my family was alcoholic. I had not slept with my father. You may wonder how I thought that anyone would be interested in what I had to say. In fact, I didn't. I never imagined anyone reading my book. When I conceived of the book, as I wrote the book, as I rewrote the chapters, I never thought about anyone but myself or imagined any readers but my tiny posterity and small band of unshakeable well-wishers. If I had, I doubt I could or would have written the book at all. Sheer stupidity, failure of imagination, freed me to write.

The writing itself was blissful. I set myself the task of writing truthfully about certain experiences that had not to my knowledge often been honestly described — among others, ambition, childbirth, the combination of arrogance and self-disgust which textures my every day. This was a deeply personal project. I was once and for all and for whatever it was worth going to tell the truth about myself. I felt no impediments to writing. Although I always enjoy writing, I wrote this book with unprecedented speed. Toward the end, I was seized with a sense of urgency. I wanted to get this all down. To some extent, this is typical at the end of any big project (the horse smells the stable), but I've never experienced it as intensely as with this book. I wasn't expecting to die in the near future, but I wanted to finish the book before I did, so that something would survive that was truly me. I recalled repeatedly Montaigne's address to his reader: "The goal I've set myself is private and domestic. I had no thought of serving you or glorifying myself. My book is intended solely for the pleasure of my relatives and friends, so that, when they have lost me (as they must soon), they will find in it some traces of my character and disposition and so keep what memory they have of me more completely and vividly alive."

The book is about the experience of reading all of Proust. But in spirit it's much closer to Montaigne and Boswell, the self-revealers, the diarists and autobiographers, than it is to Proust, the consummate novelist, consummate transformer. Onto the spine of reading Proust I hung various reminiscences from the past, both recent and distant, and many vignettes about my life in the present. The book is called *The Year of Reading Proust* and subtitled *A Memoir in Real Time*, and the idea was to combine elements of journal and diary with the memoir form, so that I would be writing about events almost as they were taking place. Since reading is central to my life, I wrote a lot about what I was reading in addition to Proust and made connections between life and art, as I have always liked to do.

I was concerned about issues of privacy that the writing of any memoir raises. Concerned isn't the right word. I was terrified. I wrote into the book a cautionary tale, a story that haunted me, of what happened to Marjorie Kinnan Rawlings, the author of the children's classic *The Yearling*, after she published in 1942 a memoir of her life in backwoods Florida, The memoir was called *Cross Creek* after the small town she lived in. She didn't want to disrupt in any way her cordial relations with her neighbors, and specifically, she wanted to avoid being sued for libel. So she went around and read chapters out loud to many of the people portrayed to make sure they weren't offended by what she'd written. No one she consulted was. People who were involved in illegal activities like poaching or running stills were especially grateful for the lengths she went to to conceal their real identities. Most local people were pleased by the book and nationally it was a great success. But one person was furious, Zelma Cason, the postmistress, who, because she was more sophisticated than most of the Cross Creek population and a closer friend, Rawlings had never worried about offending. But offended Zelma was by her four-sentence portrayal in *Cross Creek*. Rawlings described her as an "ageless spinster" who resembled an "angry and efficient canary" and claimed she didn't know if Zelma, a bossy nurturer, would have been better off as a man or a mother. Cason sued not for libel but for the very recently established tort of invasion of privacy, and after six years of court battles which went both ways, a jury found in her favor. Since no financial damage to her could be shown, Cason received merely token compensation. Nevertheless, Rawlings paid a huge price. The protracted trial ruined her concentration and destroyed her nerve. Her later work is unimpressive. She abandoned the gritty and unsentimental studies of the world of poor whites in the South which had been her strength and sought refuge in high-minded historical dramas set in distant places.

More than anything I feared spending years of my life in a law court, like Rawlings, like Janet Malcolm. It was my nightmare to have to go over every word I'd written and justify it before a literalist audience, as Rawlings had. "'Angry canary?' What exactly does that mean, Ms. Rawlings?" But the moral I saw in Rawlings's experience was not that you should be careful and check with the people you've written about—because she did check, she was careful. The moral I saw was that no matter how careful you were, you would offend someone—probably the person you least expected to offend—and on grounds you never could have imagined.

Trouble started for me when I began showing the manuscript to people I'd written about, to find out if they wanted something changed. When you do this you quickly discover that people who have never read with any seriousness in their lives, when the subject is themselves, become as acute as a Yale English professor to the tones and subtexts of a sentence. For example, in a section describing my mother's repeated emergency treatment for heart problems, I told how my sister once got my mother to the hospital after she'd collapsed. Usually, my brother did this. My sister, Susan, doesn't live as close to ground zero as my brother. Moreover, she has a hospital phobia. She has a hard time bringing herself even to visit people in the hospital. I wrote, "By the time I got to the emergency room, Susan was experiencing the exhilaration of someone who has been present at a disaster and behaved well. She went back over every minute of the crisis in appreciative detail: how she had returned from dinner and found mother gasping, how she hadn't known what to do, how she had called me and I wasn't there and Richard (our brother) was away for the weekend, how she'd finally thought to call Barbara Rubin and Barbara had come right over and called 911, how six people had arrived and how nice they'd been, how they'd rushed her to the ER, which was better than the TV show, etc. etc."

My sister didn't like my mentioning her friend, Barbara. "It makes me look like I couldn't handle it myself," she realized. Exactly my intention! Now she explained that the reason she'd had a hard time getting herself to call 911 was not administrative incompetence or hospital phobia or shirking of responsibility but moral quandary: Mother had explicitly said we were not to take her back to the hospital, no matter what happened. Susan was torn between the desire to save Mother's life and the desire to respect her wishes. So I rewrote the passage, removing Barbara Rubin and saying that Susan had a hard time getting herself to call 911 because Mother had explicitly said not to. This was, I knew, also true. It's just a question in memoirs, which truth you tell. There are so many.

Several of the people I wrote about are writers, and they invariably saw what I said as my business, asking for no changes. Annie Dillard, who is a good and valued friend of mine and who is, according to some readers, harshly portrayed in the book, merely said that in one place, where I concealed her identity, I shouldn't bother, as it was perfectly clear who she was. She herself had written a memoir and gave me some advice: if anyone is upset by their portrayal, make sure to explain that after it's changed, the earlier versions won't show through. Non-writers don't understand this. She was so professional in her response that when I later described how I had changed the text to respond to various people's objections, she felt cheated. "You mean I could have asked you to change more?"

The person hardest to accommodate was a childhood friend, my oldest friend, now a real estate broker in New York, who is wealthy herself and knows many wealthy and powerful people. I described a weekend with her in East Hampton, and she was quite unhappy with what I'd written, not because I'd revealed anything she didn't want revealed, but because, in her eyes, she came across as a loser. Her term. I didn't understand. I said she was witty and down-to-earth, one of the smartest people I knew, loved by all her friends in café society. OK, maybe café society was a put-down. I changed it to "a wide range of people. She moved in distinguished and glamorous circles." I reported telling her that I wanted to write a whole book about her, a kind of updating and Americanization of Mrs. Dalloway, and her reply, which I admired for its modesty and down-to-earth self-deprecation, was, "Believe me, there's nothing to tell." This, it emerged, was one of the things that bothered her. What a loser not to have any story in her life worth writing about. So I changed the dialogue. When I say I want to write a book about her, she replies, "Forget it." The only thing important to me was the offhand turndown, so typical of my friend's style. Still, no matter how much I tinkered with the prose, she wasn't really happy. She said, "I can't tell you to change anything else, because it's all true." "Yes," I said, "but I can change a word and give a different impression. And believe me, what was there before won't show through." So we worked on it more, but never got it entirely to her taste, and she said, "It's like seeing a photograph of yourself. You always hate them. You can't believe you look that way. I read your book, and I thought, is that vain, shallow, materialistic person me?" But then I had another conversation with my old friend and told her what I was going to write, including that I'd never understood what bothered her. So she elaborated, "We're all so insecure. We all wish we had strengths we don't have. My deepest fear is that I'm an airhead. I was hoping you'd say I was a deep intellectual. I know it's ridiculous, but that's what I wanted. A eulogy. I wanted it to be like my fantasies of attending my own funeral."

No one who I asked to vet their pages had an easy time. Some people said it was the hardest thing they'd ever done in their lives. One such was a hairdresser in Key West I call Gabriela. I have a long monologue in the book by Gabriela on the subject of how we do not let old people die. She herself had had a radical mastectomy, and when her aged grandmother was faced with the same procedure, Gabriela, although she's a devout Catholic, thought it would be better to let her go than to subject her to the procedure. I had gotten down what she said on this subject exactly right, she told me, so she couldn't object. (It's extraordinary how people think truth is its own justification.) But she would hate anyone who knew her to recognize her and she asked me if I would change her name. We picked Gabriela together, one day when she was doing my hair. At least that part was fun for her. When I did readings from the book, I often read Gabriela's monologue, which people found moving and in all too many cases relevant to their own deep concerns about parents and grandparents. I reported to Gabriela when I read her section, to say how well the audience responded, but if she got any pleasure from this she didn't show it and I soon stopped.

Gradually it became clear to me that I was making trouble for almost everyone I included and some I didn't. People do not like being forced to confront how they appear to others. Robert Burns said it's a gift "to see ourselves as others see us," but really it's a torture. We'd prefer to live with our fantasies of ourselves.

Years ago I published a memoiristic essay about my family's trips to Florida when I was a child in the fifties and the hotel life of the time, so different from now, so formal. I described getting dressed up for dinner every night and the women wearing their jewelry. A string quartet played. The piece was about shared memories — how only my family and a few others would remember this place. This is what made us a family. However, my brother was unhappy with what I'd written. It made us sound rich, he said. For whatever reason, he didn't want to sound rich. Who can argue? You either want to seem rich or you don't. I had tampered with his self-presentation, part of his autonomy.

No matter how insignificant the things revealed, people resented my having taken it upon myself to reveal them. For example, I mention being on the phone with a colleague at Wesleyan and discussing Gita Mehta, whose works I say she liked. After the book appeared, someone told me how irritated my colleague was to have me say that she liked Gita Mehta's work when she did not. Still, she went on, at least I'd said she liked Gita Mehta's work. It would have been worse if I'd revealed that she didn't. Clearly my colleague felt it was none of my business to tell the world whether or not she liked the novels of Gita Mehta.

The only thing more unpleasant than being written about is not being written about when you want to be. One friend was hurt that I hadn't mentioned her. Aren't I important in your life at all? she asked. Am I too boring? Another friend, whose scandalous doings I had tried to cover with a pseudonym, insisted on having his real name revealed. In some ways, the memoirist can't win.

My mother, about whose feelings I was most concerned, was perhaps the easiest subject to satisfy. She said, "I'm so old. Who cares if you tell all my secrets? There's no one left to be shocked." In fact, Mother, who died at ninety-three, was even then at the age at which, if her secrets were *not* known, she took it as a sign of lack of interest.

The problem with writing about your own life is that there's no way to do it without writing about other people's lives, and however tangentially you include other people, you take something from them. It's usually called their privacy. But it's more to the point, I think, to call it their opportunity for self-representation. This seems to some people who've been robbed as tangible an asset as their mutual funds. That they are not writers and cannot commercially develop the property is of no consequence. Everyone has an imagination. Everyone has fantasies of themselves that allow them to act in the world. Yet I think it's no accident that some of the people who reacted most strongly to being in my book without their consent, even though they were disguised, or who, like my old friend, were pickiest about their representation, were the wealthiest. The rich seem to understand that the power of self-representation—of having others endorse their fantasies of themselves—is one of their greatest perks and privileges.

Janet Malcolm has written brilliantly on the exploitative nature of much nonfiction, specifically of journalism and of biography. "The biographer," she said bluntly, "is a thief." I am beginning to think that the same is true of the memoirist. The memoirist is also a thief, for you cannot write about someone else, however briefly, however sympathetically, without stealing a little bit of their self-determination.

I've put off for last what for me was the most painful and problematic of the prepublication vettings. I have a long section on my husband's brother, who is a Benedictine monk in the south of France. He used to be a well-known concert pianist. He is exceptionally charming and universally beloved. I met him only once, shortly after my husband and I were married, at a place in the Pyrenees where he was at that time a hermit. We spent hours talking. He wanted me to understand why he had become a monk and then a hermit. I was fascinated by him on every level and spent the next week writing down everything I remembered of our meeting. This account I rediscovered six or seven years later, when I was writing *The Year of Reading Proust*, and I realized I wanted to include it in some form. To have my brother-in-law in my life was impossible, but to have him in my book seemed right for several reasons. Proust wrote about social life; my own life was social. Here was someone who had turned away from ordinary social contact, his central relationship being with God and the members of his religious community.

I was not expecting any problem with my brother-in-law. First of all, my husband had read the whole book and had said that he couldn't imagine any-one in his family objecting to anything. Second, the man was a monk! A one-time hermit! He spent his days in prayer and meditation! Could he possibly care what someone said about him in a language he didn't understand on the other side of the world? I planned on showing him the manuscript, but I ex-pected, if anything, to be praised. Because he had taken some seven hours to explain himself to me, I assumed he wanted to explain himself to the world at large. I thought I was doing him a service. He was in some sense the moral hero of my book, the person who turned his back on worldly success and superficial social ties and lived daily from the core of his being. That's how I thought of him, the moral core. So it was the Marjorie Rawlings and the postmistress moment when my brother-in-law telephoned from France to say that he had been sent the manuscript of my book, and he was appalled.

The ways in which he was appalled ran the gamut. He objected to many things I revealed about his life. Some were too private for other people to know and some would shock his family. He objected to things I wrote about a specific retreat and the spiritual problems of a certain brother even though they were heavily disguised, saying that people in the monastery would rec-ognize the brother nonetheless. Really, my brother-in-law didn't want to be written about at all. He had often been asked for interviews by journalists and had always turned them down. It was appalling to have been betrayed, as he saw it, by a member of his own family. Finally, he was horrified that I had not been the one to send him the manuscript. At the time, I was still working on the manuscript. I was months away from sending it to him for his okay. But my agent had an early draft for which he was trying to find a foreign publisher. I should not have released anything that wasn't ready for public viewing, but I never imagined the manuscript would go so far. In fact, it made its way with the speed of lightning or of bad news traveling fast to a remote Benedictine monastery in southwestern France. The parts my brother-in-law would find most upsetting had been translated for him into French. I hoped he would see all this as a hostile gesture. He didn't. He saw it as a kindness.

I went over every sentence with him and took out everything he objected to. Faxes and FedExes went back and forth between the monastery and my house, and at the end, after weeks of revisions, he said he could live with what was left. Nevertheless he would prefer it if I excised the whole chapter that mentioned him, though he doubted I would. I would not. I could not get out of my mind the idea that I was doing him a service, even if it was a service he hadn't requested and didn't want, even if his commitment was to silence and non-explanation, even if the French have quite a different sense of privacy from Americans and the kind of book I'd written was unthinkably intrusive in France. Brought up on humanism and Areopagitica, I believed that truth telling was good in itself, that truth would make its way, that to know all is to forgive all. My brother-in-law, I sensed, considered the whole book vulgar, tasteless, name dropping, self-congratulatory, and it disgusted him to be in it.

I don't want to dwell on this episode much longer. I stopped sleeping. Every time my mind came to rest, it returned to my brother-in-law and his pain and disgust. Short of suppressing my book, or even the chapter, I wanted to do something to make the situation better, and of course I chose the way I would, as a writer, choose — to write more — and ended by making the situation even worse.

What happened was that a magazine wanted to run the section about my brother-in-law (confirming my sense that it was one of the best parts of the book), and I gave them permission with the understanding that they let me add a paragraph. This paragraph I imagined as my apology to him, the thing that would make everything all right. It acknowledged that he had objected to my publishing the account of him, and that I had changed everything I could to accommodate him, but that I knew he would still see what I'd written as a breach of confidence and a betrayal. I wrote this by way of expiation, to confess my fault, and to give his side of the disagreement, but I was merely repeating my error — presuming to speak for him. Letters to the editor were many and uniformly hostile to me, though some people also blamed the magazine. They said they felt tricked into an immoral act: if they'd known at the start what they learned at the end — that the piece was written without the subject's approval — they wouldn't have read it. "That's the kind of prissy-ass audience that magazine has," my agent said, to calm me down. "That's why no one reads it." But guess who read it in his monastery in the south of France? And guess who was upset all over again? And guess who, never learning, wrote a reply to the letters to the editor which essentially said the same thing all over again, that a writer's nature is to reveal, which angered even more people, even some of my friends, one of whom said to me, "It sounded like you're saying that if you want to write something, you can."

All this before the book was even published. When it *was* published, I realized the mess I'd made because people started saying to me how brave I was to have written it. I know when people tell you you're brave, it means you have some fatal disease that they can only thank God they don't have. I replied to all of them what I started by saying to you, that I wasn't brave—only stupid. The extent of my stupidity became, with time, clearer and clearer to me. For one thing, a memoir is generally understood to be an assertion of self-importance. Many people think that if you've written a memoir you must think you're someone special. I don't happen to feel this way about memoirs. I feel everybody's life is worth writing and a memoir is justified not by the events described but by the quality of attention brought to those events. However, writing a memoir certainly calls attention to yourself.

As I realized that people were actually reading my book, I became increasingly appalled over what I had revealed. Trivial and serious, passages came to haunt me. Had I really announced to the world that Laurent, my husband, is allergic to garlic? Had I really written about my ex-husband's failure to pay attention to our son at the moment of his birth? Why hadn't I thought how this might affect my son? Why did I do this to my ex-husband? Why did I risk my friendship with Annie by saying anything less than fawning about her? Why did I risk trouble with my husband's family in France by saying anything about them at all? How could I have written about weighing the advantages of a Saab as opposed to a BMW, a passage which seemed to me especially important and realistic in its banality as I was writing it and which produced scathing mockery when the book was reviewed? And how, though no reviewer had the temerity to mention it, could I have been so stupid as to discuss my episiotomy?

How? How? How? Why? Why? Why? I have some answers.

There are those who argue—and I'm not sure I don't agree—that anyone who has anything to do with a writer and doesn't understand that they run the risk of being quoted or portrayed is naive, and perhaps even insulting to the writer in his or her professional capacity. If I respect (theoretically, at least) the monk's silence and concealment, shouldn't the monk respect my blabbing? People continually tell me things which assume my discretion, and I always say, "Don't." I use my own judgment about what revelations would be harmful, but with the best will, I won't remember who asked me to keep quiet and who didn't. The best way to guarantee my silence is by telling me something I don't find interesting. I say this, but people tell me things anyway. About the only person I ever met who had an appropriate sense of privacy was a conservative lady from Orange County with whom I spent two weeks traveling around Sicily, as members of the same tourist group. Trying to make conversation with her on one of our endless lunches, I inquired dutifully, "When did you meet your husband?" She snapped back, "Nosy parker! I'm not going to tell you that." In my then-state, in the wake of the memoir's publication, wounded by the wounds I felt I'd inflicted, I was delighted by her snippy reply. If everyone were as careful about what they revealed, I wouldn't have been in the mess I was. Everyone imagines their utterances in the framework of their own purposes and feels betrayed when other people use them for their purposes.

The fact is, I wrote the book I wanted to write. Candor was its reason for being. If I couldn't bring myself to talk about things other people didn't talk about, what was the point? I didn't see myself as having been harsh on anyone or even indiscreet, since I was more aware of what I refrained from saying than what I said. There were many secrets I didn't reveal, many confidences I didn't breach, many harsh judgments I did not offer. And, of course, no one would read the book anyway.

I am suspicious of using the word courage to describe acts any less physical and literally dangerous than armed combat or plunging into freezing water to save somebody's life. If writers didn't routinely have the courage to transgress and offend as they wrote, there would be little worth reading. Writers' responsibilities — so very different from those of psychiatrists or lawyers — are not to known, specific clients but to an audience which, if they're lucky, they can't even imagine and which they may actively try to convince themselves doesn't exist. Still, by the end of my experience with memoir, I began to believe that fiction, after all, was a higher form than nonfiction. Some humiliations should only befall fictional characters. Some truths about human nature should be detached from living, particular people and portrayed only in novels.

I have a history of forswearing activities in which I have just engaged. I used to be a biographer. I found the experience of writing biography so exploitative that I swore it off. I turned to memoir. Now I find memoir tainted.

I write in successive genres that I then see essential moral flaws with. I suffer guilt. I suffer, sometimes, depression. Always after the book is published. But I have written the book. So it occurs to me that the guilt and the depression are perhaps the price I make myself pay for allowing myself to so happily transgress, just as anxiety and stage fright are a price I may make myself pay for my pleasure at being in the limelight. And although I should now be even more sensitive to privacy issues than I was, in writing this I continue to invade people's privacy and co-opt their self-representation, revealing yet more about reactions of my oldest friend, my sister, my colleague, and my brother-in-law, among others. I can only suppose the old urges are still with me, and in my heart of hearts I still believe that candor is its own justification and that to know all is to forgive all.

"Had it been my purpose to win the world's favor," Montaigne said, "I would have put on better clothes. But I wanted to appear in simple, natural, and everyday dress, so my imperfections might be read to the life, and my natural form revealed as much as respect for the public allows. Had my lot been cast among those people who live under the liberty of nature's laws, I would gladly have presented myself naked."

You learn from publishing a memoir that the more you reveal of yourself the more the people who like you will like you and the more the people who hate you will hate you. The nicest part of publishing this book was to hear from old friends who said that reading it was like having a long letter from me after not hearing from me for years. But for people who dislike me—yes, yes, there are some—the book provided much material. For their sake, I will end with a story and a punch line. Years ago I went to a hairdresser who took one look at my damaged hair and couldn't bear to be associated with me in any way. I left his salon in tears and later wrote about the experience in an essay. I reported how other people said I should have responded to the humiliation, including one riposte, suggested by a playwright, whose words could be my motto—"If you think this is bad, you should see the rest of me."

The Ethics of Betrayal
Diary of a Conundrum
NANCY K. MILLER

✳ ✳

JULY 14, 2002

On the threshold of her autobiography, George Sand complained about Rousseau: "Who can forgive him for having confessed Mme de Warens while confessing himself?" It was hard for Sand to blame Rousseau because she was otherwise a huge fan of his *Confessions*. But as every autobiographer knows, you can't tell your own story, especially your love life, as though it were a solo event. George Sand, of course, did her own share of confessing others, which was something of a tradition among nineteenth-century French novelists. Not that she saw her autobiography as a novel. Just the opposite in fact. Which was her point about the ethics involved. Autobiography is a form that comes with responsibilities; just as our lives exist in human solidarity, all of us inextricably "bound up with one another," so too, Sand believed, does the genre (I, 13).

JULY 20, 2002

The end of Mme, de Warens's story, which details her lovers and her "unlimited extravagance" (198), coincides with the end of the first six books, as Rousseau brings the curtain down on his revelations with an uncharacteristic salute to future discretion:

> Such were the errors and faults of my youth. I have related the story of them with a fidelity that brings pleasure to my heart. If, in later years, I have amassed any virtues to grace my maturity, I should have declared them with equal frankness, for such was my purpose. But I must stop here. Time may lift many veils; and if my memory descends to posterity perhaps one day it will learn what there was in me to say. Then it will be understood why I am silent. (257)

More typically, Rousseau, the bad boy precursor whom French women writers ambivalently shun and admire, sets no limits on revelation: "I have only one thing to fear in this enterprise; not that I may say too much or tell untruths, but that I may not tell everything and may conceal the truth" (170).

But even with tell-all Rousseau, there is telling and telling. Not to say *enough* may betray as much as telling too much.

AUGUST 10, 2002

Philippe Lejeune has somewhere made the claim that all theorists of autobiography are closet, or at least crypto-, autobiographers. In this he generalizes from himself (a familiar autobiographical principle: me too!). Explaining his obsession with autobiography in his witty essay, "The Autobiographical Pact (bis)," Lejeune declares: "The aberrant form that my idolatry has assumed is the desire to write. I chose to work, academically, *on* autobiography, because in a parallel direction I wanted to work *on* my own autobiography" (132). Although I can't quite say that like Lejeune I knew that in working academically *on* autobiography I knew that I wanted to work on my *own* autobiography, it's certainly true that the more I worked on autobiography as a critic, the more I was tempted to write one. But I could only go there step by step (like the heroine of an eighteenth-century novel about to lose her virtue), never fully realizing where I was going. In hints. In jokes. In fragments. In the margins of criticism.

AUGUST 24, 2002

Like George Sand, Simone de Beauvoir marked off her difference from Rousseau's confessional model when she undertook her vast autobiographical project. In the preface to *The Prime of Life*, the second volume of her memoirs, for instance, Beauvoir confronts both the inevitability of telling other people's stories in sorting out the meaning of a life and her personal resistance to telling certain ones.

> It may be objected that such an inquiry concerns no one but myself. Not so; if any individual—a Pepys or a Rousseau, an exceptional or a run-of-the-mill character—reveals himself honestly, everyone, more or less, becomes involved. It is impossible for him to shed light on his own life without at some point illuminating the lives of others . . . .
>
> I described my childhood and my adolescence without any omissions . . . I cannot treat the years of my maturity in the same detached way—nor do I enjoy a similar freedom when discussing them. I have no intention of filling these pages with spiteful gossip about myself and my friends; I lack the instincts of a scandal monger. There are many things which I firmly intend to leave in obscurity. (10)

Until well into the second half of the twentieth century, French women writers continued to demonstrate a Beauvoir-like reticence about going public with their private lives—and for the most part blurred the boundaries between autobiography and fiction. That discretion was shattered by Catherine Millet's highly publicized erotic confession *The Sexual Life of Catherine M.*[1] But why should we assume that the truth of sex — it if *is* the truth — might not — if it's even the truth — might not still leave "many things . . . in obscurity" (could the initial M. not signal an eighteenth-century veil of decency)?

SEPTEMBER 2, 2002

As a theorist of autobiography, I was always kind of a literalist. Naive, even. I took the "autobiographical pact" seriously, to the letter.[2] I believed that autobiographers could and should reach unequivocally for the verifiable truth that corresponded to the events they signed their names to; that strategies of fictionalization were antithetical to autobiography. When I began my memoir, I still believed in telling a true story, but I also began to realize that there were gaps that could be filled in only by leaps of the imagination, not memory; and scenes that I could recreate through dialogues that were anything but verifiable. I could write down what I remembered; or I could craft a memoir. One *might* be the truth; the other, a good story. I'm not saying that these two processes are necessarily discrete. In fact, the two pulls are equally strong. When I sit down to reconstruct my past, I call on memory; but when memory fails, I let language lead. The words take me where I need to go.

SEPTEMBER 7, 2002

My memory of those years has been supported and challenged by what I have found in letters written by me to my parents during the years I was living in Paris. The letters offer me concrete evidence of the sort that Rousseau said he wanted to help make his "soul transparent to the reader's eye": it is not enough, he explains, for his "story to be truthful, it must be detailed as well" (169). Rousseau wasn't talking about documents, of course, but about memories; the details of the letters help me ground the story in the period, and make me believe in the truthfulness of my story. Often for the readers of my memoir, though, I've learned that what seems most truthful to them is what I least remember, or what I am least able to document: the dialogues.

Sometimes I think it's harder for me to be transparent to myself than to appear so to the reader.

Twenty years ago, a middle-aged French academic, who had been romantically involved with a close friend of mine, came upon a packet of letters my friend had received from me during a sabbatical abroad and appropriated them to construct an ending for a thinly disguised autobiographical novel he had written about their relationship and its demise. Hijacking my letters without, of course, acknowledging the theft to the reader was how the wounded author chose to document the woman's change of heart toward him; it was as if the letters proved that the narrator was justified in taking revenge in print against someone he once loved in life.

The violation of my privacy was not without effect on my life outside the text; the stain of revelation spread, embarrassing, in particular, to the man I was soon to marry. While I *might* one day have told him about aspects of my secret history chronicled in the correspondence, his discovering them in print during the early days of a new relationship, in a book friends and colleagues were bound to read, was a rather different matter. I view the appropriation of my letters as unforgivable an act today as I did then, but now that I myself am writing a memoir about a love story gone wrong—my first marriage—I better understand (while still regretting) a writer's temptation to put the material before the person, as though the letter were no more than words on paper (a mistake well understood by eighteenth-century novelists, and belatedly by their characters), as though the words no longer carried, were no longer attached to, the sender's emotions.

In addition to my letters home, I have in my possession letters written by my ex-husband to me, and also, as I've said, to my parents, who are now dead. I can't help feeling that the letters are mine, that they belong to me, to *my* family, and most of all, to my *story*. I want to tell the story as I remember the story, fully aware that I might be getting some of the details wrong. But if this is how I remember it, and it feels like my truth, then shouldn't I have the right to put it out there? Yes, but.

When as writers we expose other people, for whom are these revelations really intended? How do we justify them? Does it matter whether the person is an unknown, as in the case of my ex-husband, or a celebrity, or someone like me, known within a small but distinct circle. What, moreover, is the nature of harm in the context of a story motivated by disappointed love or sexual betrayal? Beyond the excuse of Art (I need it for my story), or Truth (it's what really happened), on what grounds is it possible to argue that readers can be served, not soiled, by the expansion of the domain subjected to the glare of publicity? What is important for a given community, at a given historical moment, to know? If it is sometimes possible to justify violating the privacy of others by telling, whom can we trust to adjudicate these acts of exposure? How can we tell whether to trust the teller?

SEPTEMBER 16, 2002

Couldn't you have sued, you ask? Yes. But beyond the expense, someone in my case would have had to "publicly identify herself as the author of the letters," as Philippe Lejeune points out in a general discussion of juridical privacy and autobiography, and thus "complete with her own hands," as he puts it, "the author's crime" (*Pour l'autobiographie*, 73).

Perhaps betrayal is contagious; I cannot name my own betrayal without producing another.

SEPTEMBER 20, 2002

All betrayals are not sexual, of course. Several years ago when I was doing readings from my book *Bequest and Betrayal*, a book that dealt with the death of parents—my own and that of others as described in memoirs (Philip Roth's *Patrimony* is probably the best known example)—someone in the audience asked me about the meaning of the word betrayal for me. While the question was being asked, I was thinking about how I had betrayed my parents by telling family secrets. But that was obvious. The question was much smarter and more insidious. Did I think that by betraying my parents, I was telling the truth? Was *betrayal* the truth? I had worked on this book for several years and never once asked myself that question. As I continue with various projects of life writing, I find myself tripping over the assumption I had unconsciously made that my truthfulness *required* betrayal. This is almost the autobiographer's credo: better to push the envelope, bring the dark into light, than to conceal. The ethics, if you like, of betrayal. "'You must not tell anyone,' my mother said, 'what I am about to tell you'": this is the first line of Maxine Hong Kingston's *The Woman Warrior: Memoirs of a Girlhood among Ghosts* (3), whose narrative flows directly from the refusal to obey that injunction. My questioner was making me wonder whether *not* telling (not telling the truth—the *whole* truth) would make for stronger ethics. What would *Patrimony* be without the scene of Roth cleaning up his father's shit (which is at the heart of "patrimony")? "Don't tell Claire," Roth senior begs, referring to his son's wife. "Nobody," Philip promises, as he details the mortification, making the scene of his father's disgrace the centerpiece of his memoir (173). Roth—as author—includes the acknowledgment of his betrayal at the end of the memoir through a dream that stands as a metaphor for his self-consciousness about his acts as a writer. He dreams he has dressed his father "for eternity in the wrong clothes" (237). Roth recognizes that in his dreams, he would forever be his father's "little son"—subject to his father's judgment; just as Kingston's memoir is marked by her debt to her mother's stories. Kingston may have become a writer, she is still her mother's daughter—and judged by her. The mother's gift for "talk-story" is her bequest to her daughter, a girl whose name in English sounds like "Ink" in Chinese (131). We autobiographers hate giving up on the really good material. *The Woman Warrior* and *Patrimony* would be much less exciting literary texts if their authors had obeyed their parents and kept silent.

SEPTEMBER 22, 2002

Whose story is it? However uncomfortable, the truth of human relations resides in the fact of relationship—and to say relation is to say relative.[3] Add memory to the mix and we can begin to see how delicate our notions about describing a relationship have to be. Any form of life writing must weigh the mix of competing interests. (The publication of my letters without permission tipped the scale of ethical standards, I think.) If, moreover, every account of the self includes relations with others, how can an autobiographer tell a story without betraying the other, without violating the other's privacy, without exposing (Sand's problem with Rousseau), without doing harm, but nonetheless telling the story *from one's own perspective*, which by virtue of being a published text exerts a certain power. You—the person whose life is being written about—enter willy-nilly into the public domain. Faithfully recorded or maliciously distorted, your story circulates, utterly outside your control. Can such publication ever be fair? Can ethics share the side of power? Can we imagine—would we want to—an ethics of betrayal? An ethical betrayal?

I don't know, even less because I find myself grappling with these questions now as a memoir writer.

My Dangerous Relations. As the working title of my memoir suggests, I'm looking back at my life through the literary legacy of eighteenth-century France, not with Roussseau's confessions but with Laclos's epistolary novel. Something about seizing the world through letters imprinted upon me at a vulnerable moment in my intellectual development—sex, letters, and a rage for freedom combined to thoroughly confuse and excite me. I went to Paris at age twenty after graduating from college. Away from home for the first time, and entranced by *nouvelle vague* movies, I tried to live what I took to be a life of total sophistication. Roger Vadim made a movie, *Les Liaisons dangereuses* (1960) from Laclos's novel. The movie wasn't very good and the complications of its erotic plots spelled doom for everyone (it did in the novel, too, of course), but I found it hard to resist the pull of the glamour, updated for what was not yet *les sixties*. I wanted—but what did I want?—to leave my nice New York Jewish girl self behind and become . . . Jeanne Moreau (no less). Failing my reincarnation as a French movie star—or even an American one like Jean Seberg (in *Breathless*—Godard's heroine represented another kind of unattainable ideal), I went to graduate school, studied French literature, wrote a Master's essay on *Les Liaisons dangereuses*, taught English, ate cheap food in bad restaurants, had adventures, and got married.

I was a fifties girl living on the cusp of the sixties and badly in need of a feminism that had yet to be invented—an analysis, or more simply a story that would help me make sense of my life.

The memoir deals with my brief marriage to a much older man I'm calling Patrick. Our second wedding anniversary was approaching. In my letters home, I had been telling my parents how happy I was, how I had made the right decision in choosing Patrick; Patrick wrote too.

Suddenly, in March, after raving endlessly about how wonderful everything in my life now is, I mention, as if in passing, that I've decided to spend Easter break in New York. My letter explains nothing: "I need a change of scene," I announce. All plans are off, including the notion that Patrick and I would spend part of the summer with my parents ("Go to the Orient," I say, "Don't count on us, I'm not sure how much money we have."). My letter explains nothing. In his letter, Patrick fleshes out the picture. He complains about the carpenter and the pace of renovations on the new apartment, offers details about the book I'm translating for a Sorbonne professor (in his view, a waste of time), reports on a scheme recording classical music he wanted my father to invest in, comments on the generosity of my aunt's birthday check to me, on Peter Gay's winning the National Book Award, requests copies of The Saturday Review *and* Business Week, *informs my father of my weight (in kilos), my health, fine, except for my being "nervous" (especially when I'm driving), and finally the "good news": that I'm planning a trip home. Writing separately to my mother and father, my husband offers a diagnosis of my condition. He tells my father (paternally) that I'm having a* crise. *I need someone to confide in, Patrick thinks. I need days of sleeping until noon, rest. I've developed a cleanliness mania, he writes, taking showers all*

the time, in draughty conditions, and now I have a cough aggravated by my obses-
sive smoking. Parisian grisaille *is getting me down; we should have taken a winter*
holiday in the snow, as the French say, but money wasn't available. Maybe I need a
vacation from him.

Uxorious is the word I want. Excessive fondness for a wife.

Even with the distance of time, I feel ventriloquized. My husband is telling my
story in my place. Three letters written on our second anniversary (Patrick asks to
borrow $100 from my father to give me an anniversary present). What happened
between us that's left out of these letters—his and mine?

I remember thinking back to this moment in my life when I read Sylvia Plath's
letters to her mother in Letters Home—*that sense of how what appears to happen*
suddenly always turns out to have been building insidiously. Aurelia Plath describes
a conversation she had with her daughter Sylvia when visiting her in England: "I
have everything in life I've ever wanted," she declared in the fifties discourse of ap-
propriate femininity we both adopted; "A wonderful husband, two adorable chil-
dren, a lovely home, and my writing" (458). But to help the readers of the diary,
Aurelia Plath fills in editorially the missing information that all was not well in the
marriage. Ted was involved with another woman. On August 27, 1962, less than
a month after her mother returned home, Sylvia wrote: "I hope you will not be too
surprised or shocked when I say I am going to try and get a legal separation from
Ted. . . . I simply cannot go on living the degraded and agonized life I have been living"
(460). The readers of Letters Home *were even more surprised since the letters had*
given no hint of the strains in the marriage. How do you "have" everything you want
and at the same time find the life you lead unendurable, degraded? Aurelia asks the
reader to recognize that Sylvia was only telling one side of a complicated situation
(459). Two sides always exist. That's the definition of marriage. What matters is that
corrosive contradiction between having and being.

What do I want? Don't I have what I want? I wanted to stay in Paris. I'm there.
I wanted to get married. I'm married. I wanted to teach. I'm a teacher. So what is
the problem? Suddenly, nothing adds up. Could this marriage have been saved? Did
I want to save it? Patrick said he did.

Reading these letters some thirty-five years later, I confess to being surprised, oc-
casionally touched, by Patrick's recognition that he might have played a role in my
crise—an acknowledgment entirely missing from our conversations as I remem-
ber them. He even imagines in these letters the need for his greater self-knowledge
and possible change. But toward the end, the blame shifts. With a touch of irony,
Patrick reminds my mother of a conversation they had in Paris, walking from the
Hôtel d'Angleterre on the rue de Rennes toward our apartment after we were just

married: "She's your problem now," my mother said to him with a cynical laugh. He thought he had solved the problem, he sighs, reaching for complicity; now he sees how abysmally he has failed. He spirals into a litany of abjection—citing his ignorance, rigidity, self-delusion. Still, whatever his faults, whatever difficulties inherent in the situation—life in France, distance from friends and family, financial constraints—somehow I am the problem.

In a way, I still seem to be the problem—this time, to me the autobiographer. I remember the scenes I describe, the affair, my despair, the trip to New York. What I have trouble understanding—and then writing about—is in a way the same thing that bewildered Patrick. How did this happen? What's in my memory that's not in his letters? As a writer, I need to figure out what must have happened. I need to create a narrative that works on its own terms. That means representing Patrick according to the demands of my story as I reconstruct it. I want to be fair to him in my memoir, yet I doubt very much that I'll make him happy when I describe our relationship. I confess that I fear the reaction of this man (with whom I've had no contact since the breakup, though I've seen his wife, who was a friend, and I occasionally have news of him through her or a mutual acquaintance). He is not a public figure about whom American law allows just about anything to be said. I've changed his name, of course, but some people—including himself—are bound to recognize him however much I disguise his traits. Patrick is in the position that I was in when my letters were stolen and I was fictionalized as the entirely recognizable object of a narrative of another's self-justification, which is the essence of all autobiographical writing.

OCTOBER 1, 2002

At the suggestion of a friend who has dealt at length with problems of legal privacy, I decided to reproduce a letter—experimentally—to see what the effect would be of using the actual letters, as opposed to paraphrasing them as I have done here.[4] I discovered that I had to fight interjecting snide comments as I typed Patrick's letter. He *sounds* so understanding and self-critical but let's not forget that in a world before the term existed, there was nothing he couldn't spin in his favor. Besides, he is constructing a self-portrait designed to please my parents: the sympathetic husband. And of course, the letters are much too long to be included in the memoir. It's not the eighteenth century; I'm not writing an epistolary novel. The letters would have to be excerpted or else broken up with commentary, as I do with my own letters to my parents and their letters to me and to Patrick. Once you cut into a letter, though, you necessarily distort its integrity, change its effect on the reader—to whom it was not destined in the first place (that distortion ranks above all the others).

Paradoxically, were I to flout the rule of intellectual copyright, I would betray the letter writer less rather than more. The bewildered husband sounds quite appealing in his own words minus the edge of caricature that I create in my paraphrase; even I feel that. So perhaps there really is such a thing as an ethical betrayal—publish the letters and let the man speak for himself.[5]

But setting aside the legal privacy conundrum, I face another, more intractable, problem. As I confessed a while back, I am no longer entirely sure about what happened thirty-five years ago. What caused the collapse of everything I had been building toward and indeed believed in—constructing a life in France with a man I thought I was in love with—I still don't know. Isn't that in part why I've written the memoir: to find out? So I ask myself the harder question: what is the truth in the name of which I choose to betray another person by revealing intimate details about his life? For me as a writer, the answer to the question of what "really" happened is literary—or at least textual. I will know only when I write it. When I write it, the truth will lie in the writing. But the writing may not be the truth—it may only look like it. To me.

NOVEMBER 13, 2002

It is not my wish to do harm, but I am forced to acknowledge that I may well cause pain—or embarrassment to others—if I also believe, as I do, in my right to tell my story. I can engage to make the memoir as honest as I can (respecting, as I started out to do, the autobiographical pact); but by the rules—or rather, the realities, of the genre, I can't promise not to impinge upon the lives of others in the process. This problem of boundaries extends even to this exercise in life writing, which contains analogous ethical constraints. I can't in fact write freely about writing the memoir. Sometimes, I have the uncomfortable feeling that the truest ethical position is closely related to silence, to self-silencing.

JANUARY 4, 2003

Among the many questions that I've left hanging, there's one—from October 1—I would like to grapple with again. "What is the truth in the name of which I choose to betray another person by revealing intimate details about his life?" More modestly, how do I justify telling the story of my marriage, and what do the letters have to do with it? It would be easier to deal with my question if I stopped using the words betrayal and truth, as though I (or any of us) knew what either of them really meant in any absolute way. Telling my story truthfully does not necessarily constitute a betrayal of the people who shared in it, even if in the telling I illuminate some of the darker moments from my point of view. Scenes from a marriage are always just that: scenes.

The letters from my ex-husband, I've come to feel, are just a shorthand for my difficulty as a writer, as a critic of autobiography turning memoirist with her head filled with theories of autobiography; and as a woman who has inherited the legacy of women writers reluctant to go public with certain stories. True, the actual language of the letters home is a temptation, but I can paraphrase or invent, if need be, now that I understand the law. The issue, finally, is not whether I should quote from the letters, but whether I have a story worth telling—and for whom. Who decides, author or reader?

JANUARY 5, 2003

Looking back at the coming of age story that I'm trying to transform into a memoir, I wish it were a better—nobler—tale. I wish that my younger self had been less lost, more self-reflective; I wish she had aimed higher than the seductions of a Françoise Sagan novel; that she wanted to be a writer and not merely a heroine. If only she had had an idea of someone to become.

In their introduction to *The Feminist Memoir Project*, the editors comment on the work of memoir in accounting for the recent feminist past, in the value of memoir as a gesture toward "making an honest and ethical attempt to restore a sense of history's specifics." Their view of what any one memoir can do, however, is neither nostalgic nor naive: "There will always be unbridgeable space between the story of the one and of the many; highlighting one memory often casts another in shadow. The past is inside us in flickering and mysterious ways that can never be fully acknowledged nor easily represented" (23). Part of what set the second wave of feminism in motion was the belief that if only our stories could be shared, our world could change. Telling those stories autobiographically required overcoming the kind of self-censorship Sand, Beauvoir, and even Colette practiced and recommended for other women writers—though it's true that they also offered in fiction clear windows onto women's and indeed their own lives.

In *My Dangerous Relations*, I am the narrator of a kind of female quest whose first movement is set in the 1960s just before the explosive effects of feminist consciousness that in the 1970s changed the stories of so many lives including my own. My emotional style then, I've come to think, was a kind of desperate unknowing as I stumbled through love affairs and their disappointments, intense hopes, and devastating betrayals; as I looked for something I could not have named. Like the heroines of so many women writers I've written about as a critic, I wanted to be happy and to live in the world. I tried to do that with Patrick and fell for (or into) the marriage plot. Unfortunately, things didn't quite work out the way I had imagined.

JANUARY 7, 2003

At a colloquium on the ethics of life writing for which I began this meditation, a participant asked (with a slight edge of disdain, or was it incredulity) why he should care about "these people"?[6] I can't say I know better now how to answer that question. If not "these people," then which people do (or should) readers of life writing care about? For some in the seminar, the sort of people readers (like writers) should care about are what have been called "vulnerable subjects," people who suffer from grave and multiple medical disabilities.[7] But ethical as well as aesthetic dilemmas arise in the telling of any narrative — not to say life — they emerge from. When we reveal our stories to others through the forms of life writing, do we not all become vulnerable subjects?

JANUARY 15, 2007

When I imagined returning to this diary, I fantasized saying more about its backstory. I relished the possibility of bringing into the open the crisis in writing that erupted when I shared an earlier version of the essay with intimates of the friend whose life had been chronicled in the novel I describe. At the time, this friend had recently died and I had imagined my essay as a kind of posthumous vindication. I believed then that by making the private wound public, I would be betraying the betrayer — outing him for his violation, puncturing his reputation. That was not how my friend's literary executor, her widower, saw the matter. He maintained, with no small anger (fulmination would be more accurate), that by reviving the old scandal (even at that point the story was twenty years past its sell-by date) I was harming my friend. Although strictly, legally, speaking he couldn't forbid me from identifying the people in my story, fleshing out the narrative, as it were, his moral indignation frightened me into silence. I capitulated to his sense of ethics and reduced my tale to a paragraph exemplary in its anonymity.

Now that I'm over the literary executor's reaction, and have the chance to return to my suppressed text, I find that I don't want to retrieve those words, name names. It's not so much that I have become virtuous, wiser as well as older with the passage of time since my friend's death; it's more that I've come to see how fatally entangled these relations are. I feel stung by George Sand's analysis of Rousseau's autobiographical flaw: I can't find a way *not* to confess my friend while confessing myself. I can't get back at the man without reinjuring the woman.

JANUARY 20, 2007

But which woman: my friend or myself? Even I can tell that I'm being too high minded, too theoretical. Looking back, I feel something more like embarrassment at the naiveté of my original project. What made me think I could accomplish anything but useless exposure? I'm reminded of that adage I've always loved about how resentment is akin to taking poison and waiting for the other person to die. Besides, what is the power of my truth against his fiction? Not much. Nothing I could say after the fact could prevent the novel from existing.

JANUARY 30, 2007

I was then in the early stages of memoir writing. I was only beginning to deal with the ethical dilemmas that memoir writers invariably confront. Five years later, as I seek to enter the literary marketplace, the problem has displaced itself. And not just because the James Frey scandal, magnified by Oprah's publicity machine, has redefined the scale of ethical violation in nonfiction. The success of his book represents the triumph of the recovery narrative as the preferred template of life writing.

FEBRUARY 1, 2007

Why should we care about "these people"? The judgment embedded in the question still rankles.

Which sort of life deserves the concern of readers? Clearly, not mine. I've only been depressed, not autistic; promiscuous, not a rape victim; the neurotic daughter of a lawyer and not the alcoholic offspring of a famous author. I've lived the wrong life for a memoir writer. Had I only been born poor or rich, and not hopelessly middle class! Readers seem to prefer the extremes, something to rise or fall from.

FEBRUARY 5, 2007
On the other hand, Hillary Clinton's presidential bid turns on her declaration that she has lived a middle-class life — which would make her like most Americans. She has also proclaimed on the campaign trail that in life there are no do-overs. The do-over might be a good definition of life writing.

Perhaps for that very reason, like many autobiographers, I can't stop trying, trying to make a better story of the past. I've become a serial autobiographer.[8] I'm back at work now on my generational fifties nice girl's story, but this time I'm also reaching back into the history of my ancestors, Eastern European immigrants, whose dream it was to become middle-class Americans. The desire to tell it is the siren song that lures me along on the ocean of memory.

MARCH 1, 2007
But is it only a story? And have I told it all?

Last week I received a letter from Nathalie, as I call her in the memoir, a friend who married my ex-husband after I left Paris (long story), telling me that Patrick had died a few months earlier, at age seventy-seven. She had just found my address. The letter from Paris arrived in New York on my birthday.

The last year of his life, she wrote, was long and difficult, but his last weeks were calm and without suffering. She did not say what Patrick — whom I haven't seen for almost forty years — had died of. But she included a recent photograph and the poem, printed on a card bordered in black, that was read by a friend at his funeral, W. B. Yeats's "The Lake Isle of Innisfree." I could not read past the first line, "I will arise and go now, and go to Innisfree," without choking with grief for the man who, like the poet, never stopped mourning the loss of an Ireland that never would be truly his. I recognized instantly in my throat that Yeats's wish to "live alone in the bee-loud glade" was Patrick's longing for a country he had never possessed, and that made the Paris he loved a poor substitute for a native land, though better than exile in America, where he had been born.

In the photograph taken at an outdoor café, Patrick — of course I now desperately want to call him by his name — is wearing a white shirt and tie, as he always did, and a black raincoat. He is heavy, heavier still than when I knew him, and his beard and hair are white. There is just a trace of reddish color in his eyebrows, the remains of his younger palette. His left hand holds the glasses he was always too vain to wear in photographs (I can see the mark of the nose pads), and his right, the silver handle of a dark-wood walking stick.

Do I know this man? Can you know someone you haven't seen in—in practically a lifetime? The pain in his eyes tells me yes, I do. Sitting in my kitchen in Manhattan, as I stare at the photograph, it strikes me that I have never gotten over the dream we shared at the beginning of our relationship: of being together the person we never were meant to be separately.

After a while, you believe the story you tell about your life. True story, the author says on the book jacket. But before it was a story, it was also real. So it really happened, I said to myself. The letter from my ex-husband's wife—is that a genre?—from my old friend proves that. She apologizes for sharing her thoughts and memories, but invites me to visit her when I come to Paris next. I know the address.

NOTES

1. When asked about her relationship to the libertine model in a *New York Times* interview, Millet took her distance from Laclos's novel: "I'm not like the characters in Laclos's *Dangerous Liaisons*, who risk hurting people to give free reign to their instincts" (June 22, 2002; E, 1). The paperback edition displayed in Paris on a bookstore table with the author full frontally naked on the cover would have made Rousseau blush. The trend toward the explicit representation of sexuality in the first person by French women writers dates from Marguerite Duras's *L'Amant* in 1984 and Annie Ernaux's *Passion Simple* in 1991.

2. Philippe Lejeune, "The Autobiographical Pact," *On Autobiography*.

3. On the interrelated questions of harm, ethics, boundaries of the self, and life writing, see Paul John Eakin's *How Our Lives Become Stories*.

4. Deborah Nelson. See her *Pursuing Privacy in Cold War America*.

5. In the United States, the letter writer (or her estate) retains the right to the *contents* of her own letter, even if the letter is in someone else's possession (this is true in France as well). If *mine*—in my possession—Patrick's letters are nonetheless not mine to quote—without permission (which I'm loathe to ask for—and which I'm certain would not be granted). What to do? Eakin pointed me (without recommending that I follow it) to the example of Melanie Thernstrom's *The Dead Girl*, the true story of the author's relationship with a friend who was murdered. Faced with the refusal of the dead girl's parents to allow her to reproduce the actual letters, Thernstrom ended up

composing imaginary letters, acknowledging her creation in a postscript to the book. If I were to make up Patrick's letters, would I be able to resist making him (even more) unsympathetic in order to justify my side of the story—to make my suffering plausible to the reader, to bind the reader to my side?

6. Indiana University, October 2002, organized by Paul John Eakin and David Smith.

7. The expression belongs to G. Thomas Couser.

8. I owe this term to Leigh Gilmore's *The Limits of Autobiography*.

WORKS CITED

Beauvoir, Simone de. *The Prime of Life*. Trans. Peter Green. New York: Paragon House, 1992.

Camhi, Leslie. "Sex Obsession By the Numbers." *New York Times* 22 June 2002: E 1, 9.

Couser, G. Thomas. *Vulnerable Subjects: Ethics and Life Writing*. Ithaca: Cornell University Press, 2004.

Du Plessis, Rachel Blau, and Ann Snitow, eds. *The Feminist Memoir Project*. New York: Three Rivers Press, 1998.

Eakin, Paul John. *How Our Lives Become Stories: Making Selves*. Ithaca and London: Cornell University Press, 1999.

Gilman, Charlotte Perkins. *The Yellow Wallpaper and Other Writings*. Rpt. New York: Bantam Books, 1989.

Gilmore, Leigh. *The Limits of Autobiography: Trauma and Testimony*. Ithaca: Cornell University Press, 2001.

Kingston, Maxine Hong. *The Woman Warrior: Memoirs of a Girlhood among Ghosts*. New York: Vintage, 1976.

Lejeune, Philippe. *On Autobiography*. Trans. Katherine Leary. Ed. Paul John Eakin. Minneapolis: University of Minnesota Press, 1989.

———. *Pour l'autobiographie*. Paris: Le Seuil, 1998.

Miller, Nancy K. *Bequest and Betrayal: Memoirs of a Parent's Death*. Oxford University Press, 1996; Rpt. paperback, Bloomington: Indiana University Press, 2000.

———. *My Dangerous Relations: Paris in the 1960s*. Ms.

———. *Subject to Change: Reading Feminist Writing*. New York: Columbia University Press, 1988.

Millet, Catherine. *The Sexual Life of Catherine M.* Trans. Adriana Hunter. New York: Grove Press, 2002.

Nelson, Deborah. *Pursuing Privacy in Cold War America*. New York: Columbia University Press, 2002.

Plath, Aurelia, ed. *Letters Home: By Sylvia Plath, Correspondence 1950 – 63*. Rpt. New York: HarperPerennial, 1992.

Roth, Philip. *Patrimony: A True Story*. New York: Simon and Schuster, 1991.

Rousseau, Jean-Jacques. *Les Confessions*. Trans. J. M. Cohen. Harmondsworth: Penguin, 1953.

Sand, George. *Histoire de ma vie*. In *Oeuvres autobiographiques*. 2 vols. Paris: Gallimard, 1970.

Thernstrom, Melanie. *The Dead Girl*. New York: Simon and Schuster, 1990.

Gowers' Memory

OLIVER SACKS

✳ ✳

In his delightful biography[1] of Sir William R. Gowers, Macdonald Critchley compares him to a naturalist (Gowers indeed wrote a small monograph on mosses):

> Gowers brought to the bedside all his skill as a natural historian. To him the neurological sick were like the flora of a tropical jungle, and his keen eye and collector's flair enabled him to identify, and classify. . . . To his botanist's bent he added the virtues of diligence and orderliness, probably to an obsessional degree.

And, of course, an extraordinary memory, as is obvious to anyone who reads his great *Manual*.[2] But exceptional though this was, Gowers felt it important, even crucial, to supplement it with extremely full (indeed verbatim) note-taking—and to this end devised a shorthand system that would enable him to write three times as much as one could in longhand, to record the actual words of his patients, the minutest details of their experiences, as well as all his own observations. The very act of writing, Gowers felt, reinforced memory, impressed things on the mind. Thus supplemented, he thought, memory should be nearly infallible—as infallible as the records of photography and phonography. He was enthusiastic to the point of evangelism about the use of shorthand (which, confusingly, he called phonography).[3] In this way, he felt, he could transcend some of the deficiencies of perception and memory.

Models comparing the operations of memory to those of mechanical recording go back to antiquity—the brain was conceived as receiving impressions like soft wax, then hardening like adamantine to hold them permanently— and were particularly popular in the late nineteenth century, when they may have drawn some of their force from the spectacular development of photography and phonography at the time. Thus it is not surprising that Gowers, when he came to write his *Manual*, accepted such ideas, and sought to see them in anatomic and physiologic terms. Memory, for Gowers, resided in structural changes in the brain, and he describes learning in almost Hebbian terms:

> There is a physical side to memory as to other mental processes. All functional action of nerve elements is attended by molecular changes in

them. . . . A state is left, for a time, in which the same functional action occurs more readily; there is a diminution of resistance in the combination of nerve-elements concerned, and this residual disposition is increased by repetition. This constitutes the basis of motor training. . . . A similar condition appears to constitute the physical basis of memory, properly so called. (*Manual*, Volume II, p. 99)

"Recollection," for Gowers, involved "a revival of the original activity . . . [a revival] of a past image." Such brain traces, he conceived, like photographic ones, were in their essence fixed and permanent, sitting in the brain, inertly, until "revived" by recollection. It is therefore intriguing and ironic that Gowers, who was so firm a believer in fixed memory-traces, on at least one occasion (and perhaps more) was to publish strikingly *different* versions, or recollections, of his own clinical experiences.

I came across such a disparity wholly by chance recently, when I had occasion to reread his descriptions of a most unusual complex seizure given in the 1881 edition of his *Epilepsy*[4]:

The patient was an intelligent man, twenty-six years of age, and all his attacks began in the same manner. First there was a sensation in the left hypochondriac region "like pain with a cramp"); then, this sensation continuing, a kind of lump seemed to pass up the side of the chest, with a "thump, thump," and when it reached the upper part of the chest it became a "knocking," which was heard as well as felt. The sensation rose up to the ear, and then was like the "hissing of a railway engine," and this seemed to "work over his head." Then he suddenly and invariably saw before him an old woman in a brown-stuff dress, who offered him something which had the smell of Tonquin beans. The old woman then disappeared, and two great lights came before him — round lights, side by side, which got nearer and nearer with a jerking motion. When the lights appeared the hissing noise ceased, and he felt a sensation in the throat, and lost consciousness in the fit, which, from the description, was undoubtedly epileptic. He also had attacks of petit mal, which consisted of a vision of a dull-red ball to the right, in the lower part of the field.

The unusualness, the richness, the exotic flavor of this seizure caused it to stick in his mind, and twenty-three years later (in his 1904 *Subjective Sensations of Sight and of Sound*[5]) he retells the story of the Tonquin seizure:

One strangely complex aura, which preceded every fit the patient had, deserves mention. It began in a simple form. First the beating of the heart was felt, and this ascended the chest to the head, where it seemed to become audible as a sound; then two lights appeared before the eyes and seemed to approach by jerks, synchronous with the pulsation. The lights then disappeared, and were replaced by the figure of an old woman in a red cloak, who offered something that had the smell of Tonquin beans; then consciousness was lost.

But now, we see, various differences have appeared. Some of these differences are trifling, but one is fundamental: the vision of the old woman, in the 1881 account, *precedes* the jerking lights, whereas, in the 1904 account, it *follows* them. Indeed Gowers emphasized this in his two accounts — commenting (in 1881) that "a visual sensation of very high specialization — a visual idea . . . gives place to a much less elaborate sensation"; but (in 1904) "the interesting fact that the more elaborate sensation, the vision of the woman, *followed* the more simple one, the two lights" (his italics). Moreover, where the beating sounds precede the jerking lights in the 1881 description, the two have become "synchronous" by 1904.

What are we to make of this striking difference between these accounts?

First, it is incompatible with the notion of fixed memory traces in the brain — if recollection consisted merely of the reactivation of these, it would be more reliable, it would not "slip" in this categorical way. But Gowers's memory *did* alter in the course of a quarter-century. His later memory, clearly, is not a reproduction; it has been transformed — it is, manifestly, a *reconstruction*. And, one must add, an unconscious reconstruction — there is no evidence that Gowers himself was aware of the change.

This indeed is what happens when remembering stories — they get changed, for better or worse, with each repetition. It was experiments with such serial storytelling, and with the remembering of pictures, that convinced F. C. Bartlett, in the 1920s and 1930s, that there is no such entity as "memory," but only the dynamic process of "remembering" (he is always at pains, in his great book *Remembering*, to avoid the noun and use the verb). He writes[6]:

Remembering is not the re-excitation of innumerable fixed, lifeless and fragmentary traces. It is an imaginative reconstruction, or construction, built out of the relation of our attitude towards a whole active mass of organized past reactions or experience. . . . It is thus hardly ever really exact . . . and it is not at all important that it should be so.

This sort of imaginative construction, or reconstruction, determined in part by attitude, forces us to think of remembering in terms very different from those of fixed traces and their revival. It forces us, instead, to think of remembering as inherently dynamic, and as determined by the individual's attitudes or "values" at the time. (This view of remembering now finds the strongest support in Gerald Edelman's neuroscientific work,[7] his demonstration of the brain as a ubiquitously active system where a constant shifting is in process, and everything is continually recategorized and updated.)

Gowers, one fancies, would have been fascinated by this later work—he died relatively young, sadly, just at the time when Sherrington and Head were revolutionizing neurology—but might have taken umbrage at Bartlett's saying that it was not important for remembering to be really exact. Certainly, in the case of the Tonquin seizure, while it was of no importance whether the old woman was wearing a cloak or dress, or whether it was red or brown, it was extremely important to know whether she appeared before or after the two lights. And it is precisely here that two descriptions, two recollections, are in contradiction. Which of the two accounts, one wonders, is the more accurate, the more reliable? Which is the closer to "truth" or "reality"? The 1881 story, or the story of twenty-three years later? One might at first suppose the original to be closer, especially if Gowers took shorthand notes. But this is not what we see. The second description has no loss of detail or information (as with the fading of a photograph); it is as sharp as the original—but it is *different*: different not just in detail, but in orientation, and in concept. And different, probably, *because* of orientation and concept.

But can one maintain that the first description is exempt from these influences, independent of any orientation or concept? Perceptions themselves are categorizations or constructs—there is no way of apprehending reality *except* by "constructing" it, and constructing it in accordance with one's views and values at the time. (This, indeed, must apply to the patient's own account and memories. Perhaps indeed in the confusion of his seizure, the patient himself never knew what came first—the hissing, the jerking lights, the old woman, the smell of beans.)

My own guess is that the second account is closer to the truth—partly because in the intervening years there was a change in Gowers' attitude. He was in a fierce, Jacksonian mood in 1881, intent on perceiving all pathology as "dissolution," as descent from higher to lower. He was much more unbuttoned, less dogmatic, twenty-three years later—perhaps, therefore, under less pressure to distort the truth. But more to the point, it sounds more plausible, in terms of the likelihood of seizure foci and seizure spread. I have presented the two accounts to several colleagues, and most of them, after reflection, come to the same conclusion. Orrin Devinsky (personal communication) hypothesizes three possible seizure routes: seizure spread from a primary occipital focus (this is suggested by the simple partial visual seizures also present); spread from a primary insular and mesial temporal focus (the rising epigastric sensation at the start of the seizure); or from a cortical region lying between these—all of which could lead to the symptom pattern described in 1904. It is less easy to account for the symptom pattern Gowers described originally.

What is certain is that Gowers' revision followed years of deepening experience and reflection (he was thirty-six years old when he published *Epilepsy*, and in his sixtieth year when *Subjective Sensations* came out) and that, not just here, but throughout his life and works, he revised, reconstructed, recategorized, to the end. It is this that gives his works their charm and unexpectedness, their sense of novelty and freshness, even (or especially) when he returns, as he loves to, to the observations of his early years. Such revision, such reconstruction, is of the essence in living memory, and what distinguishes it from any mechanical device.

One has to wonder how Gowers himself would have responded if someone (for example, Hughlings Jackson) had confronted him with his two discrepant versions. He would have been taken aback, for a moment, I think, then laughed—it would not have surprised him; it might indeed have released a flood of anecdotes about the continual entrance of imaginative elements into all of his own memories, and those of his patients and colleagues too. At a human level, as a clinician, Gowers knew this well and would have been more and more prepared to acknowledge it, to accept it, as he grew older. But even as a younger man writing the *Manual*, echoing his generation's notions about fixed memory traces, he indicates (in one of the most stunning of his contradictions) that a radically different idea of memory is also hovering in his mind. Thus in the very paragraph where he talks about "molecular changes" in nerve "elements," he seems to turn against all notions of memory as a thing-in-itself, and writes "there is probably no special faculty of memory, physical or psychical, apart from the general cerebral and intellectual processes."

Here, then, surrounded by sentences that contradict it, is a thought that is startling, and original, and new—indeed radical in the context of the mechanistic physiology of his time. For Gowers, if we are not misinterpreting his words, is here seeing memory as part of an ongoing and evolving inner life, and, as such, an activity that is anything but permanent and fixed, but one that will change, reorganize, reconstruct, endlessly, in the light of new experience, new needs. We see a glimmer here, a premonition, of what Edelman means, when he writes, "Perception is creation, memory recreation," and sees all remembering as recategorization. But such a thought was not to become explicit for a century.

ACKNOWLEDGMENT

I am most grateful to Dr. Macdonald Critchley and Dr. Orrin Devinsky, who were kind enough to read a first draft of this paper and make many suggestions.

NOTES

1. *Sir William Gowers, 1845–1915: A Biographical Appreciation*, London: Heinemann, 1949.

2. *A Manual of Diseases of the Nervous System*, facsimile edition, with new introductions by Nicolaas Arts, Nijmegen: Arts and Boeve, 1995.

3. In December 1894, Critchley notes, Gowers founded (and became the first president of) the Society of Medical Phonographers, and most of Gowers' writings between 1894 and 1902 were published, in shorthand, in the *Phonographic Record*, its journal (where, Critchley adds, they "have since remained concealed from the general medical public"). Foster Kennedy, one of his pupils, tells the following story:

> Gowers was once seen—and it probably happened often—to stop his coachman in crowded Southhampton Row, having fastened his eye on a likely-looking young man hurrying on his lawful occasions along the pavement. Gowers climbed out of his carriage, white beard waving, stumbled up to him—his gait was unsteady—clutched him by the arm, and glaring at him with his frightening flaming fierce blue eyes said, "Young man, do you write shorthand?" To which the shocked man answered, "No, I don't." Whereupon Gowers dropped his arm, saying bitterly, "You're a fool, and will fail in life." He then clambered abruptly back into his carriage. ("William Gowers, 1845–1915," in W. Haymaker and F. Schiller, eds., *The Founders of Neurology*, 2nd ed., New York: Thomas, 1970.)

4. *Epilepsy and Other Chronic Convulsive Diseases*, London: Churchill, 1881.

5. *Subjective Sensations of Sight and of Sound: A Biotrophy, and Other Lectures*, Philadelphia: Blakiston, 1904.

6. *Remembering: A Study of Experimental and Social Psychology*, Cambridge: Cambridge University Press, 1932.

7. *The Remember Present: A Biological Theory of Consciousness*, New York: Basic Books, 1989. There is a parallel here with the young Freud, who while writing in his *Project* about memory in much the same terms as Gowers, was also writing (to Fliess) about *Nachträglichkeit* (retranscription). Freud's concept of *Nachträglichkeit* and its relation to Edelman's notion of memory as "recategorization" have been explored by Arnold H. Modell in *Other times, Other Realities*, Cambridge, MA: Harvard University Press, 1990.

Mer-Mer

An Essay about How I Wish We Wrote Our Nonfictions

JOHN D'AGATA

✳ ✳

Alexis de Tocqueville once called America "a nation full of memorials."

He did this just fifty-five years after the country was founded, a decade before the Civil War had started, and about a hundred twenty years before the Second World War.

It was before we would build over two million individual war memorials to commemorate the nine wars America has fought.

It was before our 75,000 listings on the National Register of Historic Places, our 80,000 square miles of national park monuments, and our 107,000 square miles of cemeteries.

It was before the United States Geological Survey would estimate last year that the number of tombstones marking dead Americans' graves actually outnumbers how many of us there have been.

Before our highway dedication posts, our junior high school honor rolls, our handmade wooden roadside crosses.

Before our certificates of achievement, certificates of appreciation, certificates of participation, and best attendance plaques. Before memorial park benches, memorial park trees, memorial garden plots, memorial theater seats, memorial office buildings, memorial conference rooms, memorial college dorms, memorial scholarships.

Before all those bricks inscribed with people's names to help raise money to pave things; all those books in all those libraries with dedication placards; all those stars whose naming rights we have purchased for our lovers, pets, dead children, and selves from the Ministry of Federal Star Registration, the International Real Estate Star Corporation, and the Universal Star Market, three of more than a dozen Web-based American companies whose combined revenues over the past five years have totaled a quarter of a billion dollars for the naming rights to an estimated three million stars, even though there are only 6,000 stars visible in an average evening sky, and even though none of these companies actually has the authority to grant such naming rights, according to the International Astronomical Union, which does.

"Add up all the memorials we've got in this country," Bill Andrews, president of the American Institute of Commemorative Art, recently said, "and I would bet we already have enough commemorated objects in the United States to dedicate one of them to every American who's ever been alive, plus a couple generations worth of Americans yet to come."

And that doesn't even include our memoirs.

Indeed, according to literary scholars, we've been writing memoirs longer in this country than any other kind of literature.

By as early as 1639 there was a printing press established in the Massachusetts Bay Colony, just nineteen years after Puritans first arrived on the continent. For forty-three years the press primarily printed imported English poetry, paperback hymnals, and religious pamphlets by various Puritan clergy. But eventually, after years of urging by her reverend, a forty-four-year-old woman from Connecticut sent a one hundred page manuscript to the Massachusetts print house in 1682. It was a meditation on her capture by the Narragansett Indians during a raid on her village in 1676.

Sixteen of her village's residents were killed during the attack, including the author's father, the author's sister, and the author's six-year-old daughter. Twenty more of the village's residents were taken captive during the raid, thirteen of whom eventually were also killed.

The author, Mary Rowlandson, was marched barefoot through blizzards from her coastal village, through the craggled forests of New Hampshire, through the flagstone cliffs of the Berkshires. Eleven weeks later she was released near Princeton, Massachusetts, for a ransom valued at $13.

"Now away we must go with those barbarous creatures, with our bodies wounded and bleeding and our hearts no less than our bodies," Rowlandson writes in her book. Written throughout in the present tense, *The Narrative of the Captivity* was unsurpassed at the time for the immediacy of its tone. "Oh, the roaring and singing, the dancing and yelling of those black creatures in the night," she writes,

> which makes the place a lively resemblance of hell. And as miserable is the waste that is made here of horses, cattle, sheep and swine, calves, lambs, pigs, and fowls—some roasting, some lying, some burning and boiling to feed our merciless Enemies who are joyful, though we are disconsolate. . . . All for me is gone: my husband gone, my children gone, my relations and friends, our house and home, all our comforts, within doors and without,

are gone. Everything is gone, except for my life, although I do know not if in the next moment that it might go as well.

In *The New England Annals*, a late-seventeenth-century cultural history of the colonies, passages of Rowlandson's book are said to have been read aloud during New England church services, "causing the spells of several good ladies in a number of pews." Cotton Mather called the book "terrible . . . and necessary." And "a dramatic evocation of Satan Himself" is how the seventeenth-century essayist Matthew Byles described it.

At the time of its publication the book was considered a Puritan personal testament, providing clear evidence of God's grace for sparing Mary Rowlandson, while simultaneously proving that He insisted this New World be temperant, faithful, and utterly obedient.

At that time, in the Old World, the Netherlands was growing tulips. René Descartes was declaring, "I think, therefore I am." And thanks to other colonies that were established in northern Africa, soon there was so much sugar barreling into Europe that the Old World was tasting lemonade for the first time.

But here, in the New World, the settlers were still trying to settle into the land that they had come to over two and a half centuries earlier. Jamestown was abandoned. There was no gold in Florida. And the average life span of white colonists was a third shorter than that of Europeans. By the time that Mary Rowlandson's small book of faith was finally published, therefore, there was a ready audience among white settlers for a story of personal triumph.

Considering the impact that AIDS had on late-twentieth-century American culture — with 500,000 deaths by the late 1990s, or less than one-tenth of 1 percent of the population — or considering the impact that the Civil War had on mid-nineteenth-century American culture — with 600,000 deaths by the 1860s, or 2 percent of the population — or considering the impact that smallpox had on mid-eighteenth-century American culture — with 200,000 deaths in the 1740s, or 4 percent of the population — the estimated 30,000 Indian captivities that occurred by the end of the seventeenth century — in an estimated population of just 80,000 whites — surely were not experiences the average person was just aware of, but may have been, statistically speaking, experiences that the average person could have actually had.

Rowlandson's book was understandably then an immediate and popular success. Despite the fact that only 50 percent of the white male population was literate at the time — and 25 percent of white females — by the end of its first year in print Rowlandson's book had gone through four editions, with a fifth forthcoming in London, and an estimated 5,500 copies in print on both sides of the Atlantic. This at a time when the average number of copies in a book's standard printing was fewer than 600.

This, then, was America's first genuine best seller. In fact, according to Frank Luther Mott, a historian of American popular literature, there is not a single extant copy of the book's first edition because, as he theorizes, "they were all literally read to pieces." Rowlandson herself is said to have become so popular that upon her return from captivity the town in which she eventually settled, Wethersfield, Connecticut, voted to award her £30 annually for life. And the book's own importance was such that advertisements for the first American printing of Shakespeare's plays appear in later editions of the book's back pages.

In total, there have been fifty-two different editions of the book since the seventeenth century, and scholars now rank it among the top four best-selling titles in American publishing history.

Two others of which are Indian captivity narratives as well.

"Our American ancestors did not believe in the corrupting influence of fiction," R. W. G. Vail wrote in *Voices of the Old Frontier*, "so they limited themselves to true tales of horror in the form of deathbed confessions, stories of shipwrecks, piracy, plague, torture, raids, and the ever-present thrill of Indian captivities."

Indeed, the Newberry Library in Chicago holds over 2,000 individual titles of Indian captivity narratives. In California in the early eighteenth century, missionaries published a kind of literary annual, *The Jesuit Reader*, which lasted for fifty consecutive years and featured only stories of Indian captivities. The oldest existing book club in America, the Navy Club of Andover, Massachusetts, was founded in 1777 and, according to its charter, was initially devoted exclusively to reading Indian captivities. And even the McGuffey Readers, the Christian grammar books responsible for educating millions of American children, were still including examples of Indian captivities as models for effective prose as late as 1962.

The form in fact became so popular that the earliest short stories by Hawthorne, Poe, and Melville are said to be structured on Indian captivity narratives, and even popular contemporary stories like *The Last of the Mohicans*, *Lonesome Dove*, and *Dances with Wolves* are themselves essentially forms of Indian captivity.

As one contemporary scholar of the form has noted, "in lieu of fiction, these books set a trend-making formula for tales of true torment at that time . . .

establishing the roots of that peculiarly American proclivity for confessional narrative nonfiction."

In English, the term memoir comes directly from the French for memory, *mémoir*, a word that is derived from the Latin for the same, *memoria*. It has been so stable a word, in fact, that even Caesar's personal history of the Gallic wars was referred to as *memoriae* upon its publication.

"May his clear memories," Cicero wrote of his contemporary's book, "inform our own unknown futures."

Indeed, the presence of the moniker on a book today still suggests a document whose remembering we might learn from. Memoirs recount experiences from which one has survived, something since that has been digested, reconstituted, figured out, and now is being shared. This is an approach that renders experience not anew—as in the lyric tradition—nor observed—as in the narrative tradition—but historic—something poised stalwartly in the tradition of moral storytelling.

"What the divine leader himself has learned," wrote one of Caesar's readers two thousand years ago, "may we never cease to learn from as well."

Whether the memoirist is Mary McCarthy, Jean Rousseau, St. Augustine, or Julius Caesar, the foremost purpose in making a memoir, at least in terms of traditional interpretations of the form, is to report to readers about one's suffering and to instruct them how to overcome theirs.

However, more deeply rooted in the term memoir is something much less confident. For embedded in Latin's *memoria* is the ancient Greek *mérmeros*, an offshoot of the Avestic Persian *mermara*, itself a branch of the Indo-European root for all that we think about but cannot grasp: *mer-mer*, "to vividly worry," "to be anxious about," "to exhaustingly ponder." In the genuinely dusky light of real human memory there is an activity far less sure of itself than the effortlessly recounted stories of today's sculpted memoirs.

According to its roots, in other words, memoir is an assaying of ideas, images, and feelings. It is, in its best sense, an impulsive exploration. It is not storytelling, it is not moralizing, it is not knowing, learning, or owning. Rather, etymologically speaking, at the core of every memoir is anxiety and wonder and doubt.

"The portion of some is to have their afflictions by drops, now one drop and then another," Mary Rowlandson concludes in the narrative of her captivity, never assuming that she might understand what it was that her experience *meant*. "But the dregs of the Cup, the Wine of astonishment: like a sweeping rain that leaveth no food, did the Lord prepare to be my portion."

As America pushed farther west, however, and as conflicts with Indians became more frequent, the subsequent captivity narratives of the eighteenth and nineteenth centuries began to insist more overtly on the factual relevance of their memories, de-emphasizing the private redemptive experiences of their authors and emphasizing instead a more publicly relevant concern: Manifest Destiny. Memoir, in some regard, began to shill for national policy.

"As the first literary form American writers mastered," James Richards notes in his study of the form, *Captive Readers*, "it was also one of the earliest successful forms of American propaganda."

As Richards explains, Indian captivity narratives eventually lost the spiritual intimacy that Rowlandson brought to the form, and instead became vehicles through which the savagery of Native Americans could be exaggerated, and thus justifying the calls for their eventual annihilation.

Despite their popularity and prevalence, however, the Indian captivity narratives of the eighteenth and nineteenth centuries seldom represented the truth of an experience. Some authors in fact are thought to have deeply exaggerated the suffering they endured. Others invented crucial details in the arcs of their stories. And still others relayed the trials of captivities that never occurred. In fact, as one newspaper observed in 1797, "More captives seem to have stayed among the Indians than have chosen to return."

Indeed, according to a study by Alice Wright of the Smithsonian Institution, when Indians were raised among whites they almost always wanted to go back; when whites were raised among Indians, however, they almost always preferred to stay.

"The brutal stories found in captivity narratives, however numerous they appear," she reports, "probably represent the minority of actual Indian captivities. . . . [They] might have been the first authentic form of American literature, but they were rarely the most authenticated."

Here, then, is the foundation of American nonfiction.

Claims of authenticity in nonfiction have long been the form's selling point. In other genres, the idea of authenticity is something that has evolved since Aristotle into a concept that is called by most literary critics mimesis — °perhaps the most important notion engaging criticism today — yet in nonfiction the term mimesis is used almost exclusively to define a concern much less literary than that which concerns poetry, fiction, and drama. In nonfiction, mimesis primarily means veracity: are the facts in a text verifiable or not?

Several years ago, for example, the facts in *Fragments*, a best-selling memoir from Germany and the winner of the Prix Memoire de la Shoah in France and the National Jewish Book Award in America, became the latest to be debated in terms of their verifiability when Schocken Books, the memoir's European publisher, discovered that the book's author, Binjamin Wilkomirksi, was not a German Jewish orphan who had survived two Nazi death camps — as the author suggests he is in the book — but instead is a man from Switzerland named Bruno Doessekker, who was never an orphan, is not Jewish, and was born at the very end of the Second World War. Schocken immediately canceled plans to publish the book in America, pulling it from shelves throughout Germany, and promising to reimburse stores for any of their overstock. Deemed at one point a "masterpiece" by international reviewers, the book soon essentially vanished due to the fact that its facts, apparently, weren't.

But, as the author's supporters asked in a press release distributed at the Frankfurt Book Fair that year, "What does this have to do with the book's literary value?"

"It tells our story, the way most of us remember the experience," a representative of the Holocaust Child Survivors Group of Los Angeles told the *New York Times* in 1996. "It doesn't matter to us whether this was Doessekker's own experience or not."

For some readers, the details of the book — rats rummaging among human corpses, starving children sucking their fingers to the bone — illustrate something that "felt" real. But this activity — making something that is invented feel authentic — is one usually reserved exclusively for fiction writers. After all, what other differences can there be between nonfiction and fiction if both genres are engaged in the same imaginative enterprise, if both treat facts as images to be inspired by rather than as rules to be followed, and if both endeavor to attain a truth that is more felt than documented?

Such questions about the purpose of genre were never raised during the Bruno Doessekker case, however. The two sides of the debate — the one wanting to view the book as imaginatively true, and the one wanting to view the book as verifiably true — never seemed to be discussing the same literary issue. One, after all, is an aesthetic issue, and the other is primarily ethical. And in a genre that's popularly defined almost exclusively by its promise to *not* purvey *fiction*, the concern about ethics usually wins out. To this day, for example, the only versions of the text of *Fragments* that are still in print are embedded in three different critical examinations of the author's fabrications: *The Wilkomirski Affair: A Study in Biographical Truth*; *The Wilkomirski Case: Fragments or Figments?*; and *A Life in Pieces: The Making and Unmaking of Binjamin Wilkomirski*.

Could there be repercussions for treating nonfiction as a receptacle for only verifiable, reliable, and instructional information, rather than as a venue for literature, a vehicle for discovery, a place where experience can be had?

Recently, veracity was once again allowed to determine a nonfiction book's literary worth when essayist Vivian Gornick mentioned several years ago at a summer writing conference that some of the memories in her acclaimed memoir, *Fierce Attachments*, were imaginatively composed, but were not, as she clearly emphasized, entirely invented.

What she explained was that for the sake of propelling the narrative of her experience more effectively for the reader, she had in a couple of places conflated several incidents into more dramatically workable anecdotes.

"To state the case briefly," she said, "memoirs belong to the category of literature, not of journalism. It is a misunderstanding to read a memoir as though the writer owes the reader the same record of literal accuracy that is owed in newspaper reporting or in literary journalism. What the memoirist owes the reader is the ability to persuade that the narrator is trying, as honestly as possible, to get to the bottom of the experience at hand."

What she said was in fact not very different from what is said in any creative writing classroom.

Yet for some reason the creative writing classroom that Gornick happened to be in when she said this did not see things the same way.

I remember that summer receiving three different phone calls from people who were respectively "shocked" and "stunned" and "shocked" after hearing about Ms. Gornick's confession at the writing conference that summer.

Within ten days of the incident, an essay was commissioned by the Web site *Salon* in which a student from the writing conference detailed her peers' "disappointment" in Gornick, a writer they had previously considered "a beautiful writer," "a respected writer," "the grande dame of memoir writing," but one whom her peers seemed suddenly unable to respect at all.

And within about a month of that writing conference, a reviewer on National Public Radio's *Fresh Air* essentially cinched the public's new perception of Vivian Gornick's classic book when she claimed that Ms. Gornick's use of her imagination in *Fierce Attachments* was akin to plagiarism.

"This is nothing less than betrayal," the reviewer said.

In the intervening months, nonfiction writers around America sent letters to the editors of Web sites, newspapers, magazines, and radio shows responding to Ms. Gornick's confession of having engaged her experiences with her mother creatively—as a poet would, or as a fiction writer would, or as a playwright would be expected to—rather than "devoting herself," as one person put it, "more responsibly to the truth."

The phrase "moral contract" was used several times.

As was the word "trust."

The great majority of nonfiction writers who sent those letters to editors tended to also quote—with "disgust," "outrage," and "shock"—the same short portion of a letter that Ms. Gornick composed in response to readers' concerns that an imaginative interpretation of someone's own personal experiences had been brought into the world of nonfiction: "Memoir writing is still a genre in need of an informed readership," she wrote.

Consider, for example, what is called in the film industry the nonfiction rule: the phenomenon that seems to guarantee an Academy Award to whichever nominated actress portrays a real-life heroine in any given year. Most recently, for example, there have been the Oscar-winning roles of Reese Witherspoon in *Walk the Line*, Charlize Theron in *Monster*, Cate Blanchett in *The Aviator*, Nicole Kidman in *The Hours*, Jennifer Connelly in *A Beautiful Mind*, Marcia Gay Harden in *Pollock*, Julia Roberts in *Erin Brockovich*, Hillary Swank in *Boys Don't Cry*, Angelina Jolie in *Girl, Interrupted*, and Susan Sarandon in *Dead Man Walking*. Indeed, eight out of the last ten leading-actress Academy Awards have gone to actresses who have portrayed real women.

"It makes you wonder what the Academy is actually rewarding," a producer commented to *Variety* in 2002, "the particular performances these actresses have created, or the lives that they're portraying." More interesting to the issue of literature, however, are the ways in which such nonfiction performances are reviewed by some critics. Jennifer Connelly's performance of a woman who bravely endures a turbulent marriage to a schizophrenic Nobel Prize-winning theorist was described in the *New York Times* in 2001 as "brave." Julia Roberts's performance of a woman who inspires a small cancer-stricken town to sue its local power company was described in the *Chicago Tribune* in 2000 as "inspiring." And Hillary Swank's performance of a young woman whose sad secret life in a small Nebraska town leads to her heartbreaking rape and murder was described in the *Los Angeles Times* in 1999 as "heartbreaking" and "sad."

If one were to examine recent high-profile nonfiction book reviews like-wise, one might venture to argue similarly that the reception of nonfiction literature often focuses on the books' autobiographical facts—the illnesses, the rapes, the poverty, the depression, the heartbreak, the confessions, etc.—rather than on the strategies employed to dramatize those facts.

Dave Eggers's writing in his popular memoir about the conviction with which he raised his younger brother after the deaths of their parents, for example, was described by the *Toronto Star* in 2000 as having "gorgeous conviction." Mary Karr's writing in her popular memoir about growing up in the rough east Texas town of Leechfield among the tough-minded family and friends who raised her was described in the *Nation* in 1997 as "rough and tough." Frank McCourt's writing in his popular memoir about the searing conditions of his childhood in Limerick, Ireland, was described in the *Detroit Free Press* in 1995 as "searing." In fact, nearly every review describing memoirs like Frank McCourt's seems to insist on linking the qualities of the prose directly to the condition of the childhood, as the *Clarion Ledger* did in its review of *Angela's Ashes*—"Frank McCourt has seen hell, but he's found angels in his prose"—or as *USA Today* did—"McCourt has an astonishing gift for remembering the details of his dreary childhood"   or as the *Boston Globe* did—"A story so immediate, so gripping in its daily despairs, stolen smokes, and blessed humor, that you want to thank God that young Frankie McCourt survived so he could write it."

In some ways, this of course is insidious to all literary genres. But only nonfiction's reception seems to be limited almost exclusively to such fact-based value judgments. For example, one needn't even examine nonfiction book reviews in order to conclude that these texts are sold, read, and primarily judged based on the information that's contained in them. Instead, one needs only to consider the way in which nonfiction is packaged, and how it therefore is intended to be received. After all, when was the last time there appeared a subtitle on a Philip Roth novel? Or a Don DeLillo novel? Or a Cormac McCarthy novel?

"Reading a novel," explained a well-known fiction writer who directed a well-known writing program, "is about going on a journey of discovery with the author, and experiencing what he experiences, feeling what he does"—an explanation that suggests of course that a subtitle would therefore ruin the vicarious thrill of sharing the emotional and intellectual drama of a novel, but a distinction that also seems to suggest that none of those experiences are to be expected or are even possible in nonfiction.

No doubt this is the same reason why there has never been a subtitle on any of John Ashbery's poetry collections. Nor even on Jewel's, Paul McCartney's, former president Jimmy Carter's.

Certainly *The Waste Land: A Meditation on the Disarray of Our Contemporary Lives* does not appropriately capture the experience of journeying with that book into the limits of meaning and perception. Likewise, *The Odyssey: Finding Your Way Home through a Journey of Spiritual Growth* could not effectively summarize the experience of that book. Ditto *Beowulf: How to Survive*.

So, why then *A True Story*?

Or, *Based on a True Story*?

Inspired by Real Events?

Taken Actual History?

Based on the Letters Written to the Wives of Genuine American Heroes?

Why *An Account of Two Women and Their Historic Journey Hiking across Antarctica*?

A Memoir of One Man's Struggle to Find His Sexual Identity and the Pleasures of Forbidden Love?

And *A True History of the Captivity and Restoration of a Minister's Wife in New England, Wherein Is Set Forth the Cruel and Inhumane Usage She Underwent amongst the Heathens for Eleven Weeks' Time, Including Her Deliverance from Them, Written by Her Own Hand, for Her Own Private Use, and Now Made Public at the Earnest Desire of Some Friends for the Benefit of the Afflicted, Whereunto Is Annexed a Sermon on the Possibility of God's Forsaking a People That Have Been Near and Dear to Him, Preached by Mr. Joseph Rowlandson, Husband to the Author*?

Reality, Persona

DAVID SHIELDS

❋ ❋

Reality

1

These are the facts, my friend, and I must have faith in them.

2

What is a fact? What's a lie, for that matter? What, exactly, constitutes an essay or a story or a poem or even an experience? What happens when we can no longer freeze the shifting phantasmagoria which is our actual experience?

3

During the middle of a gig, Sonny Rollins sometimes used to wander outside and add the sound of his horn to the cacophony of passing cabs.

4

Have you ever heard a record that makes you feel as good as Stevie Wonder's *Fingertips—Part 2*? I haven't. It's so *real*. When you listen to the record, you can hear a guy in the band yelling, "What key? What key?" He's lost. But then he finds the key, and *boom*. Every time I hear that guy yelling, "What key?" I get excited.

5

Soul is the music people understand. Sure, it's basic and it's simple, but it's something else 'cause it's honest. There's no fuckin' bullshit. It sticks its neck out and says it straight from the heart. It grabs you by the balls.

6

The most essential gift for a good writer is a built-in, shock-proof shit detector.

7

Ichiro Suzuki, the first Japanese position player in the major leagues, has unusually good eyesight and hand-eye coordination and works extremely hard at his craft, but his main gift is that he's present in reality. If he's chasing a fly ball, he doesn't sort of watch the ball; he really, really, really watches the ball. When sportswriters ask him questions, he inevitably empties out the bromide upon which the question is based. Once, after running deep into foul territory to make an extraordinary catch to preserve a victory, he was asked, "When did you know you were going to catch the ball?" Ichiro said, "When I caught it."

8
Don't waste your time; get to the real thing.

9
Jennicam first went up in 1996; it went offline several years later. Every two minutes of every hour of every day, an image from a camera in Jenni's apartment was loaded onto the Web. In her FAQ, Jenni said, "The cam has been there long enough that now I ignore it. So whatever you're seeing isn't staged or faked. While I don't claim to be the most interesting person in the world, I do think there's something compelling about real life that staging it wouldn't bring to the medium."

10
Act naturally.

11
Somewhere I had come up with the notion that one's personal life had nothing to do with fiction, whereas the truth, as everybody knows, is nearly the direct opposite. Moreover, contrary evidence was all around me, though I chose to ignore it, for in fact the fiction both published and unpublished that moved and pleased me then as now was precisely that which had been made luminous, undeniably authentic by having been found and taken up, always at a cost, from deeper, more shared levels of the life we all really live.

12
People are always asking me when I'm going to make "real movies." These are my real movies. Nothing could be more real than the movies I make.

13
Making up a story or characters feels like driving a car in a clown suit.

14

Only the truth is funny (comedy is not pretty; definition of comedy: pulling Socrates off his pedestal).

15

Nicholson Baker is a comic personal essayist disguised, sometimes, as a novelist. His work is most appealing when he lavishes more attention upon a subject than it can possibly bear: broken shoelaces, say, in *The Mezzanine* or an innocuous line of Updike's in *U and I*. It wouldn't work if, instead of a shoelace, it was the Brooklyn Bridge, or if, instead of Updike, it was Proust: Baker's excessive elaboration wouldn't be funny or interesting. His style feeds upon farcical and foppish topics (e.g., his essay on the history of the comma). Baker is an unapologetic celebrant of gadgets, appliances, contraptions, machines, feats of engineering. His pseudoscientific lyricism serves him well—seems oddly illuminating—when he's overanalyzing the physics of straws or the opening of *Pigeon Feathers*. His point appears to be that nothing is beneath interest.

16

Attention equals life or is its only evidence.

17

"Why do you take photographs so constantly, so obsessively? Why do you collect other people's photographs? Why do you scavenge in secondhand shops and buy old albums of other people's pasts?"

"So that I'll see what I've seen."

18

We are poor passing facts,
warned by that to give
each figure in the photograph
his living name.

19

In the end I missed the pleasure of a fully imagined work in which the impulse to shape experience seems as strong as the impulse to reveal it.

20

Plot, like erected scaffolding, is torn down and what stands in its place is the thing itself.

21

— praise for matter in its simplest state, as fact.

22

There isn't any story. It's not the story. It's just this breathtaking world — that's the point. The story's not important; what's important is the way the world looks. That's what makes you feel stuff. That's what puts you there.

23

Shooting must be done on location, and props and sets must not be brought in (if a particular prop is necessary for the story, a location must be chosen where this prop is to be found); the sound must never be produced apart from the images or vice versa (music must not be used unless it occurs where the scene is being shot); the camera must be hand held; the film must be in color, and special lighting is not acceptable; optical work and filters are forbidden; the film must not contain superficial action (murders, etc. must not occur); temporal and geographical alienation are forbidden (that is to say, the film takes place here and now); genre movies are not acceptable; the director must not be credited.

24

The most political thing I can do is try to render people's lives, including my own, in a way that makes other people interested, empathetic, questioning, or even antipathetic to what they're seeing — but that somehow engages them to look at life as it's really lived and react to it.

25

Verboten thematic: secular Jews, laureates of the real, tend to be better at analyzing reality than re-creating it: Lauren Slater, *Lying*; Harold Brodkey, most of the essays; Phillip Lopate's introduction to *The Art of the Personal Essay*; Vivian Gornick, pretty much everything; Leonard Michaels, nearly everything; Melanie Thernstrom, *The Dead Girl*; Wallace Shawn, *My Dinner with André*; Jonathan Safran Foer, "Primer for the Punctuation of Heart Disease"; Salinger's later, consciousness-drenched work (I know I'll love the Buddhist-inspired meditations he's been writing the last forty years in his bunker). Less recently, e.g., Marx, Proust, Freud, Wittgenstein, Einstein.

26

The first resurrection of Christ is the heart of the backstory for the holiday of Easter and the original deification of Jesus. On the cross, he said that he would rise three days after his death. After he died of crucifixion, disbelieving Pilate and the Romans placed him in a cave and sealed the door with a boulder. On the third day, the boulder moved, Christ emerged, told his followers thank for your devotedness, etc. This is where Doubting Thomas gets his due. The risen Christ has Thomas actually feel the mortal wound (see the painting by Caravaggio for visualization). Jesus proves to all disbelievers that he really is the son of God. He will return on Judgment Day. Up to heaven and he hasn't been heard from since. (The last Christian died on the cross.)

27

The writing class has met every Wednesday afternoon for the past few years: twenty women, a retired dentist, and my father, now ninety-six. Although he's been plagued by manic-depression for fifty years and has received electroshock therapy countless times, in almost every piece he presents himself as a balanced okaynik, Mr. Bonhomie. He's always thrown a stone at every dog that bites, but in one story he sagely advises his friend, "You can't throw a stone at every dog that bites." His children from his first marriage, from whom he's estranged, didn't attend his ninetieth birthday party, but now they do, bearing gifts. He's been bald since he was forty, but now his hair is only "nearly gone." My mother, who died at fifty-one, dies at sixty. His voice in these stories is that of a successful tough guy: "She was dressed to the nines in flame-red shorts and a low-cut halter that showed her heart was in the right place." My dad, Sam Spade. His Waterloo was failing ever to see or call his childhood sweetheart, Pearl, after he had lost his virginity with a woman he met at a Catskills resort (the woman who became his first wife). In real life, at age sixty-eight, when he was visiting his sister, Fay, in Queens, Fay bumped into Pearl at the Queens Center Mall, got Pearl's number, and suggested that my dad call her. Again, he couldn't bring himself to call—which is a great, sad story. But in the story he wrote, he calls her, they get together, and "Eleanor" tells "Herb": "Please don't be so hard on yourself. It happened. It's all water under the bridge now. You did what you thought was right for you then. I understand. Maybe I didn't then. But it's all over now. That year, Joe and I got married, so I guess it's all worked out for the best, right?" This was, according to my father, the "toughest thing I've ever written—painful. It hurt deep down just to write it, more than fifty-three years after it happened." I want it to hurt more. My father and mother divorced shortly before her death thirty years ago, and they had, by common consent, an extremely bad relationship. But it's now a "solid-as-Gibraltar marriage." My father, asking for time off from his boss, tells him, "I'm faced with a palace revolution, and the three revolutionaries at home are getting ready to depose the king." The king he wasn't. I want him to write about forever having to polish the queen's crown according to her ever changing and exacting specifications. I want to ask him, What did that feel like? What is it like inside his skin? What is it like inside that bald, ill dome? No aerial views or airy glibness. Please, Dad, I want to say: only ground level, which at least holds the promise of grit.

28
Daniel Johnston, a manic-depressive singer and songwriter whose early songs were recorded on a $60 stereo, has a cult following (recipient of praise from Kurt Cobain and Eddie Vedder), due primarily to the unglamorous, raw, low quality production of his music, which chronicles his mental illness.

29
All the best stories are true.

30
That person over there? He's doing one thing, thinking something else. Life is never false, and acting can be. Any person who comes in here as a customer is not phony, whereas if a guy comes in posing as a customer, there might be something phony about it, and the reason it's phony is if he's really thinking, "How am I doing? Do they like me?"

31
He is to be accepted and forgiven because his faults are the sad, lovable, honorable faults of reality itself.

32
A didactic white arrow is superimposed on the left- and right-hand panels, pointing almost sardonically at the dying man. (These arrows, Francis Bacon's favorite distancing device, are sometimes explained as merely formal ways of preventing the viewer from reading the image too literally. In reality, they do just the opposite and insist that one treat the image as hyperexem-

plary, as though it came from a medical textbook.) The grief in the painting is intensified by the coolness of its layout and the detachment of its gaze. It was Bacon's insight that it is precisely such seeming detachment—the rhetoric of the documentary, the film strip, and the medical textbook—that has provided the elegiac language of the last forty years.

33
Life isn't about saying the right thing, and it's certainly not about tape recording everything so you have to endure it more than once. Life is about failing. It's about letting the tape play. Boswell, *Life of Johnson*. Jean Stein, *Edie*. *The Education of Henry Adams*. Geoffrey Wolff, *The Duke of Deception*. Julian Barnes, *Flaubert's Parrot*.

34
If you were hit by a truck and were lying out in that gutter dying, and you had time to sing one song, one song people would remember before you're dirt, one song that would let God know what you felt about your time here on earth, one song that would sum you up, you're telling me that's the song you'd sing? That same Jimmie Davis tune we hear on the radio all day? About your peace within and how it's real and how you're gonna shout it? Or would you sing something different? Something real, something you felt? Because I'm telling you right now: that's the kind of song people want to hear. That's the kind of song that truly saves people. It ain't got nothing to do with believing in God, Mr. Cash. It has to do with believing in yourself.

35
Reality-based art is a metaphor for the fact that this is all there is, there ain't no more.

36
The world is everything that is the case.

Persona

37
And I shall essay to be.

38
The book is written in the first person, but that "I" is the most deceptive, tricky pronoun. There are two of us. I'm a chronicler of this character at the center who is, but in the necessary sense not, me. He doesn't have my retrospect nor my leisure. He doesn't know what's around the next bend. He's ignorant of consequences. He moves through the book in a state of innocence about the future, whereas of course I as the writer, from the time I begin writing the first paragraph, do know what the future holds. I know how the story is going to turn out.

39
Painting myself for others, I have painted my inward self with colors clearer than my original ones. I have no more made my book than my book has made me.

40
Cinéma vérité looks for performers in everyday life; without them, you really haven't got footage. Some people have whatever that quality it is that makes them interesting on film—a kind of self-confidence or self-assuredness mixed, perhaps, with a degree of vulnerability—and other people don't have it, but as a filmmaker you know it when you see it. You have to sense that there's something real behind the so-called performance.

41
Johnny Carson, asked to describe the difference between himself and Robert Redford, said, "I'm playing me."

42
In *Essays of Elia*, Charles Lamb turned the reader's attention to the persona, the unreliable mask of the "I," not as an immutable fact of literature but as a tool of the essayist in particular, who, if he or she wants to get personal, must first choose what to conceal. These peculiarities—the theatrical reticence,

the archaism, the nostalgia, the celebration of oddity for its own sake—are regular features of Lamb's essays, and they helped to change the English (and American) idea of what an essay should be. Even when personal essayists don't flaunt their power to mislead us, even when we no longer expect belletrists to write old-fashioned prose, we still expect essays to deliver that same Elian tension between the personal and the truly private and to tell stories that are digressive and inconclusive. Most of all, we expect personal essayists to speak to us from behind a stylized version of themselves, rather than give us the whole man—as Montaigne or Lamb's favorite devotional writers seem to do—or a more-or-less representative man like the *Spectator* of Addison and Steele. Lamb wasn't the only romantic essayist who wrote this way; Hazlitt soon followed suit, so did De Quincey and Hunt. But Lamb was the first. Ever since Elia, eccentricity has been the rule.

43
Autobiography can be naively understood as pure self-revelation or more cannily recognized as cleverly wrought subterfuge.

44
When I state myself, as the Representative of the Verse—it does not mean—me—but a supposed person.

45
I'm not interested in myself per se. I'm interested in myself as theme carrier, as host.

46
A novelist-friend, who can't not write fiction but is flummoxed whenever he tries to write nonfiction directly about his own experience, said he was impressed (alarmed?) by my willingness to say nearly anything about myself: "It's all about you and yet somehow it's not about you at all. How can that be?"

47
One is not important, except insofar as one's example can serve to elucidate a more widespread human trait and make readers feel a little less lonely and freakish.

48

"The soul must become its own betrayer, its own deliverer, the one activ-ity, the mirror turn lamp"—which could and should serve as epigraph to Alphonse Daudet, *In the Land of Pain*; Fernando Pessoa, *The Book of Dis-quiet*; Michel Leiris, *Manhood: A Journey from Childhood into the Fierce Order of Virility*.

49

Andy Kaufman went way beyond blurring the distinction between performer and persona, past the point where you wondered what separated the actor from the character; you wondered if he himself knew anymore where the boundaries were drawn. What did he get out of such performances? The joy of not telling the audience how to react, giving that decision—or maybe just the illusion of such decision making—back to the audience. Afterward, he typically stayed in character when among fellow performers, who resented being treated like civilians. On his ABC special, the vertical hold kept rolling, which the network hated because it didn't want viewers to think there was anything wrong with their TV sets when in fact the problem was by design.

50

In Lorrie Moore's story "People Like That Are the Only People Here," the pu-tatively fictional account of a writer whose toddler is diagnosed with cancer, characters are named only by the roles they play: the Mother, Husband, Baby, Surgeon, Radiologist, Oncologist. The Mother discusses the possibility (the Husband emphasizes the financial necessity) of writing about the experience. When the story was published as fiction in the *New Yorker*, it was accompa-nied by a photo of Moore and a caption, "No, I can't. Not this! I write fiction. This isn't fiction." About the story, Moore has said, "It's fiction. Things didn't happen exactly that way; I reimagined everything. And that's what fiction does. Fiction can come from real-life events and still be fiction." The Mother is a writer and teacher who is already writing each scene as she experiences it. If this isn't a story about Moore and her baby, what is it about? The deep ambivalence writers have about using their personal lives to make a living. Even as the Mother agonizes about taking notes, she's diligently observing the environment, gathering data about cancer that will both help her child and (bonus!) make the story she'll write a better one. God, embodied as the manager of Marshall Field's, informs the Mother that "to know the narrative in advance is to turn yourself into a machine. What makes humans human is precisely that they do not know the future." The writer, of course, writing the story, does know what the ending will be, has planned it, lived through it. And the Mother also knows the future. When they leave the hospital with their baby, the Husband expresses gratitude for the people they've met, and the Mother responds, "For as long as I live, I never want to see any of these people again." The Mother will see those people, over and over again: she'll spend a great deal of time and effort re-creating them; writing the story, she insures that those people will always be with her. The Mother is angry at the world for paying to read such a story, but she's also angry at herself for profiting from not only her own life and pain but that of her family and all the families who shared their time in the pediatric oncology ward with her. She's angry that she can't leave these people behind, or the worry behind, or the fundamental truth that a part of living, of breathing, of surviving, is to exploit those human relationships in order to make our own stories, in order to live.

51
The source of my crush on Sarah Silverman? Her willingness to say unsettling things about herself, position herself as a fuck-me/fuck-you figure, a bad-good girl, a JAP who takes her JAPpiness and pushes it until it becomes the culture's grotesquerie: "I was raped by a doctor—which is, you know, so bittersweet for a Jewish girl." "I don't care if you think I'm racist; I only care if you think I'm thin." "Obviously, I'm not trying to belittle the events of September 11; they were devastating, they were beyond devastating, and I don't want to say especially for these people or especially for these people, but especially for me, because it happened to be the same exact day that I found out that the soy chai latte was, like, 900 calories."

52
A Hero of Our Time, gentlemen, is in fact a portrait, but not of an individual; it is the aggregate of the vices of our whole generation in their fullest expression.

53
The man who writes about himself and his time is the man who writes about all people and all time.

54
Was Keats a confessional poet? When he talks about youth that grows "pale and specter-thin, and dies," he's talking about his kid brother Tom, who died

of tuberculosis. But he's talking about more than that. The word confessional implies the need to purge oneself and to receive forgiveness for one's life. I don't think that's what confessional poetry is about at all. I think it's a poetry that comes out of the stuff of the poet's personal life, but he's trying to render this experience in more general and inclusive, or what used to be called universal, terms. He's presenting himself as a representative human being. He's saying, "This is what happens to us as human beings in this flawed and difficult world, where joy is rare." Sylvia Path is certainly one of the outstanding confessional poets, but when Path entitles a poem "Lady Lazarus," she's trying to connect herself to the whole tradition of pain and death and resurrection. She's not presenting herself as Sylvia Plath, but as part of a larger pattern.

55
This is the wager, isn't it? It's by remaining faithful to the contingencies and peculiarities of your own experience and the vagaries of your own nature that you stand the greatest chance of conveying something universal.

56
Self-study of any seriousness aspires to myth. Thus do we endlessly inscribe and magnify ourselves.

57
A man's life of any worth is a continual allegory.

58
What is true for you in your private heart is true for all men.

59
All our stories are the same.

60
Every man has within himself the entire human condition.

61
Deep down you know you're him.

Trying Truth

NANCY MAIRS

> Tell all the Truth but tell it slant
> — EMILY DICKINSON

✳ ✳ ✳ ✳ ✳ ✳ ✳ ✳ ✳ ✳ ✳ ✳ ✳ ✳ ✳ ✳ ✳ ✳ ✳ ✳

Some years ago, when I was writing my second book of essays, *Remembering the Bone House*, I asked my mother to read the earliest material. This was a sharp departure from my usual practice — no one but my husband ever reads my first drafts — but these essays formed a memoir, and I was recording some of my earliest memories. Mother might be able to correct details of fact. I am pretty strict about these. When I write a piece labeled nonfiction, I make an implicit contract with the reader, who reads with a set of expectations different from the ones fiction elicits. What I'm telling you here, I imply by calling my work nonfiction, really did happen; these people actually live, or at least did once; I really believe in the ideas I put forth, or at least did once. Invention lies in the language, not in the reporting — a distinction not always observed, recent instances reveal about writers for such prominent publications as the *New York Times*, the *Washington Post*, the *New Republic*, and the *Boston Globe*, as well as several wildly popular memoirists. Since my work is literary nonfiction rather than reportage, perhaps I could have gotten away with some embellishment of the facts and my own popularity would have soared, but I'd have strayed from my aim of plumbing the significance of ordinary human experience.

After reading the essay set during the period when she was piecing together a life for herself and two little girls following my father's death, Mother telephoned me and said, "I think this is fine. But you know the place where you tell about getting lost on the Swazey Parkway location my sister Sally and I had been forbidden to approach? I don't think that was you. The only one who could have told us for sure was Granna, because she was there. But I think it was Sally." We wound down the conversation and I returned to Sally, with whom I was spending the afternoon.

"You know that part where I get lost on the Swazey Parkway?" I asked her. "Mother says that was you, not me."

"It was? I don't remember that." We laughed. Who did the memory belong to, the sister to whom the adventure might *really* have happened but who couldn't remember it or the sister who had carried the recollection around with her for forty years? In either case, my grandmother, the witness who could have verified ownership of it, was long dead. Where could the truth be found? I finally decided that, since recalling the incident had acted on my consciousness for so long, I had some right to it, and so I included it in the essay. But I learned from this dilemma that even when I was writing in the best of faith, invention might be taking place beneath the surface. The only claim I can make is that I'm telling the truth as I know it. Doubt or believe me as you will.

Because I write personal essays, most of my material comes out of the perceptions and interpretations I make of the events of my life and the creatures that populate it. A lot of my readers remark upon the candor with which I discuss these and often ask how I dare to speak so openly about intimate matters. Good grief, I want to say, you'd think I was twirling on a trapeze with no net instead of reflecting on issues I've encountered in the course of my life as a highly educated middle-class radical Catholic feminist heterosexual white married woman with children and grandchildren living in a little green house at the edge of downtown Tucson who has spent most of her years crippled by multiple sclerosis and dogged by depression. Many of these issues, I've discovered, are pretty common, though some of them, like infidelity, are seldom acknowledged, let alone explored, out loud.

As a child in a large, tight-lipped family, I found the matters not spoken of frightening and hurtful. Maybe forthrightness became my antidote to the sense of shame secrets so often instill. Even after I learned that one grandfather was an alcoholic and the other had shot himself dead before I was born, they were spoken of curtly in lowered voices. Eventually I came to feel not ashamed but cheated. Their stories were part of my story, and I was deprived of the opportunity to know them — and, in a sense, myself — more fully. Mine was a platitudinous family, and "honesty is the best policy" was intoned any number of times, but emotionally it was violated as a rule. I think my outrage trumped my fear of reprisals. I became plainspoken.

I don't mean that I strip myself naked in my writing. It only appears that way because I examine closely matters that have long been debarred from polite conversation: sex, politics, and religion, common wisdom has it. Over the years, I have also had a good deal to say about cats, but I suspect that readers don't have them in mind when they refer to my frankness. Truth to tell, I am a private person, and that frankness is something of a ruse. When you see how open I am, you figure I couldn't possibly reveal more, and so you don't ask me questions about subjects I don't care to talk about. I have secrets, but they tend to be about other people, not myself; except for a couple of regrettable slips, I am quite a good secret-keeper. There are no falsehoods in my writing, but there are secrets; and these, I suppose, twist the truth in ways I don't even recognize.

At first, the response of some readers to my truth telling startled me. "You put my feelings into words," I heard time and again. Although the details I use in building my essays are intensely personal, I gradually realized, they resonated with details in the lives of others and aroused similar responses, thus bearing out Ralph Waldo Emerson's observation in *The American Scholar* that "in going down into the secrets of his own mind, he has descended into the secrets of all minds"; indeed, "the deeper he dives into his privatest, secretest presentiment, to his wonder he finds this is the most acceptable, most public, and most universally true. The people delight in it; the better part of every man feels, This is my music; this is myself." Truth to self rings true to others.

To this point I've been speaking the plain truth — but not the only truth. In the early days of my essay writing, I recall, George would virtually gnash his teeth in frustration at my account of some incident from our shared life: "I don't see it like that." "I'm not speaking for you," I would reply. "I'm writing about the way I see things. If you want people to understand your perspective, go write your own book." After a while, he decided he didn't want to write a book, but he also came to grasp the point I was getting at: we are each the stories we tell ourselves about ourselves, and no one of us can authentically tell another's story. If you want to know George qua George, don't come to me. He may or may not tell it to you, but either way, it's his truth.

An essay is not the same as reportage, although it may subsume reportage as it may do poetry and narrative also. As a writer, I like best the flexibility of the essay, its stylistic inclusiveness. It may recount facts one moment, sing about them lyrically or raucously in the next, weave them into stories, transform them into lessons, toss them aside in the end. Strictly speaking, an essay is just what Michel de Montaigne meant when he named the genre: a test or trial of an idea, which may lead to a firm, unambiguous conclusion but probably, in my experience, will not. In short, although an essay may offer insights into the truths of human being, it will never yield the capital-t Truth, for the not-so-simple reason that no such entity exists.

This kind of relativism is not especially popular these days. Believe me, as a practicing Catholic of a divergent stripe, I know. The more fundamentalist religious belief becomes, the more rigidly it insists on belief in the Absolute

Truth dictated by a deity or deities and the more strictly it imposes rules devised on the basis of that belief. Nonbelievers view these in various lights. Some of the rules seem practical: filter your water before you drink it. Others seem superstitious: don't pee outside after dark or *ndoki* will travel up the stream and bewitch you. Others seem cruel: wrap a spiked chain around your thigh in order to earn salvation from eternal torment. Some seem downright mad: take the afterbirth of a black she-cat, the offspring of a black she-cat, the first born of a first born, roast it in fire and grind it to powder, then put some into your eye, and you will see the thousand demons on your left hand and the ten thousand on your right. Only one injunction has ever struck me as qualified to be absolute: take care of each other.

So, then, no Truth—but as much truth as I am capable of telling. It may not seem like much of a bargain, but if I'm going to be true to myself and to you, it's the best I can do.

The Observer Observing
Some Notes on the Personal Essay
LEONARD KRIEGEL

✳ ✳ ✳ ✳ ✳ ✳ ✳ ✳ ✳ ✳ ✳ ✳ ✳ ✳ ✳ ✳ ✳ ✳ ✳ ✳

The great appeal of the personal essay, at least for writers, is that it allows us to draw a line in the sand between self and world. The attractiveness of the "I" that stares out at the world is that it knows two things: the first is that it is unsheltered, the second is that it is the writer's own eye that must measure what it sees in that world. Should the writer choose to thrust his or her "I" against the world, it amounts to a confession that he is willing to match his angle of vision against the skepticism of his readers. This confession is made with the very first word he puts on the page. The personal essay depends upon his eye, for it is with this eye that he casts himself across the world. How that eye sees and what it chooses to look at is central to what the writer of the personal essay does. The essay as a form asks the writer to concern himself not with character or plot or even with the beauty of words but with how he sees and, even more important, what he is willing to look at. In this respect, personal essays differ even from the most autobiographical fiction. No essayist needs to be told that his is a different craft from that of writing stories or novels. For the essayist, Fitzgerald's insistence that character as action can be safely ignored. Character is the act of seeing — and from the essayist's perspective, character is to be measured by how honestly the writer handles what he sees. His "I" must serve both as witness to and functionary of the world he observes, the world he has chosen to write of. At its most honest, the personal essay offers the reader a chance to observe the observer in the act of observing. The essayist's challenge is to make sense of what the eye sees.

For the essayist, then, the world is a reflection of the self he sends into it. And for the essayist, history is nothing if it is not personal. This is true even if the essayist is a historian himself. To read William Manchester's great essay on the fortieth anniversary of the Battle of Okinawa is to absorb history into the personal in ways that even the greatest of war fictions do not do. In Manchester's essay, "Okinawa: The Bloodiest Battle of All," the very sentences spring as much from the young marine — who the author was forty years before Okinawa became a "topic" he was asked to write about — as they do from the distinguished historian and essayist that marine ultimately evolved into.

Re-reading this essay I am struck by how hollow our rhetoric about war has become. Manchester certainly needed no reminders that, as we were constantly being told in the sixties and seventies, the personal is political. A glib if soporific accuracy, it turns out—yet read Manchester's essay and you are left with little doubt that, glib or not, cliché or not, it is true. Only the essayist is able to turn that around, as Manchester does, and remind readers that the personal is, first and foremost, personal. And if the writer is working out of a memory so scarred that it cannot age into peace, the personal is also unrelenting and unforgiving.

The aging Japanese man whom Manchester had met ten years earlier on a return trip to Guadalcanal, where he also had fought, evokes in him not a mutual sense of shared tragedy but a simmering rage. For him, the enemy is still visible. The essayist discovers that memory is recollected in anything but tranquility. The enemy is still there, in front of a young, terrified William Manchester. And the enemy still possesses a physical presence. In the ex-marine's mind, his job remains what it was, and he wants to destroy this enemy soldier who still wants to destroy him. In some corner of his deeply civilized consciousness, a highly skilled journalist and historian still views an aging Japanese man as the enemy. Because the personal really is political, William Manchester does not feel that he must feed us the usual banalities about war as hell. That is a given. But the complexity of what memory has deeded is a reflection of what the writer sees on his return to the South Pacific. And that complexity absorbs us, eyeball-to-eyeball, so that a brief essay about the fortieth anniversary of a key battle in the Pacific War, "Okinawa: The Bloodiest Battle of All," leaves us scarred with the knowledge that, for this writer at least, the personal will never be anything but political. And it will remain political in ways that would horrify those who urge their banalities upon us. *Make love, not war* was another slogan of the late sixties. But it takes the essayist's probing eye to show that this is not the choice we face. Viewed through the eye of the "I," neither making love nor war has meaning if all we can do is to reduce them to slogans. Like T. S. Eliot's Sweeney, the essayist must use words, since there is nothing else with which he can express his rage and anguish. Here is Manchester describing his encounter with that Japanese man eight years before his visit to Okinawa.

I trembled, suppressing the sudden, startling surge of primitive rage within. And I could see, from his expression, that this was difficult for him, too. Nations may make peace. It is harder for fighting men. On simultaneous impulse we both turned and walked away.

The accomplished personal essayist forces us to see ourselves as we do not necessarily want to see ourselves. One can argue, of course, that this is the function of all good writing. Yet few other genres commit the writer's "I" so relentlessly and few other genres are able to force the writer to confront himself so absolutely. The personal essay allows writers to discover their own complexity—and that includes their hatreds, as well as the rawness and sustainability of their wounds. Among the legacies of the personal essay is that it has been used to describe so many different kinds of pain and self-discovery. I can think of few better examples of the personal being political than that which is provided us by William Manchester in this essay. Few writers have evoked the counter memories that make clichés like "War is hell" so embarrassing. It is impossible to read this essay (as it is impossible to read the remarkable memoir, *Goodbye, Darkness*, which this essay serves as a kind of coda) and not succumb to the grinding, overwhelming horror of combat, the sheer unadorned shittiness of the fear and trembling that is so much a part of the denuded world one enters in war. In the hands of the essayist, the reality of the hell of war is woven into each sentence, so that we feel not the movement of troops or historical forces but the power of the personal, a power that is made physical because of one writer's willingness to focus the eye of his "I" not on the world's ills but on the terror a single human being is forced to relive. Manchester's task, the task of the writer of personal essays, is not only to tell us what happened to him but to show us how what happened to him was transformed by memory. The personal essay is at its most powerful when it gives us the writer realizing how he has been permanently, inextricably, changed by all that he has witnessed. The eye he casts upon the world will never again see as it saw before consciousness itself was changed. In re-living the scenes that fathered his words, the writer demonstrates, both to himself and to his readers, that not only is the political personal but that it changes the nature of what is personal. History focuses the eye that searches the past so that the "I" can see.

Whether it is an aging historian describing his return to the warring fields of the South Pacific that still vividly reside in memory or George Orwell forcing his childhood beneath time's microscope in "Such, Such Were the Joys," the personal essay imposes this peculiar awareness upon the writer—he must recognize himself as the observer in the act of observing. When the writer looks at his past, he is like a man who has been forcibly removed from his own body. Told to stand outside it and describe what he sees, he is controlled not by what he has become but by that old witness still lurking in memory, the voice that he cannot shake free. His view of the world he now lives in is fused to his view of life in that earlier world. It is not enough to point out that many, if not most, personal essays are ego-driven, that the writer is caught trying to make what he has witnessed as interesting and personal to the reader as it is to him. Whatever skin he seeks to shed, whether that of the timid class-conscious Eric Blair at an English public school or that of the aging ex-marine for whom the carnage witnessed decades ago has so seared memory that it is more real than anything he can see before him, the one thing he knows for sure is that it is his skin that is being shed. He may find himself forced back into the Harlem of the young, black, and angry James Baldwin, once again forced to pit his sense of being the unwanted native son against the death of a tyrannical father and the prospect of a future to be lived in an America whose racial categorizations he is expected to accommodate himself to. Or he may be seized by the nervous skepticism of Joan Didion determined to "keep in touch" with the California she has already transformed into a metaphor for the naked wackiness of the rest of America.

Whatever haunts the eye of memory, it is loyalty to perception that must be wrested from the past before it can be returned, reshaped, and reinvigorated, to the reader. The essayist's vision defines his success — along, of course, with the language with which he evokes that vision. "The hallmark of the personal essay," writes Phillip Lopate in his introduction to *The Art of the Personal Essay*, "is its intimacy." It is an intimacy that pits the writer against specific memories — which is, I suspect, why Gore Vidal is so much more interesting writing about Tennessee Williams in Rome in 1948 than he is when he plays the grand master of the novel and gives us fictional re-creations of history. No one can question Vidal's learning or scholarship. He not only possesses a historical sense but seems to have read and absorbed everything written on, say, Lincoln and the Civil War. Yet in spite of his formidable intelligence and his storytelling talents, his Lincoln is never as real as the Tennessee Williams we meet in his essay, "Some Memories of the Glorious Bird." One cannot explain this simply by saying that Vidal is one of the most talented essayists America has produced or by pointing out that none of his novels rise to the level of the ambitions he has set for himself. All one can do is to point out that Vidal takes possession of the personal essay form as he never quite seems able to do in his novels and stories. Like Baldwin's, his essays command a distinctive personal voice, a singular voice. And it is that voice that one misses in his fiction. His novels may be skillfully written, yet they offer readers nothing as engaging as the intimately caustic eye we expect from Vidal the essayist. And that lack of an intimate voice depletes his fiction, until even the sentences, like the characters, strike the reader as curiously isolated. Much the same can be said of Baldwin, whose novels and stories seem to strain against the verbal power of those remarkable essays he wrote in the fifties and sixties. Nothing in Baldwin's fiction possesses the coiled passion of the essays collected in *Notes of a Native Son* and *Nobody Knows My Name*.

I do not mean to suggest that the personal essay will ever replace fiction. I simply mean to point out that the musings the essayist brings to ordinary life, even when they are abstract, can be transformed into art. The writer cannot willingly disfigure those musings, since his success depends upon his ability to follow their lead as faithfully as possible. The personal essay rarely attains the economy of scale or the tightness of structure that writers are taught to admire in graduate programs in creative writing. The true essayist is so completely involved with what he sees that he finds it relatively easy to let go of the ego that drives him. To read Orwell's "Such, Such Were the Joys" is to watch a writer close in on his past with all the intensity of some hunter tracking his prey. Orwell's Crossgates is not intended to stand for all schools or even for all English public schools. It is this specific school that haunts the writer because it is this school that haunted the young Eric Blair. The essayist cannot allow himself to become the victim of his own ego. Revenge is not in the cards for him. It isn't even in the sentences he writes. How interesting that Hemingway, who wrote a good deal of nonfiction, avoided what we think of as the personal essay. It was an intelligent decision on his part, for one suspects that he would not have been successful in the personal essay for the same reason that his nonfiction fails to capture us the way his stories and novels do. God knows, no writer could be more ego driven. Yet it is precisely his ego that gets in his way. His desire to rework the past and make it conform to his idea of who he is and what he believes he has achieved clamps down even on the best of his nonfiction, the posthumously published *A Moveable Feast*, so that reading it leaves readers with a sense of intimate falsity. Getting even with the past overwhelmed Hemingway's ability to let his eye roam free and absorb as honestly as possible what it saw.

Of course, Hemingway never really attempted the personal essay. He had too sharp a sense of both his strengths and his limitations as a writer. Yet all essayists — and this is true of anyone who has mined the genre — secretly want to force their past into a container, to make it conform to the image they have of who they are and what they have accomplished. The writer can have a sense of both his strengths and his limitations without allowing them to define him. If the unexamined life really isn't worth living, then the life that has been cast beneath the lens is worth writing about only when the ego is free of cant. Freud is praised for having had the courage to do a self-analysis. Montaigne, on the other hand, is made into a kind of bucolic, intelligent uncle. Yet Montaigne's stoic sallies into self and world reflect the power of the observer observing—and he does that as well as the Viennese physician who had put himself on the couch. The father of the essay placed the world on the couch, and in seeing it he saw himself. Three hundred years before Freud's self-analysis, Montaigne's *Essays* offer the introspection of a skeptical humanist able to understand that the only unbreakable rule of writing is that the writer cannot restrict his roaming eye. One must seek out the world one inhabits. This is the only obligation the essayist cannot get beyond. In the essay about Tennessee Williams, Vidal is as catty and as intent as Hemingway on getting even for old slights. He joyously goes about peeling Harold Acton's English skin from his soul, as if he has been saving up for thirty years to take his revenge for what seems, at most, a minor slight. Yet the reader trusts Vidal's cattiness because he senses that the one thing Vidal will not allow his cattiness to do is to permit his ego to interfere with memory. The personal essayist can be nasty; he can be vengeful; but he cannot be untruthful. Orwell may wish every conceivable socialist plague on the titled and untitled wealthy whom he recalls as having made his life at Crossgates hell. Yet that does not interfere with the pleasure we take in his depiction of Crossgates, nor does it keep us from recognizing that Orwell has written a remarkable essay. Readers understand what the personal essay can give them, and they are willing to accept Eric Blair and his tormentors for who and what they are. Orwell does not need to elevate his status by making a Crossgates that exists only to feed his desire for revenge.

If the future of the personal essay is as bright as its practitioners believe, then the demands the form will make on both the essayist and the reader are clear. The greatest danger the essay faces is, peculiarly enough, how popular the form has become over the past two decades. In America, at least, it now threatens the hegemony of the novel. Why this is the case is not altogether clear. But the personal essay, along with the memoir, has suddenly and mysteriously evolved into fashion. To be part of a fashionable literary genre is a rare experience for essayists, and they should approach their new popularity gingerly. Being in fashion offers any number of temptations, none of them particularly appealing in a culture as susceptible to celebrity orchestration as the American literary world. It is quite possible that the personal essay will overwhelm the novel because of the intimacy that is so integral to it. Good personal essays offer a distinctive voice—and it is precisely the voice that seems so absent in contemporary fiction. The essays in a magazine like the *New Yorker* are today far more individual than are the magazine's stories. What makes the essays singular is the integrity of the eye. Of course, it is not enough to serve as witness. We read essays—and I suspect this is behind the genre's growing popularity—because we seek what is human in ourselves. This is what readers used to seek in novels and stories. The apparent simplicity of the essay as a form, its very randomness, may also account for its growing popularity. There is nothing luxurious about the form. It is not experimental, and it reflects the kind of established order a novelist would have no difficulty moving beyond. But the observer observing remains the strength of this simplest of literary genres. Let us hope that observer, in all his quirkiness, manages to keep the essay free of the many temptations offered by its new popularity. Let the observer observe—and let his vision remain singular.

Occasional Desire
On the Essay and the Memoir
DAVID LAZAR

* *

1. MEMORY AND DESIRE

The allusion in my subtitle is obviously to *The Waste Land*, and less obviously to Montaigne, whose "On Some Verses of Virgil" is one of the great demonstrations of the possiblity of the essay.

> April is the cruelest month
> Breeding lilacs out of the dead land
> Mixing memory with desire

Familiar lines, of course. But why am I invoking them here, what do I want to claim that they say now? Among other things, April is the cruelest month because, as a time of transition, it stirs memory in with the desire that is emerging—memories of, perhaps, other desires, older ones. This season, spring, personified in the form of this month, April, is a kind of demiurge, which creates confusion because it throws us back, in the direction of memory, at the same time as we are thawing forward—such is desire. Mixing desire in with memory makes no schematic sense in winter, after we and our memories are covered "with forgetful snow."

Spring is profane, as is desire.

And we might consider December, winter, sacred, in its depths of spiritual or inner consideration. We might, but in "The Burial of the Dead," the sacred languishes into corruption.

Still, does Eliot mean, to extend, to extrapolate the metaphor, that memory is sacred?

Well, memory may be sacred, which is to say experienced as such. Anything might be. In *The Waste Land*, we plunge into parodic, nostalgic recollection, a half-sweet half-curdled memory of youthful winter pleasures, when Europe *seemed* whole—before the land was wasted, was laid waste to. Wholeness, we know, and the reclamation of European culture, and of course that inscrutably benevolent monarch God, would increasingly fill Eliot's desires, which mixed with his memory, and reversed the equation I suggested above: in *Four Quartets*, desire seems mixed with memory in an ultimately painful ecstasy: "There is only the fight to recover what has been lost / And found and lost again and again . . ." And in the last stanza, "We shall not cease from exploration / And the end of all our exploring / Will be to arrive where we started / And know the place for the first time." Desire for the transcendent knowledge of God will take Eliot back . . . his perception utterly changed, changed utterly. His desire makes memory dynamic.

All of this is to suggest that memory and desire swirl around each other, or take turns riding one another, or perhaps they're symbiotic, parasite and host exchanging places as time allows or demands. Luckily, metaphors for memory and desire are inexhaustible (see David Bromwich's *The Past Is a Foreign Country*, or *Metaphors of Memory* by Douwe Draaisma) or we'd all be in a pretty pickle, a pinch, a box. But my real question, in case you doubted I had one, is how do we and how might we think of the relationship of memory and desire with regard to autobiographical writing, more specifically autobiographical prose?

What kind of bedfellows can memory and desire be? How is memory colored by desire? How does desire inflect and infect memory? How do they joust, caress, repel, or require one another?

To this I have a simple answer: I'd love to remember if I ever knew, but since I don't, I'm forced to believe that the answer is escapable. In other words, thinking I know that this relationship is too complex to unravel or solve, I have to resist simplification, forced resolution, merely incidental connection, and glib disentanglements. In other words, I have to approach the subject as I approach most others: as an essayist; my desire to understand this subject and any invocation of the past should be instruments that I use warily and strategically. Let me cut to the chase (a phrase I remember fondly from my days in Brooklyn schoolyards — Marie, hold on?): when we are in memory mode, when we remember, we almost always have an ulterior motive, even when we have an anterior one. I remember my mother on a day, let's say spring, in 1963, when I was six (and April wasn't cruel). Why? Why do I perform this memory? How do I perform this memory? Do I engage in a process of duplication, trying to re-create a memory I've envisaged before? Or am I approaching it differently this time, circling around my mother from the left instead of the right as she sits on the stoop and smokes? Is her housedress plaid, hemline right at the center of the knee? (Do I dare to eat a peach?) Or is she dressed in the vague halos, the fogs of memory that fill in the details we aren't focusing on? Is the memory static, or a mnemonic changeling, a shape-shifting child of Mnemosyne, mother of the muses. Here I'm thrown back to Henri Bergson (is my memory thawing or cooling into intellection?), a significant influence on Eliot, coincidentally enough (is it?). Bergson speaks of mechanical time and dulled senses, the object we vaguely see, but do not go past the familiarity of, do not vitally register. When we're in this sensually dulled-out state, we're far from what he called the *élan vital*, which in Bergson's description sounds like a fugue state with a view. To simplify: too often we treat memory blandly and with a kind of willfully perverse reification. This makes for autobiographical writing that pays homage to unexamined lives, our own and others'.

Why do I want to remember my mother in 1963? This is the $64,000 question, in a chronological accident (is it an accident?). Is it because in missing the long dead, one salves one's wounds through re-creation? Or am I rubbing a wound, seeing how much it hurts, or whether it does? Why did I just change pronouns, from the personal "I" to the impersonal "one"? And why the change back again? Is there something I need to know about my mother? About my mother in 1963? About me in 1963? About my mother and me in 1963? Or is the question, like dreamwork, off to the side, hiding behind the couch, in the broom closet, in my repressed desire or my self-conscious but incomplete desire? In short, what do I want? And, an important distinction for me: am I invoking a memory, a simulacrum of what happened that I have thought of as static, or performing a more active act of remembering, holding it, the memory, in my hands (Marie, hold on tight) and turning it around, upside down?

Generically, this question, for me, speaks profoundly to the differences in autobiographical writing, most intensely, but not exclusively, the difference between the essay and the memoir.

Some further complications: many of the memoirs being published today are what might be called collections of autobiographical essays that are more or less chronological—but many of these lack the tension, the structural and organizational complexity, and a resistance to the possibilities of the personal or lyric essay voice that give the genre its credibility. Other books sold as essays may be philosophy-*lite* (psychobabbling brooks of watery promise) or sequential autobiographical narratives that insist on a tiresome comical intensity or Dickensian disaster motifs (sentiment scrubbed or smudged). There is a version of the column—the short comic essay, urban if not urbane, comedies of manners, whose essayistic personae forget that they are not Molière, but his characters. Essayists such as W. S. Trow, Alphonso Lingis,

D. J. Waldie, or Susan Griffin hold our line against the onslaught of collections that dilute our sense of what the essay is. There is a difference between the democratic and the digestible (think NPR essays). I'm enamored of writers of the sparkling limited output, like James Agee, Robert Burton, Elizabeth Smart, Charlotte Delbo, Joe Brainard . . . But I digress . . . .

The autobiographical essay, the personal essay proper, whose lineage is Hazlittian, Lambian, Woolfian, Montaignian ("Any topic is equally fertile for me. . . . Let me begin with whatever subject I please, for all subjects are linked with one another," "On Some Verses Of Virgil") usually contains or contrasts memory and desire, producing resistance through friction: this is what I'd like to believe, and this is what I think is true, albeit contingently. There is a profound difference between Nancy Mairs or Phillip Lopate or Richard Rodriguez or Edward Hoagland and the light essay or short piece of memoir (we need terms for such work: memoirette? autobiografillies? memory prose?). And the difference comes down (rises?) to the centrality of ideas.

The rise in interest in the lyric essay is too large a subject to really breach here. It's exciting, as it was when Basho and Pascal and Weil and Benjamin in the *Arcades Project* were writing them, and a handful of people are writing them now brilliantly. The form seems a tonic, generally, to the overwrought and underthought autobiographical essays I've seen too much of. On the other hand, ideas and opacity, difficulty and impenetrability, seem to be lines that get routinely crossed. As an editor I'm seeing lyric essays that are really just autobiographical essays with the transitions taken out. Uh-oh. But the essay regains its exploratory footing with the "lyric" essay (part of me longs for the return of the simple "essay"), which is all for the good.

The memoir, in long or short form, is usually content heavy, narratively driven, and in the American literary marketplace today, usually dependent upon a hook: substance abuse, physical abuse, strange adventures, exotic backgrounds, any aspect of what Nancy Mairs has called "the literature of personal disaster." The short or long memoir frequently sees a memory as sacred, immutable, or transcendent, mistily mysterious even if seemingly understandable. Of course, if a memoir were to question every moment it rendered, it would bog down in infinite regressions, as the narrator of John Barth's *Floating Opera* suggests: to write my autobiography, I must write my father's, and so on. . . . On the other hand, in not questioning enough, the memoir risks nostalgia, or white-washing, or a kind of fictional re-creation that may have more to do with . . . some desires — to re-create, to publish, to burnish, to enshrine—than others: to demystify, to consider, to enlarge one's subject, to self-investigate. The memoir frequently performs memory for its audience of voyeurs, who vicariously enter the narrative. The memoir wants to entertain the reader—needs, craves our interest in its foretold story. As such, it can be a bit whorish. And you thought the sentimental whore died with Camille? The memoir's occasion is frequently quite simple: this is a good story to tell, with lively characters given a vervy charge by having actually existed. It may record, valuably, a period of time, a place, a place in time. Memoirists are usually lyrical—after all, heaven knows they've got time.

The essay, in contrast, is voice driven, question filled, metaphysically complex. Ultimately, its questions always threaten to overwhelm any possible answers. The essay not only asks "what happened," it wants to know "what did it mean?" and "why am I remembering it?" and "what does that say about me?" and "where can we go from here?" If memoirs perform narrative, most often a linear view of the past, then the essay performs in a hall of mirrors that is also a room with a view, but the view may be anything. Sound paradoxical? Welcome to the essay. The essay leans toward the profane, toward a severe attitude concerning memory, and the persona performing it. It mixes memory and desire, and tries to separate them, to disinfect the effects of fearful or dubious desires. It desires to understand its desire. It threatens to sink the narrative ship, to send chronology rolling away down a steep hill, while it stops and argues with itself. The essayist accepts the reader looking over her shoulder—or it may enlist the reader as an accomplice, an intimate, in the process of self-examination, in the processes of asking difficult questions of any subject it turns to. But in its classic form, the essay doesn't quite know where the hell it's going to go from the outset. The essay's occasion, an implicit or explicit question, is a grain of sand disturbing the oyster, the writer's complacency in whatever form it may have taken or be taking. If essayists sometimes sound querulous, it is because they frequently have a rock in their shoe. Or the essayist may at times seem a bit manic, digressing in a flailing way, as a way of trying to get somewhere, anywhere. Joseph Epstein, an essayist whom I am convinced was a curmudgeonly child, has written a book of essays called *The Middle of My Tether*.

One generic difficulty in contrasting the contemporary essay to the short memoir is that the essay as practiced and taught in creative writing programs seems to me too dominated by autobiography. The idea of using a personal voice to discuss a subject, whether it's Schubert, or baseball, or say that good old Montaignian chestnut friendship, or a new *Three Guineas* on our current sense of war sometimes seems a drop in the bucket of contemporary creative nonfiction. Robert Nozick, Hannah Arendt, Martha Nussbaum, Richard Selzer, Andrea Dworkin, Adam Phillips . . . these are precisely the kinds of essayists that my students haven't read and whom I don't see much discussed. Even Oliver Sacks has faded from discussion in the academy as he has been chased out by more watery memoirists whose truths are more easily available. Let me overload my case while I'm at it: Seneca, Carlyle, Pater, Stendhal, Anatole France, Nietzsche, Adorno, and M. F. K. Fisher have drifted away from many of the current academic practitioners of the form as models for discussion — were they ever? I confess there are days when I can barely respond to the overwhelming sameness of autobiographical tastes many students bring from the essay: David Sedaris, Annie Dillard, David Sedaris, David Sedaris, David Sedaris. I've certainly been guilty of writing my share of autobiographical essays (*j'accuse* should begin at home), though I've also inflicted on readers essays on film and photography and painting. I'm not arguing that essayists should not use or write their experiences, but that the self can turn in two directions. I think, I sense, that many writers, especially young writers, venturing into the essay form have been raised on the autobiographical essay rather too exclusively. But it's giving me gout, not them. It's my teacherly concern. This is to say they don't have a thorough education in the form. Why be polite? Many writers of autobiographical essays couldn't tell a Montaigne from a Bacon, a Browne from a Donne, a Hellman from a McCarthy. But they can remember lyrically and ruefully, evocatively.

Which is why I'm so fiercely fond of Rachel Blau DuPlessis' work on the essay in *The Pink Guitar* and her essay "f-Words: An Essay on the Essay." While DuPlessis is much more displeased than I at the very thought of autobiographical writing, in the narrative sense, her work is a corrective, a tonic, to the sloppy thought and easy lyricism that passes for essays these days. How can anyone, I wonder, not trust enough to listen to a writer who says the following:

> But if essays are works of "reading," they are also works "wrought," a thinking that occurs through the material fabrication of language, a work and a working in language, not simply a working through intellectually or emotionally — language not as a summary of findings but as the inventor of findings. Wrought is the past participle of work, but I had always thought (wrongly, but willfully) that wreaking was a related word. Reading and wreaking make a euphonious pair. However, wreaking in its real meaning

is at the extreme end of the essay—its wrath, its venting of anger, its drive. But I think if a wreaking could be sweetened just somewhat—its propulsions made positive instead of vengeful—one would have the sense of the energy of the essay, its wayward reach into utopic desires. ("f-words")

Clearly, anything is possible within the fugitive reader, as well as the fugitive writer. But DuPlessis reminds us that essays that are lamely belletristic, that are "too nice," are probably not using the form actively enough (E. B. White, hold on tight). And stirringly, she also makes the case for the essay's adoption as a form of feminine écriture (in the largest sense), that in its avoidance of linear movement, conventional wisdom, and complacencies of the pen, it has always had the qualities of an "excessive writing practice," "forever skeptical, forever alert, forever yearning." (Rachel—here's my list of essay descriptions, fond as I am of d's: desire, disruption, discovery, dyspepsia, disturbing, disturbed, distemper, dissonant, disquietude, disgraceful, discursive, discomfiture, dereliction, Daedalian, doubt, DuPlessian . . .).

I've discussed the memoirization of the essay, but there are certainly cases of the essayification of the memoir or autobiography. Nathalie Sarraute understood the essay mode beautifully in her autobiographical *Childhood* (*Enfances*). She divides herself into two voices (it could be ten, of course, or one with more integrated selves. One voice is the lyrical voice of memory: it is filled with desire, it wants things to have turned out all right. The second voice, profane, is slightly demonic or daemonic, pushing the first voice around, questioning her interpretations, impatient with the beautification of memory. It provides resistance, driving a necessary wedge between memory and desire.

Listen to these two in one, this one in two voices with it, Sarraute's object and ostensible subject, her childhood:

—That's just it: what I'm afraid of, this time, is that it isn't trembling . . . not enough . . . that it has become fixed once and for all, "a sure thing," decided in advance . . .

—Don't worry about it having been decided in advance . . . it's still vacillating, no written word, no word of any sort has yet touched it, I think it is still faintly quivering . . . outside words . . . as usual . . . little bits of something still alive . . . I would like . . . before they disappear . . . let me . . .

—Right. I won't say any more . . . and in any case, we know very well that when something starts haunting you . . .

— Yes, and this time, it's hardly believable, but it was you who prompted me, for some time now you have been inciting me . . .

—I?

— Yes, you, by your admonitions, your warnings . . . you conjure it up, you immerse me in it . . . [ellipses in original]

What emerges is a meditation on memory, a theory of memory by necessity incomplete. And this is where Sarraute (and Georges Perec and Michel Leiris and Christa Wolf . . .) differs from most contemporary memoirists: not just the thing itself (memory), but ideas about the thing, a process more common to the essay than to conventional autobiography.

My mother's housedress must sit in the closet. I'm afraid it isn't germane to this essay, no matter how much it might be to something else, anything else, I might write. Avoidance, led by the leash of decorum, can be exemplary, or at least A-OK.

This essay is marked by some modernist allusions; like most writers who are interested in the postmodern: as in the incomplete, the contingent, the fragmentary, unresolved and unsystematized . . . I'm really a late modernist at heart. And I feel that the essay, rather than the narrative memoir (memoiritty? memza?) best suits my interests, my intellectual and emotional temperament. Narrative without resistance, memory and desire unacknowledged as cohorts try to use wholeness to shore against their fragments. These ruin things for me; I just can't buy the work.

The best essay's sheets are rumpled, askew; it sits on the corner of the bed with one eyebrow raised. Memoir, too often, stands at the window in white linen; it gazes out wistfully, not admitting it wants a large greasy breakfast.

2. ON THE OCCASIONAL

Nothing seems to me more central than the idea and execution of the occasion of an autobiographical work. But the occasion has a different function depending on the kind of book one is writing. As I mention in the essay, the occasion of an autobiographical work may be rather simple, even when the book itself is complex. Of course, the book may also be equally simple.

For example: *Riding in Cars with Boys*—the occasion: Beverly Donofrio, in taking her son to college wonders how she could have raised such a normal child. Her last twenty years, therefore, don't quite jive with her first twenty, and she's going to tell us why.

In *Truth*, by Ellen Douglas, the occasion is in the subtitle: *Four Stories I Am Finally Old Enough to Tell*. The implication is clear—her memories, some of her memories, are painful or shocking, family revelations that may have felt like betrayals at an earlier stage in life. Here, by the by, we might remember Joan Didion's warning at the beginning of *Slouching Towards Bethlehem* that writers are always selling somebody out. The occasion that reveals family secrets always sells the family out, no matter how justified, necessary, or balanced.

Treetops, by Susan Cheever, has a split occasion: the genially general memoir occasion of capturing a time and place, the eponymous Treetops. And she tells us that after writing *Home Before Dark*, "I began to see that I had told only half the story—my father's story. The myths he created about himself were part of a larger family legacy: a history passed on and embroidered to serve its members." So, the second occasion is the desire for balance, an occasion that is self-generated, since the world in all likelihood does not register that only half a story has been told. And here I must digress to discuss this intermingling of public and private motive. Certainly one's memories performed/rehashed/explored in writing always entails this mix. But I always find it interesting and curious when the writer asserts that the record needed to be set straight. Of course it didn't. As readers, we couldn't care less about the imbalance of revealed family history, unless of course it *reads* as imbalanced, as skewed or self-deceiving or protectively partial. When my students ask about bending facts (*What if we decided to lie and completely revised the ending of an autobiographical narrative?*) I answer them with this: no one would probably know, though your own process would be compromised, and might not lead you to the most important truths you want to reach. This doesn't mean the work would lack admirable literary qualities. In the supreme court of my autobiographical writing, I'm a rather strict constructionist. My politics are another question.

And perhaps this is where we need to meditate on the case of Lillian Hellman. In 1971, Mary McCarthy was on the Dick Cavett Show, and was opining on the relative merits of American writers who were "overrated." To be fair, she was asked the question, and in retrospect it seems something of a setup, though also to be fair (and here I lean the other way like a tottering ship) one must point out that McCarthy was no innocent lured into error by a worldlier interviewer. She took the bait, when Cavett asked her about Lillian Hellman. Now, Hellman and McCarthy were the twin doyennes of the New York literary world, approximate contemporaries in their sixties; Hellman represented the unreconstructed left, and McCarthy the liberal anticommunist brigade. In other words, the Cain and Abel of political siblings. What about Lillian Hellman? McCarthy replied, "Every word she's ever written is a lie, including and and the." The next day, in New York Civil Court, Hellman sued McCarthy for slander, a suit that would drag on and only reach its final conclusion when Hellman died. What happened in the interim, however, was consequential attention given to the autobiographical prose works that Hellman had been writing to great acclaim: *An Unfinished Woman, Scoundrel Time.* (In which Hellman talks of her experience with another McCarthy, Joseph, who sent her emphysemic partner, Dashiell Hammett, to prison, and prompted Hellman to write to the committee, when they requested that she testify, a line that should be infamous: "I will not cut my conscience to fit this year's fashions.") Alas, it would seem that some years later Hellman did. The middle essay of her third collection, *Pentimento*, the central essay in fact, is called "Julia," which was made into a film starring Jane Fonda and Vanessa Redgrave, directed by Fred Zinnemann, movingly middlebrow stuff. And the only essay I can think of to be turned into a film, though I think Chaplin was contemplating "Death of the Moth," by Virginia Woolf, until he decided that it wasn't written yet. Seriously, though, the essay is about serious stuff: Hellman smuggles money into Berlin in the late thirties so her lifelong friend, almost inamorata, can help save Jews, Catholics, others in peril. The mission is a success, but Julia, Vanessa Redgrave, begins to languish, is imprisoned, etc. . . . Hellman returns, and eventually, in the afterglow of her career, writes this concentrated, moving, amazing chronicle. Amazingly moving. Movingly amazing. Never happened.

No need for a readerly double take. Hellman essentially made the whole thing up, including the woman formerly known as Julia, who was based on an actual person whom Hellman didn't know, but whose life she freely appropriated from. And the lawsuit was the machina that set the discovery in motion. To which we might ask:

Is the book now sold as fiction? No.

Did Hellman ever admit the fabrications? No. (And note the force of nonfictive gullibility among readers: why did anyone believe that a Jewish American playwright went on a covert mission to Berlin in the late thirties?)

Do we know less about Hellman as a consequence? No, ironically, we know more, since we know how she would, how she did construct a narrative so propelled by her desire—that word again—that she, in writing, lived the lie, performed a preferred life. Along with much other material whose veracity is unquestioned or tested.

What is the occasion of a narrative that never happened? For our purposes, I would say that this was the $64,000 question if a) that, too, hadn't been a hoax, b) anyone cared to pay that much for the corpus delicti of an essay, and c) again, desire, to be other than who one is.

Most of us, though, are simply not important enough for anyone to bother to check on our facts. In any case, no matter what kind of literary nonfiction, the facts are never the primary importance of the work. Facts are self-sufficient. They don't need literature. It is the interpretation of fact that all literary non-fiction is based on. Here I might remind you of Philip Roth's autobiographical *The Facts*. After a rather quick and listless recitation of his memory's salient moments, Roth's book is critiqued, in an afterward by his autobiographical character, Zuckerman. Problem is that Zuckerman is, in my opinion, quite right about the defects of the book, and the cleverness of imitative form is never sufficient—we don't want to read a bad performance for the comedy of the critique. In *Operation Shylock*, Roth, with the occasion of recovery from Halcion-induced mania, performs a much more deft dance on the borderlines of fiction and nonfiction, that region where the literary pale begins.

Back to occasions. Much more convincing than because it was, or because I am, as an excuse for autobiographical excursions, is: because I am because it was. Or he, she, or they. The author has reached a point in life where difficult questions can be asked, where the self is complicated enough in adult history and knowledge of the world (including literary knowledge) to be able to undertake an exploration. This is similar to Ellen Douglas's *Truth*, but perhaps less delayed, less an endgame. One can, or one must summon the past, to put ghosts to rest, or raise the restless spirits, or both. Edward Dahlberg, at the beginning of *Because I Was Flesh*, writes: "Kansas City was the city of my youth, and the burial ground of my poor mother's hopes; her blood, like Abel's, cries out to me from every cobblestone, building, flat, and street." There is no way of predicting, until the end of this most Oedipal of narratives, that Dahlberg will arrive at the deliriously excessive lyricism of his final invocation: "and when I regard her wild tatters, I know that not even Solomon in his lilied raiment was so glorious as my mother in her rags." Apologies, but Frank McCourt please step aside; the title of *Angela's Ashes* predicts exactly where the memoir will go, and the portrait of Angela seems relatively static to me.

Occasions are of course limitless. But these classics that recur: I must tell this story, to 1) try to find out what really happened, 2) try to find out what it meant, 3) make sure that an important element of our culture is not forgotten, 4) exorcise the demons that sit on the edge of these experiences like fallen angels, and 5) because it represents a set of experiences that has never been captured. This latter has of course fueled the rise of memoir in the United States over the last thirty years, as memoirs by women, African-Americans, Mexican-Americans, Asian-Americans . . . flock to shelves that had once been closed to them, like restricted country clubs. There they join the memoirs of personal disaster I alluded to above, which have also been in short supply thanks to cultural ignorance, or censorship of the Puritan or Victorian or more vaguely squeamish variety. As a representative phenomenon, I can't stress enough how important this movement has been, with many works of outstanding autobiographical literature. But this doesn't elide my argument that current American creative nonfiction has buried the essay, its most interesting form, under a generic mountain of autobiographical narrative.

But to reiterate, or perhaps to iterate, your occasion is an act of deference of sorts. I am here telling you about myself for a reason. And the reason is . . . even if the reason is that I need to try to find out what the reason is.

An occasion may, of course, be complex and multiple, and frequently bury the lead, even heaven help us, if it's burying the dead. My students at Ohio University working on the essay were hard-pressed to not write about the World Trade Center in Manhattan. Their occasion might seem laughably obvious, ostensibly. We were citizens of a country in crisis, an Orwellian grand occasion (leading to *Grand Illusion*) if there ever was one. But why the specific writer — we know what might bring anyone to want to write about this subject, but what brings this writer to it, around it? If I were writing it, other associations would suggest themselves easily. My family used to dine frequently at Windows on the World, the restaurant at the top of the Center. I remember one Christmas, my brother's birthday, watching the snow fall and gradually cover the city, my city, now so distantly, so gradually indistinctly, below me. A very different covering, a more innocent veil, than the one of those not made for TV nightmare images. Or I might have something to say about the Towers being completed when I was thirteen, when my lower Manhattan started vying with my upper Manhattan for dominance. It's the Manhattan project of pubescence, or something of the sort. But I'd probably want to speak about a lost city, ultimately — the way we lose things larger than us. A secondary occasion would have to be at the center of the essay's exploration, since an event is not really a promising central occasion, but may be an ostensible one, the thing that gets you going. The occasion is my need to write that essay in the shadow, to evoke Art Spiegelman, of all that happened. It is about me and larger than me.

And my students from Sandusky, or Youngstown, or Worthington, what was their personal occasion, if they hadn't the rhetorical gifts of Christopher Hitchens, the political insight and panache of the writers I cut my teeth with: Ellen Willis, Nat Hentoff, Tom Wicker, Orwell? Seeing the second plane slam into Tower Two on a TV screen in the student center, or their disaster of an apartment could set off a chain of essaying about language — disaster, let's say, or center (has it ever *really* held?) — or a mediation on how that student was driven inward, away from the body politic, by the mass media's hype about war, which she had never had the opportunity to experience fully as a member of the American polity, etc. . . . That the personal is rarely at odds with the political, is true, in fact, only as a statement of extreme alienation, which is in itself a potentially useful, informative, chilling, or heartbreaking statement on the state of our culture in microcosm.

It is for this reason that on the evening of September 11, 2001, in teaching my shocked class for fifteen minutes or so, I read them the following snippets from Orwell, this first from his essay "England Your England":

> As I write, highly civilized human beings are flying overhead, trying to kill me. They do not feel any enmity against me as an individual, nor I against them. They are "only doing their duty," as the saying goes. Most of them, I have no doubt, are kind-hearted law-abiding men who would never dream of committing murder in private life. On the other hand, if one of them succeeds in blowing to pieces with a well-placed bomb, he will never sleep any the worse for it. He is serving his country, which has the power to absolve him from evil. One cannot see the modern world as it is unless one recognizes the overwhelming strength of patriotism, national loyalty. In certain circumstances it can break down, at certain levels of civilization it does not exist, but as a positive force there is nothing to set beside it. Christianity and international socialism are as weak as straw in comparison with it. Hitler and Mussolini rose to power in their own countries very largely because they could grasp this fact and their opponents could not.

Orwell extends his consideration to the idea that there really are considerable differences in people from culture to culture, an idea that seems both contrary to certain kinds of humanistic sentimentality, and self-evident. He writes, "in fact anyone able to use his eyes knows that the average of human behavior differs enormously from country to country. Things that could happen in one country could not happen in another. Hitler's June Purge, for instance, could not have happened in England." Just so, despite my most cynical liberal bona fides, I would argue that there are limits to even my paranoia—I may argue that the feds can grab anyone off the streets, but I usually don't fear it myself. That may mark the limitations of white middle-class self-interest. I spend too much time thinking about what has grabbed my dear departed. I white knuckle death and sadness (mourning and melancholia?—Is the month of my mother's death the cruelest?) more than anything. But I try to think about them when writing about them.

Orwell moves to a discussion of what makes the English different, arriving first at the feeling that, "When you come back to England from any foreign country, you have immediately the sensation of breathing a different air." What follows is typical Orwell—memorable images that embody character-istics and ideology and progressive counter-myths masquerading as unbiased analysis, utterly convincing along the way. But to return to my larger subject, which is to say the one I began with, Orwell moves from his immediate oc-casion in the moment of writing (the chance of a bomb landing on his head, real, though unlikely) to a more general sense of who the hypothetical victim and perpetrator are, to the national differences of countries, to his analysis of what make the English who they are—the relationship of character and char-acteristic. The occasion is that a way of life is at stake: morally complex and frequently stupid, slow to change with more hurried change on the horizon, classist, devoted to the domestic pleasure of gardening. . . . The occasion has moved from what might happen to me to what might happen to us. He essays where the occasional action is for him. For other writers, that first line, that ostensible occasion, could lead to all kinds of variety on the road, or cul-de-sac, of truth.

As you may have noticed, I have moved from autobiography and memoir to the essay. Surprised? Am I not performing my own desire in this essay, the oc-casion being, among other things, a response to autobiography's seeming he-gemony in the world of creative nonfiction? Perhaps we need a separate camp, of destructive nonfiction, a wider, wilder, grayer zone, in which the essay and other fugitive forms, known and as yet undiscovered, can ply their wayward trades, following those occasional desires into open forms which—like the figure of my mother in 1963, for me—challenge facets of the imagination be-yond the complacencies of memory's narratives.

The Rape of Rusty

WAYNE KOESTENBAUM

> So perhaps whatever beauty of life still remains to me is contained in some moment of surrender, abasement, and humiliation.
> — OSCAR WILDE, *De Profundis*

✳ ✳

1

I used to jerk off while reading scenes from Gore Vidal's *Myra Breckinridge*.

I found it on my mother's shelf. I was ten, eleven, twelve, thirteen.

On the novel's black cover, a jubilant mannequin wore white cowboy boots, one knee raised, as if marching in place.

2

Myra Breckinridge notices—relishes—her student Rusty's body hair.

She strips him, fingers his hole, probes his prostate, rapes him with a dildo.

She performs a spontaneous, unlicensed doctor's exam on him.

The inspection is protracted, unwanted.

She arouses his nipples. She lowers his undershorts. She observes peach fuzz on his buttocks. Eventually she opens his hole to her sadistic, cinephilic inspection.

3

Words from *Myra Breckinridge*:

The total unveiling of the buttocks.

I beat the meat to the tune of this scene, a student's humiliation at the hands of a dildo-wielding transsexual.

I can't remember whether I brought the book into the bathroom, or read it in the living room, memorized the relevant chunks, and then retreated to our carpeted sanctum, a lavatory I could lock.

I sought the parts in *Myra* where she notices Rusty's body hair and humiliates him as if in retribution for his physical maturity.

Did I identify with shamed Rusty? Or did I identify with punitive Myra, questing for erotic information?

I don't want to pretend to stand at an objective distance from these experiences.

4

My third grade teacher ordered a disobedient boy to pull down his pants in front of the class. She paddled his naked ass. He was crying and trembling.

Call him Robbie. Call her Mrs. Fact.

5

Myra rapes Rusty, though I never called it rape when I was a kid—I imagined merely that Myra was a scientist, a quester for information about how boys matured into men.

A teacher, posing as a nurse, Myra wanted to discover what Rusty's body hair looked like. She wanted to touch the tufts.

I knew a Myra once. She was the mother of my friend—a prematurely gigantic kid with an unpleasantly raucous manner. This Myra was a typist, tall, blonde. I associate her with a comedic undertone and an abundance of paper clips.

6

Raquel Welch starred in *Myra Breckinridge* (the film); Mae West costarred. On my bedroom wall, I taped a poster of Raquel in *One Million Years B.C.*, and a poster of Mae in *Every Day's a Holiday*.

I performed an ordinary displacement, extracting erotic energy from Rusty (as written by Vidal) and transplanting it onto Welch and West.

I, like Welch and West, was a "W," a Wayne.

I drank Welch's grape juice. I lived in the West.

I read Mae West's autobiography, *Goodness Had Nothing to Do With It*, largely because she appeared in *Myra*.

The movie was rated X.

A circle around the X was prohibition's trademark, like the ring around the copyright sign's C.

7

Myra Breckinridge was playing at Century 25, a bulbous theater a few blocks away from our tract house.

I begged my father to sneak me into the show, as if he had the power.

I convinced him to ask the theater manager to make an exception to the adults only rule and to admit me, a juvenile, to *Myra Breckinridge*. The manager refused.

I didn't see the film until, at age thirty, I bought a VCR player.

The first video I rented was *Faster, Pussycat! Kill! Kill!* The second was *Myra Breckinridge*. Both films parody female sadism.

8

In memory, permanent, this image: Rusty's rear, as seen by Myra.

We watch the buttocks unfold, like plot.

Myra says, upon first beholding his genitals: "Poor Mary Ann. That's a boy's equipment."

I had a boy's equipment.

Rusty's girlfriend was named Mary Ann. So was my first girlfriend.

I met my Mary Ann in kindergarten.

By the time I first read *Myra Breckinridge*, I had already betrayed Mary Ann, rejected her, treated her unkindly — so ungenerously that her older brother, Greg, threatened to beat me up.

9

I understood what Myra wanted — to place herself in a cinematic pantheon, and to get revenge against cute hairy guys who'd snubbed her when she was a boy. She exacted retribution by sexually humiliating them — teaching them that their buttocks were erotic fodder.

10

Myra, a connoisseur, understood certain facts: "Like so many young males, he has a relatively hairless torso with heavily furred legs. Myron was the same. With age, however, the legs lose much of this adolescent growth, while the torso's pelt grows heavier."

I loved Myra's knowledgeable tone — her understanding of the consistency, amid variety, or men's secondary sexual characteristics.

She approached men's bodies as a researcher, an empirically minded pervert, a film scholar, a fan of Parker Tyler's writings.

More than once my prose has been accused of bearing resemblance to Parker Tyler's.

11

Myra Breckinridge was my mother's book, a hardcover, shelved under "V."

I helped alphabetize her library.

She paid me, per hour, for this service.

Fifty cents?

A good fee.

I enjoyed helping my mother classify.

Among the sorted items were D. H. Lawrence's *Lady Chatterley's Lover,* a prized source of passages describing men's furred bodies.

Escutcheon-like, hair exposed men to humiliation but gave them secret immunity from their captors.

Myra was attracted to Rusty's body hair, but she also wished to punish him for it.

12

Critics panned the movie *Myra Breckinridge.*

I read the reviews.

I remember being awestruck by the negativity of the critics.

How was it possible to hate so strongly, so self-confidently?

How was it possible to criticize Mae West from such an assured position of vantage?

I was fascinated by point of view — Myra's point of view on Rusty, the critic's point of view on the movie *Myra Breckinridge.*

This position of knowledgeability seemed an arcane and inscrutable pedigree.

13

Breck's shampoo was never far from my mind as I saw or said the word "Breckinridge."

I knew the thick smell of Breck's: bubbly, coppery, marketable, synthetic yet agricultural, like modern poppies.

14

Rereading *Myra Breckinridge* today, I choose to interpret it as an oblique riposte to Susan Sontag's "Notes on 'Camp'" (first published four years before Vidal's novel). Myra is a scholar of camp taste, an ambulatory encyclopedia (as Andy Warhol might have put it) of Hollywood ephemera. Significantly, Myra/Myron's psychoanalyst is named Montag. Myra, in her invincible smartness, her unplaceable eroticism, and her political ambivalence, is Sontag-like.

Sontag/Montag: S/M.

This present essay is, obviously, a montage, a manner Sontag perfected.

The second chapterette of *Myra* begins with a Sontagesque sneer against retrograde realism: "The novel being dead, there is no point to writing made-up stories. Look at the French who will not and the Americans who cannot."

Vidal dedicates *Myra* to Christopher Isherwood, in whose work the word "camp" (in its queer sense) made its first printed appearance, according to Sontag herself, who calls his sketch, in a punishing adjective, "lazy."

15

Says Myra, "Deliberately I took the Jockey shorts by the elastic waistband and pulled them slowly, slowly down, enjoying each station of his shame."

Prose divides shame into stations.

In stations, we watch Rusty's shame, or Robbie's — Robbie, whose pants were pulled down in Mrs. Fact's class, because, as I recall, he'd made the mistake of saying "Hell" or "Goddamn it," a verbal infraction.

Disobedience ran in families. Two or three disobedient dynasties dominated our school — cartels of brothers who talked back.

I feared I would be Mrs. Fact's next victim. I, like Robbie, liked to talk back.

16

Our teacher had conspicuous swaying breasts and a slight mustache.

She loved her paddle.

It hung by the drinking fountain in the back of the classroom.

The paddle was inscribed with an aphorism about how punishment makes men wise.

Wisdom came also from the intercom, a broadcasting contraption, mounted on the classroom wall. This intercom — as opaque, silver monstrance — reminded me of the mask a fencer wears to protect the face.

17

Mrs. Fact divided our third grade class into two reading groups: advanced and regular.

I belonged to the advanced reading group.

Robbie belonged to the regular.

We in the advanced group stayed after class for an extra hour of accelerated reading.

That was our gift, our prerogative — our literacy lessons took place after the rest of the students, the ordinary ones, left for home. Robbie was a slow reader. But he'd said "Hell" or "Goddamn it," so he stayed late, after the others in his middling group had departed.

18

Mrs. Fact said to him, "Do you want to pull down your underpants here, in the classroom, or outside, where the fourth graders can see?"

The fourth graders were playing soccer on the lawn.

I weighed the two options. Which was more humiliating—to strip in front of the advanced reading group, or in front of the soccer players?

Robbie chose to be punished indoors.

19

Robbie was wearing white underwear. I remember it as Carter's, because that was the brand I wore.

Palpitating, he pulled it down himself.

I recall his buttocks as red and pimply.

How I could see pimples from across the room?

His tears made him seem an idiot, a goat, dog.

A slow reader.

In two years I'd be advanced enough to read *Myra Breckinridge*.

20

As Mrs. Fact paddled Robbie's buttocks, I saw his small, prepubescent, hairless penis, available for our inspection—we, the accelerated readers, gathered in a frightened circle, supposedly staring at our books, but instead riveted by the spectacle of a boy whose Carter's underwear had been pulled down; he had lowered it himself, when the teacher insisted, a pretty woman, young, recently married, formerly Miss Fancy, now Mrs. Fact.

21

I can't help replaying this scene, a remake spawning multiple remakes, *Beyond the Valley of Myra Breckinridge*, *The Return of Myra Breckinridge*, *Myra III* . . . .

I replay the punishment scene—Mrs. Fact paddling Robbie's naked ass—whenever I write, or speak in public, or lecture to a class, even if the seminar is called (in an abreactive gesture) "Humiliation," a graduate course I recently taught. We read *King Lear*, *Jane Eyre*, Kristeva's *Powers of Horror*, Sade's *120 Days of Sodom*, Wilde's *De Profundis*, Wright's *Black Boy*, Artaud's "To Have Done with the Judgement of God," Genet's *Funeral Rites*, Levi's *Survival in Auschwitz*, Plath's *Ariel*, Saramago's *Blindness*, Jelinek's *The Piano Teacher*, and essays on shame by Silvan Tomkins; we saw Fassbinder's *The Bitter Tears of Petra von Kant*. These exemplary texts were stations of our rediscovery and reclamation of humiliation—its magnetism, and what I call "the *eccola* effect," epitomized by the moment that Lucia di Lammermoor (in Donizetti's opera) comes onstage for her mad scene. Lucia, wearing her bloodied nightgown, holds a knife; she has just finished slaying her bridegroom Arturo. As she enters, the chaplain Raimondo says "*Eccola!*" There she is! There is the madwoman, ready for her big number! This is her moment of glory but also her moment of humiliation, because no one wants to be caught sleepwalking, no one wants to be caught on stage with soiled nightclothes.

Eccola! That might have been what the bystanders said when Oscar Wilde appeared at the train station while he was being moved from one prison to another. For a half hour in the rain, he was exposed to the mocking crowd, who spat and jeered. He considered it the most humiliating moment of his entire life.

He was being pointed out.

He was being seen.

Eccola, we say, and point.

We recognize this man at his nadir, naked, soiled, jeered at, rained upon, with a thermometer shoved up his ass, Myra's anal thermometer, Keats's "Pleasure Thermometer."

22

"It sets before me at once the gradations of Happiness even like a kind of Pleasure Thermometer . . ." (John Keats, letter to John Taylor, 30 January 1818).

Happiness or humiliation.

23

Two good girls in my third grade class saw Robbie's penis. I remember my sense of horror that the small panicked item between his legs (a slack or stiff appendage best hidden inside Carter's underwear) was being observed by girls—innocents, straight-A students, pianists. One of these good girls would later in the year perform "Für Elise" for our class.

24

Says Myra, of Rusty: "He leaned rigidly, all of a piece, to one side and grabbed the fallen trousers. Had he slightly squatted—the normal thing to do in his position—I might have caught a glimpse of the heart of the mystery from the rear, an unflattering angle which, paradoxically, has always excited me, possibly because it is in some way involved with my passion for 'backstage,' for observing what is magic from the unusual, privileged angle."

I, like Myra, value backstage vantage.

I appreciate the back room, the backyard, the back street, the back door — the anterior meaning, the obscured scene, the oblique entrance to revelation.

In the back room, culture's caretakers store the junky and the obsolete, the broken and the mannered, the prose of Parker Tyler, the films of Rose Hobart, artifacts for which no profitable use has yet been found.

25

When I was in first grade, someone set my elementary school on fire.

My older brother was in the third grade when the fire occurred.

He described to me the melting intercom on his classroom wall.

The heat from the fourth grade room traveled through the wall and melted the intercom on the third grade side.

About the liquefying intercom (like a timepiece in Salvador Dalí's painting *The Persistence of Memory*), my brother said: "That's how I knew the school was on fire. The intercom was melting."

Each classroom had an intercom, near the Seth Thomas clock and the unfinished portrait of George Washington by Gilbert Stuart.

Intercoms transmitted the voice of the principal announcing recess, the pledge of allegiance, assemblies, emergencies.

The intercom was a silver, speckled screen, a communicative surface, cold and heartless, neutrally releasing information, originating nothing of its own.

26

Supposedly, a local arsonist — a boy — set the elementary school on fire.

I'm not sure the authorities ever caught him.

He might have been merely a rumor.

Rumor or reality, he set several fires in the neighborhood.

The elementary school didn't burn down. It merely suffered minor charring. And a melting intercom.

27

I've saved this secret, this story of Robbie's punishment, for decades. Magical possessions belong backstage, husbanded in privacy — like fondled texts, books circulated apart from customary channels of publication.

I like disseminations to take place privately, in back rooms, in grottoes, in antechambers, saunas, stalls, basements, places where one might be surprised by a foreman from the front room suddenly appearing and turning on the light to shout, "*Eccola!*"

28

The slowness of Myra's act of stripping Rusty, or forcing him to undress himself, in her office, showed me that fantasies, and acts of literary production, may be slow; that analysis may be protracted; that reminiscence may crawl, not run. I took Myra's gradual rape of Rusty as a lesson in how desire proceeds incrementally through its stations and stages, never rushing to colonize its prey, but proceeding, like a fugue, layering the information a step at a time, sometimes repeating the figures, never apologizing for the repetition—for in life, as in any invention, or any work of literature, however lofty or pedestrian, there exists a fixed set of dominating themes, and mere diligence cannot increase their number or alter their nature. Their substance, if not their sequence, remains incorrigibly the same.

29

When I returned home from school, the day of Robbie's martyrdom, I told my mother what had happened. We stood in our side yard, beside the bamboo. I don't think my tale shocked her.

Of our bamboo I remember not the stalks but the thin leaves that fell compulsively and made a dry, papery sound when walked upon. The bamboo hugged the house's side wall. The leaves, which seemed happier to fall than to remain hanging on their stalks, were either brownish yellow or greenish yellow, an unattractive color. Our redwood fence, near the bamboo, left rust red stains on the hands if you were foolish enough to touch its always contagious surface.

The Bed of the Fairy Princess

JOANNA FRUEH

✳ ✳

Once upon a time in a magical city not too far away from yours, a fairy princess began a new life. She had purchased a house from a fairy man of exquisite taste, and she loved her new home, her new neighborhood, and the city itself, which dazzled in a desert filled with prickly pears and chollas, saguaros and agaves, oleander and ocotillo. The sun shone most days, in a sky whose multitude of blues would swallow your heart, if you were ready for the healing of heaven. When her friends from not too far away asked the princess about her new home, she told them, simply, the truth: "I am in heaven." ("That can't be true. It can't be real." So said unfriendly spirits. You know how they populate the planet with beliefs about the necessary suffering of human beings. Skeptical, nay-saying spirits cast the human lot to hell.) The magical desert city was known far and wide for its summer heat, and the fairy princess had moved there when, day after day, the temperature was over 105 degrees. Then the monsoons came. Their short torrents brought the desert into bloom, and all over town a shrub called Texas ranger thrilled the inhabitants with profusions of purple blossoms; and in some gardens roses sweetened a viewer's vision.

Fairy prince, she prayed, come stretch your legs out in my bed. It is adorned in Dionysian beauty. Grape vines and clusters are waiting to surround our pleasure. Come heal me in my blue sheets, the color of this desert sky when it is moving into monsoon mood. Fairy prince, I am in a homecoming, a heartwarming. Come warm your heart with mine.

Becoming acquainted with her neighborhood on morning walks around 6 A.M., before the heat went too much to her head, the fairy princess lingered to smell the roses here and there. In traditional fairy tales, the rose is the narrators' favored flower. It blooms in Hans Christian Andersen's Garden of Eden, where, at sunset, lilies turn rose red; and in his story "The Wild Swans," millions of red roses, which proclaim the innocence of a princess, perfume the air and eyes of a crowd whose jeers give way to the joyous pealing of church bells. ("That can't be true. It can't be real. The voice of dumb and hostile masses: it will never ring out in love." The labor of torn-hearted beings consists of wringing the spirit out of spirituality.)

Fairy prince, she sang, come to my searching lips, which I have colored a long-lasting rose red. The lipstick tube reads Power House. Here, at home, we seek the powers of red and purple, the grapey colors loved by Dionysus and his girls.

The fairy man whose home the fairy princess bought sold her a bed that drew a Wow! a Cool! a Beautiful! from everyone who saw it — any man or woman of any age or station. Designed by a desert artisan and fashioned of steel — leaves painted dusty green, grapes a soft magenta, vines weathering into golds and coppers — the frame sat almost three feet off the ground, so that the bed seemed to be levitating, and the vines rose up to five feet on every side. The princess found a footstool so that she could easily climb into the covers and so that the prince she called and sang to would feel welcomed in her fairy bed. At first she said to people about the bed, It's so feminine! She thought that men wouldn't like it — so voluptuously undulating, so frankly vegetal. Then she let men's enthusiasm about the structure of the bed change her mind. Indeed, it was sturdy and spaciously proportioned — well built. She realized that its fine structure allowed the men to speak responsively without having to reveal their attraction to its intoxicating sensuousness.

Fairy prince, come to my bed. Climb out of that car you bought to glide along Pacific highways, to glide into this desert: that silvery-blue Jaguar. I am your cat, whose paws and tongue know where to linger where you like them.

People living in other cities asked the fairy princess how she managed in the heat. She responded, "I slow down." Luxuriating in that slowness, she saw and lived life at a manageable pace. The rush — to nothing — of contemporary life passed her by, and, walking one early morning, she thought, "I live in a neighborhood of palaces and trash. Big houses that are well maintained and walled off from the street. Small ones — some cared for and some unadorned by love. I live in a city where residential streets are as big as boulevards, so they make you want to speed in your car. Fifty miles an hour. More." Uninhibited ease; gliding: that is the way she imagined speeding, so that, oddly enough, swiftness and slowness were, in her mind, equivalents.

"Welcome, neighbor!" the mailman greeted her the first time they met.

"Humanitarian Aid Is Never a Crime," read placards in many front yards, both trashed and palatial.

Artists had decorated roundabouts: she stepped into a painted patch of huge prickly pears on the street itself; she studied the figures on a picture mounted like a stop sign. The composition reminded her of Masaccio's angel driving Eve and Adam from the Garden, but here, in her neighborhood, an angel on a bicycle, above, was urging on angels below. The princess took herself to be a fellow angel, helped by this humanitarian image, into Go: forward—fast and easy, slow and steady. ("That isn't true—the fast and slow as one pace. This princess clings to paradox, the kind we see in mystic texts, where, in Christian absurdity, the meek inherit the earth and, in Taoist nonsense, learning comes from unlearning the things you know.")

She noticed many churches in her neighborhood as she walked through it at a graceful pace. Some of the churches had become private residences, some were in use for their congregations, and one was undergoing renovation. She crossed the street from another, Holy Name, to stand in front of the Redeemed Art Gallery. It was not associated with any church, and this early in the day it was not open. Brightly colored metal sculptures—abstract, playful—filled both the gallery's interior and the fenced-in yard. The fairy princess cried. Right there, right then, the desert and its trash and palaces, its purple, pink, and rose-red flowers, its rains and its reasons—for being beautiful, for simply being—were releasing her into a humanity of limitless heart, into the holy name that belonged to everywoman and everyman: angel. All that *angel* means is messenger, and in this desert garden she was feeling more and more able to sustain and communicate its heavenly effects. (The skeptic spirits cannot bear any language that seems to them impractical. They define impracticality as falsehood, and so they chorus wildly, "Jeez, get down from that high horse you can only ride in heaven!")

The fairy princess listened to the parakeets that sang in the front yard of the house at the corner of her street. Like the princesses in famous fairy tales, her long hair gleamed, and she was beautiful. But, unlike them, she was not a girl in years, she did not miss the sometimes gloomy shade of the northern European forests that were home to her sisters in those stories, and she was not a virgin untouched by man, unused to sexual intercourse. She had slept with more than enough men; and she was a virgin in ancient, pagan terms. She was virgin territory, "fiercely independent," as a young male friend had called her, native soil for new ideas, fresh perspectives, and new men. ("No one enters her adulthood that unspoiled," the jaded skeptics sneer. "No woman, neither old nor young maid, lives life long without a subdued body and a substantially splayed heart. This is the story of a woman spinning tricks in order to muster romantic diversions from reality.")

Although she loved sexual pleasure and had never hidden that from friends or lovers, she had not been easy in her loves with men. Nor slow. Rushing into sexual relations, her emotional closeness with her partners could have flourished more; and her rush to orgasm—a peak that arrived quickly and many times—often precluded the connection that she prayed for now, in which the embrace of a thoughtful, giving, kind, intelligent, and loving fairy prince would break her resistance to the intimacy that only love can free. ("That can't be true. That can't be real. 'True love': it is an epithet. The ones who wield that phrase imperil their own sanity. Truth is something you can prove. It is a fact, like fire on the stove, not in the eyes, and the heat of a desert, not in the loins. Truth: it is uncomfortable, and the uncomfortable truth of 'true love' is that it ruins the 'true lover's' perception of reality.") Of course, she hadn't demanded immediate intercourse with soon-to-be lovers, but she could have explored—in simultaneously more conscious, intimate, and intuitive ways—the save and savor of tongue on clitoris and tip of cock and within her vagina; of fingers stroking forearm, calf, or belly; of eye to eye for as far as eyes can see; of kisses paused and then continued with a conversation theorizing a preference for penetration from the rear or from the front. The fairy princess was philosophically as well as erotically inclined. In fact, she could not separate philosophy from eros, and relaxed, alone, in her new home, she knew she had been missing the meaning of *making love*.

Fairy prince, please demand nothing of me. It is the only way to break this spell, of fucking rather than making love.

Orgasm is high pleasure, and in the goal oriented culture in which the fairy princess lived, fucking was the way to get to orgasm. But orgasm accomplished by fucking, and, indeed, orgasm itself, is not the only high pleasure of physical intimacy. Hedonistic intimacies multiply in the embraces of true lovers of each other's soul-and-mind-inseparable-from-body. Hedonism derives from the Greek *hedone*, pleasure, and the fairy princess's dictionary gave the usage of the word by philosophers as: "the ethical doctrine that pleasure, variously conceived of in terms of happiness of the individual or of society, is the principal good and proper aim of action." Long ago a friend had called the fairy princess a hedonist, and she had declined what she now perceived as an honor: to be seen as a person who pursues happiness through pleasure. She wanted the happy pleasure of love with a fairy prince who would be a companion. They would accompany one another through life, they would share speed and roses. (The spirits of misery mocked happiness itself. They laughed to their gloomy rhyme, "a lie, a lie, pie in the sky.")

Honey prince, eat at my house, all the dessert that you've been wanting. Lie down in this desert garden, this flower bed, and I will join you in singing for our supper. Panther, pussy, pussycat, O now I lay me down to sleep.

Fucking could be a form of her resistance, sensationally exciting though it was. Fucking, the word and the act, had been her flash of poetry in the mundane world of must do this and must do that, of whaddya know? and why don't you think? As the philosopher Norman O. Brown wrote, "There is only poetry," and so, the fairy princess thought, we must take it any way and anywhere we can. Yet, a poem can be an ideology and a body can be a wall.

Let me be like water, soft and flowing, prayed the fairy princess. It brings out all the white and pink and purple in my garden. Help me to release the ideology that fucking is the only purity of sexual encounter.

Cover me in sweat and ecstasy. You know as well as I that maenads bleeding wine from every pore were sweating for their Dionysus.

The princess waited for the monsoon rains. In a trance produced by desert heat and stillness she remembered someone's surprise when she had said in another city and close to a decade ago, "I'm not staying here forever." How could she when a wand had waved its sparkle over her and given her directions to the magical city not too far away from yours? Although she had not been observant enough to see the stars that whirled and drifted from the sparkle or to feel the breeze that it created all around her or to trust what she was seeking, the princess gradually began to know where she was going. To a living room and dining room that protected her with earth tones, the colors of a cave. To neighbor dogs whose muzzles she petted when watering aloes on the patio. To a huge stone head of Buddha in the corner of a backyard and the plastic pink flamingo, Buddha's friend, that stood nearby. To dew point and brow sweat. To palo verde beetles whose presence signaled that the rains were on their way. To the place that welcomed her with spirits saying, "You are home and it will introduce you to your fairy prince."

He arrived.

He brought her gifts: his thoughtfulness and generosity, his kindness and experience, his love and his intelligence. He seduced her masterfully, because he saw who she was. Seduction can seem sweet, even when it's malevolent. Seeing her truly, the fairy prince seduced her with beneficence, true sweetness. And speed. Together, they were wizards of romance. Together, in love, they cruised, brakes off, into each other's innocence. White as the wings of the brothers, turned into swans by a bad queen's spell, in "The Wild Swans." White: it was the color of a string bikini that he gave her because he knew the shapes of her body and the size of her heart. She said, "I can't wear that." He wondered why and disagreed: "I want you to see yourself as I do. I want you to see how incredible you are." She felt so seen that she feared herself, but she had become tired of her resistance to intimacy; and intimacy was all he wanted. The prince energized the princess, taking away her tiredness, which was a spell she had cast on herself. The bikini fit her perfectly, and the fairy princess cried when she modeled it for her prince. She cried because in his sight, and now in hers, she was all and only who she was, and that made love easy. He gave her black goods, too, and purple, *violet*, he called it, the color of the Texas ranger that they saw through the windows from the fairy bed. The goods were lingerie whose transparencies and lace brought her heart into focus. "For-me more than fuck-me," was her thought. Enamored, he disarmed her of her fears.

Thank you, Aphrodite and other divinities of love, for revealing my heart in its every operation. I am in catharsis, and the burden of an inability to receive love melts away. Thank you, companion who sees me clearly and who loves the essence and elaborations of that vision. Our love making is the conversation embedded in the rose.

At first she couldn't imagine making love with him. He was so different from bygone lovers. He wanted everything from her and made her giving it so easy. The fairy princess told a friend about her feelings and about a dinner date at which she and the fairy prince ate and drank and talked for five hours without looking at any clock. Her friend said, with a little smile, "You've been making love for five hours." How gentle the practice of love became as the fairy princess and her companion prepared in their imaginations and unconsciously to climb into her high high bed.

He did not sweep her off her feet or turn her head over heels. Simply, he set her on solid ground. His love came from reason moderating passion. Aristotle advised the moderation of passion by reason. Perhaps that philosopher, the teacher of a boy who became Alexander the Great, guided his pupil on such a path of sanity.

The fairy princess and the prince kissed and touched, then talked philosophy. Aristotle, Nietzsche. They kissed again, and her bare foot found his thighs. They talked some more. Kierkegaard on seduction. Metaphysics and fucking. Craving and satisfaction. Happiness and ethics. Had Alexander lost all reason when he took on Persian ways?

She no longer looked for the consuming—the consumptive—passion of crazy-making love, the throes that made Tristan and Isolde famous. The fairy princess heard her companion saying, "You're so reasonable," not because she agreed with him on this or that, but rather because she didn't argue from stale emotion or from constipated principles. ("The truth hurts," repeated the tedious spirits ad nauseam.)

The fairy princess and her prince shared orgasms and catharses, but those were not their goals. They came to, in a consciousness bedazzled by the naked truth, which was as simple as their bodies. Long ago, the princess had learned that one of the oldest meanings of the unclothed body is naked truth. They sobbed together in her Dionysian palace of a bed. He cried in sadness over his recently deceased father. She cried because he called her on her coolness, which proceeded from fear. "I don't think that you understand men: they want sex, they need sex. It's physiological." So that she wouldn't have to talk anymore, she said, "I'm fried," and turned away from him. He said, "That's a silly subterfuge." She said, "You're right." Then, still not turning toward him, she offered, "I do understand men. And I don't care." They listened and they spoke, and their intention, put into practice not achievement, was clear: making love, again and always, in a continuity of conversation. To converse with belly laughs and wisdom, mojitos and mimosas, while walking or watching movies, while cooking meals or sharing a chocolate malt, on all occasions, high in the fairy bed or witnessing the streaming light after a driving rain was to delight in consummations, each one woven into the others.

In one catharsis, she thought, "I can never fuck again," because she was getting so close to the fairy prince, so close to the truth, that she remembered sex with bygone lovers when, though sensation was pouring into her, fucking alienated her from romance, which was blooming now, like the purple ranger and the red red rose, in the erotic conversation between her and the fairy prince. ("Romantic love is for the young. Or for the foolish—just like the princess.")

In the desert the princess noticed many men, from young to older, with shaved heads, and those men looked good. Maybe the fairy prince would be shaved-head sexy. In actuality, his dark, thick hair was going silver, just like hers. Surprising himself one day in the mirror, he asked himself, "Who *is* that young and handsome guy?" Like any man who's called a fairy prince, he *was* just a guy. He became a fairy prince in the bed of the fairy princess, so any frog he'd been was gone. Just as the princess knew that his kisses and his touch would heal her—she told him so after their first kiss—the prince felt renewed by her red red lips, her smooth smooth skin, which he called silk, and her soft soft labia, which he called petals. ("You call this true? This language that succumbs to corniness?") He had not imagined her unpredictability. She surprised him by calling "new" emotions that she experienced in his love, and those emotions renewed him. He had not imagined the innocence of her responsiveness to experiences—which, really, was her responsiveness to *him*. That innocence smoothed everything, from his skin to his daily life.

He awakened her with roses and truffles, and, like any right-minded and full-hearted prince, he kissed this Sleeping Beauty not so that she could be his, but rather so that she could be her own true self.

The fairy princess told her friends that she was undergoing "a radical re-awakening," as if she had been asleep to one and another aspect of her joy. "He awakens me in every way," she said to some, "from soul to mind to body," and to herself she said, "I reevaluate everything. From the hair on my head and lower lips to the colors of the sky and the shapes of the clouds; every-thing that is in this desert heaven." ("You cannot use metaphor as truth. That elevates the prose of everyday reality and can even give it the appearance of the sacred.")

Faith once had been a word that mystified her. She would have walked the other way after a date with the fairy prince; because she was unable to have faith in the breadth of the smiles he brought to her lips or the depths that had opened from the tears she wept with him. Now, in active beauty she thought, "A fairy tale is a story of faith," and in a magical city, what other kind of story could be told?

As poetry in motion filled her mind and moved it, all the voices that cursed people into apathy and apprehensiveness, that dissuaded them from love, argued till they choked. From choked, they changed to choking back, then choked up, and as the very poem that was the fairy princess changed, the voices changed too, into a chorus of roses that were singing in the wind that whipped through the neighborhood of trash and palaces.

The wind blew tree branches sideways and broke them too. The fairy prin-cess watched its effects and smelled the freshness that the wind brought. She heard the song of once unfriendly spirits, those who had recovered from their suffering:

> The wind is as wild as a fairy tale
> Listen, hearts, you cannot fail
> We wish you peace and merriment
> And everything that's heaven-sent

"The wind was wild," the fairy princess said to a friend of hers the next day. Her friend responded, "The wind was violent."

Flowers and animals were wild. Thoughts and feelings were wild. Violence twisted, wrenched, and forced. Violence destroyed things, it was extreme wildness, and though the wind had broken trees and blown their parts, with papers and loose objects, all along the wide streets, the princess did not feel hurt by it. Her friend, she sensed, felt violated by the wind, because her friend, she felt, regularly perceived violations. And her friend had not heard the friendly spirits' voices. Differences in observation and perception produced different truths, about the everyday as well as what philosophers call the Absolute. The fairy prince and princess made peace and merriment their foundation, and they built on it their palace of pleasure, a stately architecture where reason and passion, fucking and lovemaking were at home. Filled with thought and poetry, and voided, through their intention, of alienated energies, fucking entered their practice. Fucking, as word and action, excited them, and in a revelation that arrived while fucking the fairy prince, the fairy princess heard these words, "Making love, it rhymes with dove."

The fairy prince called his princess poet, seer, scholar, goddess, pin-up, peer. *Prince* can mean a good fellow or a preeminent male in any field. *Princess* can mean a graceful and accomplished female or one who's snobby, arrogant, and pampered. The terms are not equivalent. In conventional definitions, a prince and princess are not peers.

The prince's names for his princess suggested truths that he perceived, and he felt comfortable with them. Truth allows people, including prince and princess peers, to relax, into freedom, never complacency. Truth is comfortable; it comforts people: the fairy princess in the white bikini and black lingerie. Black and white: what could be clearer? Discomfort, the floating anxiety of faithlessness in all its vagueness, does not free the heart.

In the bed of the fairy princess, the loving peers embroidered the truth by attending to their inclinations. They embroidered, in order to make their feelings as clear as they could be. They embroidered in order to reveal consciousness, which was a place, like the bed of the fairy princess, where truth and faith were one.

And so, in the naked truth of love stitched through and intoxicated with grapey hues and flavors, the fairy prince said, in his reasonable and easy way, "We don't need more orgasms." Through her ears, she heard this: we don't *need* more orgasms; and she agreed, for pleasure had no number. In all consciousness, they loved the depths of penetration and all the unpredictable and limitless enchantments, the kind that came from the healing of heaven.

The Kazakh Eagle

ALPHONSO LINGIS

✳ ✳

When I was twelve I persuaded the old man to buy a purebred bull calf. Our cows were a mixed lot, bought at auctions on the cheap. The old man had come over from Lithuania and was more a peasant than an American farmer. He liked Guernseys, their orange and white color that makes them look more gentle than the black and white Holsteins and Brown Swiss we had in the herd.

A couple of miles up the road the three Peck sisters raised purebred Guernsey cattle. And Merino sheep whose skin, twice again too big for their bodies, bunched in wrinkles over them. Their wool was very fine between those wrinkles, not that there was any special market for extra-fine wool. The Peck sisters were middle aged and had wrinkles all over their faces. They had no hired man, and we saw pigeons flying in and out of broken windows on the second floor of their house. They were dressed in overalls and high rubber boots as they strode through the manure of the cow lot to corner and rope the calf.

Gentle they may look, Guernsey bulls grow up ornery; you hear of more farmers gored by Guernseys than by the much bigger Holsteins or Brown Swiss. But I persuaded the old man not to saw off the horns of the purebred calf. I saw myself exhibiting him in the county fair.

After the morning milking of the cows I led the bull on a leash to drink at the outside water tank, and again after the evening milking. At the tank I stroked his flanks as he swung his muzzle across the water, slurped and snorted. I sensed his force in the hopeful musculature of my puny body and his lusts inflamed mine. I was also lining up my body with boys of my age who guffawed and bragged about the manhood we were trying to fit into. But I was a farm kid among those town boys whose ideas of virility came from sports and movies and porn magazines. In two years the bull weighed probably near a ton, and I continued to lead him on a leash outside twice a day. He could have gored me just by turning his massive head.

The old man had come from the old country and spent twenty years working in factories until he could buy this farm that I would take over from him. But I left and became an academic. When he died the farm was sold. The Guernsey bull had been shipped off to the stockyards years ago.

Ken is an academic too; he teaches education theory in a university in another city. He's into critical theory—Paulo Freire, Pierre Bourdieu, Stuart Hall, Henry Giroux, Slavoj Žižek, that kind of thing. Thing about academics, you get the whole summer to make contact with reality, learn something. This time we talked about Mongolia.

"Mongolia was a Soviet satellite with military installations. I had looked into it once," I said; "couldn't get a tourist visa."

"Shamans," he came up with. "A shaman falls into a spell, maybe with a little help from our green and yellow friends, becomes a wolverine, a leopard, an eagle. It happens in Haiti, Nigeria, Bali, among the Native Americans. But the word shaman comes from the shamanism of Siberia and Mongolia." In fact Ken is allergic to religion, spiritism, animism, fetishism. None of that would stand up against critical theory.

"Tartars," I said. "In Lithuania the Mongols are called Tartars. Some Lithuanians told me my old man looked like he had some Tartar blood in him."

Ken is a big guy, strong as a horse, and he told me once that there was some talk in his family of Cossacks that raped in the area of Central Europe where his family came from. "In the Altai Mountains in the I think far east of Mongolia," Ken had read on some Web site, "there's a population of nomadic Kazakhs. It is only one theory," he said, "that the Cossacks are related to the Kazakhs."

So we took the flight from Ulaanbaatar to Bayan Olgii, in the Altai Mountains in the far west of Mongolia. At the airport we met a departing British NGO worker who said that bubonic plague had killed two people in the region and that the province would be closed to outsiders, quarantined, as soon the bureaucracy got all its papers stamped. "It happens regularly," he told us. "The virus is in the marmots. When they come out of hibernation at the end of winter, wolves and people hunt them for food."

In the fourteenth century the Mongols brought that virus to Europe and a third of the population died. The Black Death.

We asked the innkeeper if he knew someone with a vehicle who could take us for a round in the area. Shortly a young man came to our room, identifying himself as the English teacher at the high school here. He explained the nomads do not speak English and we would need a translator. The price would depend on how much gas would be used and what the driver wanted. He said he understood how visitors are distrustful of nomads in Mongolia, they think that once out in the distances they could be taken advantage of. He said he would write up a contract detailing what we would receive for the price; we would all sign it. He left to go locate a vehicle and driver.

Ken said, "I'm going to visit this dude's school. I bet they are ready to go charter, run the place for profit."

"We could give them some brochures, direct them to some Web sites," I said. "Do something useful on a trip for once."

The innkeeper had a boy take us to a small mud brick house on the edge of town where we met Canat. He threw sheepskins over a bench along the wall, invited us to sit and served us tea. He was small and lean, a boyish body with quick movements; on his oval face his dark eyes remained impenetrable as he grinned or laughed showing perfect teeth. His nose was long and thin like the beak of a bird of prey. He said he could take us, tomorrow if we wanted. He pointed to a four-wheel drive outside whose cracked windshield swirled glints from the setting sun. He spoke rapidly in stumbling English, throwing in Russian words instead of slowing down to fish for the English. Often the rush of mismatched words seized up, and he fell back and yukked. I realized how much I wanted to spend the next week in the radius of his black eyes and sizzling energy. I glanced at Ken who nodded.

We left at dawn. The four-wheel drive, of Russian make, which looked to me like a Jeep though less stylish, lurched across rocky slopes and sloshed through rivers. Canat relaxed expansively when we were far in the mountains and sighed with pleasure at the sight of the sweeping valleys that came into view as the jeepovich heaved over a mountain ridge. He sang songs in Kazakh, looked at us and laughed.

The snows had retreated up, and on the mountain flanks were scattered herds of horses, Bactrian camels, sheep and goats, and always two or three men or boys accompanying them. "Look at those horses," Ken turned to me. "This, dude, is where it all started. The herdsmen who as the last ice age was melting down drove their herds northward and pushed the peoples up north yet more northward and over the Bering Strait to dribble down into our American hemisphere. These are the horses on which the warrior-nomads thundered westward to push and shove the Teutonic barbarians who overran and trashed the Roman Empire." Remembering my old man's mastodonic work horses, these horses looked like ponies to me. "On these horses the hordes of Chinggis Khan raced over to Korea, across China, down to Java, over to Hungary. Closing off the Silk Road and forcing the silk-coveting and spice-hungry Europeans to their boats to circumnavigate the Cape of Good Hope to overrun India and Indonesia and cross the Atlantic to plunder the Aztecs, Maya, and Inca."

"And rape. Rape during slack moments of history," I muttered lest Canat caught that.

Canat told us the Kazakhs here were the Dzuuz Clan. Mostly it was enough to look at the treeless mountains, the people, their gear, and their animals to catch on the patterns and rhythms of activity. As a kid I spent whole days hanging out with the cattle and horses in the pastures.

Canat knew everyone we saw, and each time stopped to exchange news and gossip. Ken asked how he knew English. "In Moscow," he said. "When I finished high school I was picked out to go to the Soviet Union and study engineering. After two years they had me specialize in nuclear engineering."

"And you worked there as a nuclear engineer?"

"Lots of places. We never knew where they were. We would be seated in cargo planes where we couldn't look out the windows. When we got out there was no town, just a base camp."

So he had been at the launch centers in the last days of the thermonuclear arms race. When the US and Soviet Union had stockpiled enough thermonuclear weapons to destroy a Hiroshima-sized city every day for the next 550 years. (When I taught ethics I used to bring that up.) I had never even been in the army and looked at him as somebody out of a Star Wars movie. Couldn't even think of a question to ask him about those weapons or about the scenarios they rehearsed for their use. I wondered if he might have been in Cuba during the missile crisis.

"When the Soviet Union broke up," he said, "the foreigners in the military were sent home. My military education was useless in Ulaanbaatar, but I did know Russian and English, and passable Chinese, and got jobs, you know with export-import companies."

"Now you are staying here?" Ken asked.

"After two years, I came back here. I am staying here."

"You transport stuff with this four-wheel drive?"

"Yeah, the meat and skins the nomads have to sell. To Ulaanbaatar. Or to Siberia."

Siberia—that was a place I heard talk of a lot when I was a kid. Under the Czar, when my old man grew up there, troublemaking Lithuanians would be shipped off to Siberia. He had left Lithuania, crossing into East Prussia hidden in a hay wagon, in order to avoid being drafted into the Czarist army. The émigrés that came over after the war would tell of troublemakers being shipped to Siberia under the Soviets.

Canat swung the vehicle around rocks, improvising charges into mountains that looked impervious to motorized vehicles. I thought he must have driven military vehicles across terrains as forbidding. Ken asked, "Are you still in touch with the Russian military specialists you had been teamed up with?"

"Yeah," he said. "We get together. They call me Bad Dog," he laughed. "I go to Moscow once or twice a year. I can drive there in four or five days."

At day's end, we came to a ger camp. "Ger" is the word you use: "yurt" is a Russian word and not used by the Kazakhs or the Mongols. A ger, we saw, is some 15 feet in diameter; the circular wall is made of a wooden lattice frame that can be collapsed together for transport, the roof made of 90 to 110 spokes like a Chinese umbrella, the whole covered with felt made of wool pounded into sheets. Inside, the ground was covered with carpets, the walls with embroidered hangings in bright reds, purples, greens, and yellows. There were intricately carved chests. There was a Buddhist shrine veiled with the smoke of incense sticks.

A low table was immediately covered with salted milk tea, breads, cheeses, curds, and pastries for us. Soon the ger was crowded with people, each addressing us ceremonious words of greeting we did not understand. Chunks of dried dung were lit in the iron stove in the center with a chimney pipe that extended up and out, pots of rice were cooked, lamb or goat stewed. We can tell nothing of our wanderings and encounters, but they, regularly refreshed with glasses of fermented mare's milk, recount, shout, laugh. A young man played a stringed instrument rather like a mandolin. They were still drinking fermented mare's milk and telling tales when sleep overtook us.

In the chill morning the sheep, goats, and horses were milked. The sheep and goat milk will be made into cheeses; the mare's milk fermented to drink. Then the animals went off to graze and we climbed into a Tovarich Jeep. Ken and Canat talk cars. Ken has had nineteen cars since he got his driver's license, on average a car every six months. Bought on the cheap, no purebreds, so he knows every engine part that can blister, buckle, burst, blast. Ken starts talking about buying a Russian motorcycle and driving across Kazakhstan with Canat.

In the late afternoon of the third day, we approached a group of four ger on the side of a robust stream. Canat told us his wife's parents were here. He said his father-in-law had been the Communist governor of the province. They greeted us, and a young woman with them at once spread a low table with salted milk tea, breads, curds, cheeses. On the wall there was a painting of Lenin and a framed photo of the governor and his wife in formal Mongol dress. I asked the old man if he had been to the Soviet Union. Canat translated. Yes, he had, a number of times. He had also been to Poland, Hungary, Romania, Bulgaria, Latvia, Estonia, Lithuania. I said my parents had come from Lithuania.

Ken asked what he thought of the government in Mongolia now. "Things change," he said. "There are good things and there are bad things. Things do not stay the same."

I asked him if this is where they live now. "In the summer," he said. "In the winter we go down to the lower valleys where there is grazing for the animals."

When Canat made signs of leaving, I asked if I could take a photo of them. The old man opened a chest and took out a formal Mongol coat and waist sash, as his wife put on an embroidered shawl. They sat together and Canat and the young woman stood behind them, posed for a very formal picture.

That night we drove on higher. In the morning, we watched Aralbai, his wife, and his two adolescent sons milk the flocks and send them off to graze and wander. Aralbai returned to the ger, opened a chest and took out a white shirt, black trousers, and a long black coat with silver buttons. He fastened a broad belt of silver. Finally he put on a hat made, Canat murmured to us, of the tails of fifty mink.

We followed him outside to a stone corral on the flank of the mountain nearby where an eagle stood on a stump. She was tethered, we saw, with a stout cord fastened to one leg. Aralbai approached her, put on a leather sleeve and glove, untied the cord from her leg and she stepped on his hand. Canat translated his answers to my questions. The eagles are taken young from the cliff nests. It is female golden eagles that are taken, for they are the stronger hunters. A hawk is also kept and trained as a falcon; it will bring back hares and marmots to feed the eagle. When winter comes and the animals are in new thick fur, the hunters mount their horses and climb the mountains to release the eagles who soar over the mountains and return with foxes, lynx, even wolves. Eagles live forty or fifty years; after ten years the hunters release their eagles into nature so that they can find mates and reproduce. The eagle hunters wear this dress and these hats made of the tails of fifty mink. There are about two hundred of them in the Altai Mountains.

Aralbai held the eagle on his arm and gazed expressionless and long in the distances. In that gaze I saw the fierce intent, patience, and love of the high mountains of the eagle. Then he shouted and raised his arm and the eagle spread her wings and plunged upward into the sky. She rose higher in spirals until I could hardly see her in the whiteout of the sky. After some twenty minutes she was overhead and then dove down, talons stretched for Aralbai's arm.

The eagle's eyes were dark and impenetrable and her black beak edged with gold gleamed like a dagger. Ken, who grew up and lives in a city, stood well back from her. Aralbai gave me a thick leather glove and sleeve and passed the eagle to me. She gripped my sleeved arm with her talons; I felt she weighed twenty pounds; I propped up my arm with my other arm. I felt her fierce heart beating for the mountains and the skies. She turned her yellow eyes on me. She relaxed her talons so that they did not cut into the glove. After awhile she opened her wings, they spread wider than I am tall, but she did not crouch to dive skyward. I loosened my arm and stroked her tail, then her wings, then her head.

When we left, Aralbai looked long at me in the eyes and held my hand. Canat told me he had said, "Come back in winter, when the animals are in fur."

Like penguins, zebras, and buffalo, humans are gregarious animals. Penguins, zebras, and buffalo act as though what the other penguins, zebras, and buffalo have in their minds is plain to see, and they even act as though what skuas, lions, and wolves have on their minds is clear. Humans, especially educated ones, academics, postmodern postcolonial academics, talk as though what others have on their minds is opaque and hypothetical. Don't we have the everyday experience that people looking at me, talking about me or to me are only addressing some role I occupy in a society, some pantomime I am performing, some set of clothes and haircut I am wearing: they see and address the dentist, the suburban housewife, the decently dressed restaurant client, or the American. And I—this individual me—think for myself and act on my own, behind that image they see. Doesn't it work the other way too? The agent or agency inside my head listening and interpreting is decoding according to its own code. So we have to be made to recognize this, and examine that code, its class, race, and gender categories and paradigms. When we go to different places inhabited by members of our biological species, is not what our eyes see of them but tourist images—facial contours, complexions, and garb that look exotic only to us? And when someone there is standing before us, speaking directly to us, we have been cautioned that he is not speaking with his own voice but speaking the language of his gender, his family, his class, his education, his culture, his economic and political interests, his unconscious drives, indeed his state of physical health and alertness. The effort to know him gets detoured into efforts, ever more evidently fragmentary and superficial, to know all these layers. Today the professionals who study these things write books exposing how superficial and deluded have been the efforts of the experts: exposing the imperialist, the Christian, Victorian, romantic, or Orientalist fables written by those people who left their homelands and fell in love in some remote place, married, and never returned; the positivist, Freudian, or Marxist fables of the last generation of cultural anthropologists; the rationalist, structuralist, or postmodern fables of the current generation.

So everything we experience we experience *as*—we interpret. The things are recognized and identified with words. Tree, arbol, Baum—the words are arbitrary signs, without natural relationship with what we take them to designate. We interpret words, translating terms into other terms already familiar to us. For that matter, we interpret sounds as words, and indeed we interpret vibrations in our nervous circuitry as sounds.

From a distance we interpret, decode, or translate what we hear or see of another. In interpreting, decoding, or translating we maintain the other at a distance, as other.

With our friends we do not interpret, decode, translate, analyze, deconstruct.

The word "tact" designates a light touch, supple and agile, a holding back. It contrasts with the touch involved in the apprehension, comprehension, appropriation of others. Tact, which holds back one's forces and intentions, is the sensitive form of receptivity. It's the body in the room that imposes tact! In tactful dealings with someone we are aware of his or her anxieties, rage, shame, shyness, and secrecy.

In ordinary language we refer to tactful behavior—tactful ways of approaching someone or keeping at a distance from him or her, and especially speak of tactful language. There is a speaking that from a distance makes contact with the heartache, fury, mortification, wariness, and secrecy of a body.

And in the contact with someone's vulnerability and mortality, but also inmost wellsprings of energies and exhilarations, tact is made of silence. The silence that is listening in, receptivity, sensitivity to what the other feels and dreams. In fact this silence, this listening is in all the words we say, it modulates their tone, it puts forth whatever we say as subject to the other's consideration, judgment, refusal, and assent.

We do succeed in finding the right touch, the right words, the right tone, or the right silences when speaking with someone whose complex situation and confusion we touch. We can see this tact in practice among refugees, among victims of famine and of the plagues, among peasants laboring on harsh lands in uncertain climates. We can see this tact in practice in every friendship. It begins every friendship, be it the friendship of a week or of an evening.

Tact, that finding the right words and the right silences, is not only a relationship with real people; it is also a relationship with real things. The language that seeks to make contact and stay in touch with real things, with the Colca Canyon, with the baobab plains of the Sahel, with Angel Falls, with the Kalahari desert, with a hamlet glowing in the Himalayan twilight, finds the right tone and the right silences and is laconic. It is not the Web site that stores everything anyone has been able to say about them, but poetry, words of a song, that keeps us in touch with the real things with which we have made contact. Unrestrained garrulousness is as much a lack of tact about things as it is about people. How coming into the real presence of hummingbirds, opals, fossils silences us.

We go off, to the nearby or far-off forests, to the mountains, the glaciers, the beaches, the oceans. Look at our feet, Bruce Chatwin said, they are long and set parallel; they are made to move on ahead. We make our way across mountains and continents as the continental plates collide and buckle up these mountains that freeze the west winds and dry out these deserts. We descend into the Grand Canyon and the Quebrada de Humahuaca, treading the eons that deposited these fifty strata of petrified sediment. In the crystal nights of deserts and mountains our gaze travels the light-years of the stars. We visit excavations and monitor the millions of years from algae to dinosaurs. We trip through the savannah with the wildebeest and the impalas and stroll the beach tacking the waves with the plovers. We make contact with people far away and long ago.

Stepping across the splashes of tinted light in forests we fine tune to the scale of the rustling leaves and the silence plucked with the small songs of shy insects and birds. Climbing the mountains we step into the winds and onto the immemorial stillness or imminent freefall of the stones. Diving the oceans we abandon the movements of the human upright posture and steer in the surge with our fins like the fish. We find ourselves welcome in the penguin rookeries of Antarctica as long as we pick up the movements, concentrations, currents of the colony and do not come with the moments of predator orcas or skuas. Among the crowds in the streets of Calcutta, in a Tuareg camp in the Sahara, in the rice terraces of Java, we catch on to the periodicities, the rhythms, the frenetic or feline force of movements before we catch on to the meaning of the things being said—when we cannot understand anything being said.

You hear travelers say the best way to learn a language is in bed—get yourself a girlfriend or boyfriend. (What you really pick up there is a feel for the color of the skin and the baby down or kinkiness of the hair, the boldness or timidity of movements, the tempo of gestures and rejoinders, the kinds of sensations triggered and idled in, the momentum and urgency of cravings, the abandon to strangers in the night.) Every traveler knows he or she has communicated more deeply and intensely with someone met on the night train than with people that have been neighbors for twenty years. Fallen in love with that someone.

Long ago and far away a hunter acquires the sharp eyes, wariness, stealth movement, speed, readiness to spring and race, and the exhilaration of the beast he hunts—which are available for stalking prey but also for gamboling down the hills into the river, dancing, and sexual contests. In the forest the woodman's body does not become ligneous and stiff, but he stands tall, looks skyward, and becomes laconic. A forager is bent upon the earth, is herself imbued with the damp and smell of the ground, and acquires the patience of plants. And the prey animal contracts the speed and direction of movement of the hunter; the plants protect themselves with thorns and toxins from foragers and recover after their passage.

Long ago and far away, in trance and in delirium a shaman is possessed by a wolverine, leopard, or eagle. He is not imitating them or identifying with them; he is not acquiring the structures and organs of other organisms. He is contracting certain forms of their behavior and cries, behaviors without objective or termination, since they are susceptible of extending in the most varied situations. He will move as a leopard moves among leopards, among antelope, among men, in storms and in the night sky. He will look over mountains and valleys with eagle eyes.

The True Frame of the Prose Poem

RAY GONZÁLEZ

✳ ✳

When I write prose poems, the main truth I confront is the fact that the paragraph I am trying to bring to life is a poetic form in itself, though one that gives me an odd freedom to write away from lyrical stanzas, line breaks, and the isolation of individual words. This kind of truth magnetizes form and subject, until the prose poem forces me to be honest toward its composition into one or more paragraphs. This honesty means each prose poem I write has to sustain its form through the cluster of sentences it is allowing. When the sentences work in grammatical and lyrical methods, the factor of surprise is heightened. Truth in prose poetry forces me to maintain the paragraph in a poetic atmosphere, while I attempt to break out of its boundaries. This is done through a language that speaks both within and outside the block form.

Zbigniew Herbert, the great Polish poet, approached truth in his prose poem, "Wall." While the content and lyricism can be found in a poem built in stanzas, this block form allows the poet's higher measures of eternity to rise above the sentences:

WALL

We stand against the wall. Our youth has been taken from us like a condemned man's shirt. We wait. Before the fat bullet lodges itself in our necks, ten or twenty years pass. The wall is high and strong. Behind the wall there are a tree and a star. The tree is lifting the wall with its roots. The star is nibbling the stone like a mouse. In a hundred, two hundred years there will be a little window.

To look beyond the lines that form the wall and allow the creation of the window is the approach of a truth that applies to any prose poem of integrity. Herbert opens the world of war and tragedy by compressing time and its moments of revelation. In a way, the poem reads like a note, a reminder to the reader and the eternal survivor that there may be a way into the poem and an exit toward life. This journey is through the window of time, revelation, and human understanding. Again, these are universal truths one can find in traditional poetic forms yet, what Herbert accomplishes on a higher level is pushed into the paragraph function of the prose poem because the paragraph is a timeless concept that reinforces truth telling by the way it uses words whose visual and linear characteristics are not bound by set patterns. Yes, the paragraph is a pattern, but its words within are constantly moving across a kaleidoscope that enlarges the poem.

Herbert's influence on my own prose poems is hard to measure, not because it is transparent or subjective, but because the prose poetry of "little windows" contains a poetic power that allows true strains of the self to be woven into a text that stands on its own, carries the measure of influence, and composes a fresh stage. In other words, a prose poem written in response to great prose poets like Herbert, or Charles Baudelaire, Russell Edson, or Charles Simic is the kind of paragraph that announces it is constructed out of a truth telling that bridges the elements of poetry and nonfiction. And, in the case of prose poetry, the element of nonfiction applies to real details, setting, and even the psychic makeup of the poet. The lyrical or poetic strain comes through the imagination, the influence, and responses to the world through the multi-layered plains of language. It is not an ideal marriage because Herbert's little window is constantly tempted to close, completely shutting off the poet from his material. This is where the freedom of the prose poem comes into the picture — the prose poet does not allow the text to fail or remain incomplete because the uncanny form of a poem-in-paragraph propels the writer beyond the trappings of a lyrical tradition that often make the poet stop writing. The window stays wide open and the truth of the poem emerges because a poem as paragraph is a living text without boundaries placed on thought and meaning.

My prose poem "Sticky Monkey Flowers, Monterey Bay" is not about the violence between men and their centuries, as the Herbert poem, though it was influenced by "Wall" in the way it looks beyond the obvious and attempts to find a way out of vision — a way of seeing that focuses on the present moment, even as the poet acknowledges what has come before is never going to alight itself right in front of his eyes:

STICKY MONKEY FLOWERS, MONTEREY BAY
Blossoms scrambled in the eye of tomorrow, bright little fires outlining the shape of secrecy, actual light of measure wounded by consequence, given color against argument, in favor of remorse as the flower is handled without letting go of its green veins — fragile lines toward the surf hitting shore as if something were thrown out there long ago. When flight kept track of that line of pelicans, there was a roar across the bay, distant white specks in the sky vanishing like the seeds of this nourishment, their cold pardons

a combination of infinite movement and the words for the kindest news. Sticky monkey flowers spreading into sunlit nerves, moving in the mist like a distant yellow horizon taking its time coming back. Blossoms lifting, small and untroubled, given their green moisture to fill the eye after the fever breaks, after sands drift into hidden coves of disaster, one lone pelican making it back in time to avoid the shape moving across the plants that twist sand with wind, flower scent with muscle, leaving the unknown out of the garden, the unspoken out of the rising drifts of what has been.

My complete truths are hidden in the poem and its block density invites the readers' interpretations because its character attracts such dissection. My reality is revealed through the details that a piece of nonfiction commonly builds upon. This is a prose poem because I am showing what I see and I am inside the poem and outside of it. It is nonfiction, and some readers argue that many prose poems are miniature essays because any kind of movement through the text is completely on the level surface of experience and understanding, despite certain unrevealed mysteries that could take the piece in other directions. This is what a prose poem does—joins the poetic shadows of deception and clarity with the sunlit, open windows of a nonfictional confrontation with what lies in front of the writer for any reader to see. At this point, I must repeat myself and demand that attention be paid to the fact, once again, that these things are being done in sentences and paragraphs and the prose poet has said farewell to the line break and stanza in the same manner that Herbert's wall is lifted by the roots of the tree.

The immense waters that line the horizon of Monterey Bay blink toward a distant line of pelicans as they approach the beach. I stand in clusters of sticky monkey flowers and smell the fresh oblivion of a distance only a poet can imagine, capture, and realign on the page. These acts naturally condense into paragraph form because what I see across the bay and the affirming approach of the huge, white birds creates questions whose answers have woven a prose response even before I know I am going to react in that style. The prose poem is suited for this experience because the visual aspects of what I see are layers of perception, emotion, and detailed awareness whose weight collapses in early attempts at the traditional poem. They fall into themselves, perhaps having entered through the little window I have been given because the poet standing alone on the beach gathers the immensity of their being and recreates how they fall upon each other in a coagulating syntax that wants nothing to do with the same, old poetic patterns.

This means the prose poem evolved before its author even realized it. This flavor of truth, and the idea that poetry is already there and the poet goes to it, is not mysterious or has anything to do with a sense of the Muse. The pre-arranged prose poem, moving in my direction in the shape of the immense Monterey waters and the captivating pelicans, comes into my awareness only after I step out of the sticky monkey flowers to thwart the impulse toward stanzas. The truth of the prose poem is given, not felt. The actuality of a linear, lined poem is felt and not given. The Monterey Bay experience is given to me in a very honest manner because the prose telling, the prose journey, and the prose magnet of words were already there, waiting to be identified by standing on the beach and contemplating the world. These conclusions often cause some of the sharpest debates over the prose poem. I pronounce them because the window of accepting my experience at Monterey and being able to write about it in a truthful manner hung over the salty waters until I went and plucked them in the same, awkward manner some of those pelicans picked fish out of the water. The "actual light of manner wounded in consequence" I recognize along the shore is a moment when I admit I cannot lie about what I see or what the shoreline makes me ponder. It is a complex recognition that arrives in a paragraph that stays with me before I set it down on paper. When I write the words, "Blossoms lifting, small and untroubled, given their green moisture to fill the eye after the fever breaks," I allow these temperatures of knowing and trust to pattern themselves into sentences, "leaving the unknown out of the garden, the unspoken out of the rising drifts of what has been." My prose poem has done this because what it contains is exactly what I want to say and I will not hide behind vague poetic dimensions to say it. The block of words does not allow me to hide behind grammatical curtains.

One of the most important sentences in Herbert's "Wall" is, "The star is nibbling the stone like a mouse." It is crucial in understanding truth in a prose poem because this demand for existence and knowledge cannot be measured through the immensity of established patterns of poetic discourse. The star will completely absorb the stone in the same manner my blossoms lift, small and untroubled, after the fever of experience has ended. They rise out of the paragraph and give off their powerful scent because I have confessed. As I finish writing the prose poem, this confession burns with a temperature that cannot be measured because a line, then a sentence, and finally — a paragraph have been identified in the shape of a prose poem whose window is unlocked and about to be shattered.

Tender Fictions

BARBARA HAMMER

> "Construct an autobiography before someone does it for you. From Peoria
> to Hollywood, this is a story of a second generation Ukrainian daughter."
>
> "Study everything."

All quotes in italics are text or narration from Tender Fictions, 55 minutes, 16 mm. film, 1995.

✳ ✳

I am a filmmaker because I can embrace multiple disciplines: painting, collage/montage, poetry, architecture, and photography together with feminist, queer, and cultural studies. Documentary film as a genre can use elements from all of these categories and can be a challenge of ideas, of contradictions, of wonder. I work in a smaller subcategory of documentary called the essay film or the metadocumentary, a genre that is about ideas and questions, proposes various possibilities and points of view, and, is often self-reflexive. I work in this field because nonfiction films can negotiate cultural values and meaning in Western culture; they can disseminate information and misinformation; they can prompt social change and engender significant cultural debate. I ask my audience to stretch and embrace new forms with each new work. Form is as important as content and, indeed, is content itself.

The way images are structured, arranged, presented, or performed provides particular meanings to the understanding or reading of the film. No matter how original the images or interviews in a documentary film are, if the form of the film does not stretch beyond the traditional approach, the meaning will only be understood in conventional terms. It will lie within our neat ideas of things we already know. The film will subjugate new information into our existing ideologies. To question the concept of truth in nonfiction filmmaking is to question the very form of the documentary itself. New meaning requires new form.

My film practice turned to the essay documentary in 1991 when I made my first feature length film, *Nitrate Kisses* (1992). This film presents ideas on history and how history is made, asks questions about who makes history and

Barbara and Shirley Temple, from *Tender Fictions*. Courtesy of Barbara Hammer.

who is left out, and recognizes the loss of lesbian and gay histories. At the end of the film, Joan Nestle, the lesbian writer, implores the audience to save every scrap of paper, every grocery list, all ephemera in order to document lesbian history for the coming generations. I began to search my own mental and physical archives for memories and personal film scraps that I could use in making an auto/bio/graphy that would question truth making in nonfiction film. *Tender Fictions* became the second in a trilogy of films on lesbian, gay, and queer histories whose goal was to make the invisible, visible: *Nitrate Kisses* (1992), *Tender Fictions* (1995), and *History Lessons* (2000).

"I invented myself as an artist by reading autobiographies of famous artists, poets, painters. None of these were by or about lesbians."

"Fictionalize yourself."

"Violate chronology."

Tender Fictions investigates the literary genre of biography and autobiography and the consequent implications for filmmaking. The film challenges the traditional modes of personal history storytelling using a wide variety of tactics to destabilize the hegemonic narrative that implies truth, not fiction. My investigation began with an inquiry into feminist, anthropological, and cultural studies texts on the ideology of truth and fiction in autobiography. Authors repeated over and over in a variety of ways that there was no truth, that everything was fiction, that the most we could do was circle the subject, recognize multiple truths, and always remember that the person reading the text influenced and changed that very text through their presence. I gathered quotes from these texts and I assembled a series of 8 and S8 mm film from my own archive. I telephoned my friends and asked for their memories of me as a lesbian. I digitally manipulated educational movies on 1950s family life. I rifled and rephotographed the family photo album including yellowing scraps of newsprint found among the pictures. I put these together without chronology, objective narrator, establishing shots, reinforcing music, or authoritative interviews. I would use my individual voice to intervene in an attempt to remake a genre.

The viewer would become the archeologist, the historian, and decide what was true and what was fiction and bring a type of agency to the film encounter. The viewer could rely on a collection of dialectics between language and image using memory as a database of illuminations stimulated by narrative, image, smell, and touch. The film became a meta-autobiography with questions of truth or fiction central to both the processes of making and viewing.

"I promise not to tell the truth, the whole truth, and nothing but the truth."

"Editing is fictionalizing."

The illusory seamlessness of autobiography based on chronology and the "truthful" narrator are thrown into question by editing juxtapositions of image, text, story, and sound. By suggesting that some of the voice-over stories were suspect I could destabilize the narrative by suggesting that the power of retrospect be rooted in illusion. I wanted to undermine notions of historical portraiture and I didn't need to construct lesbian heroes, including myself. There is pleasure in simultaneously reclaiming and questioning histories and the processes of making them. As the audience became biographers stitching and seaming the film's evidence into their own narratives, they claimed the power of making.

"The smell of diesel fuel brings back the early mornings driving the Lambretta through Turkey, Syria, Iraq before he fell... before she fell... before you fell... before I fell from the machine weakened by jaundice hepatitis picked up from the aluminum tent poles he/she/you/I bought secondhand in Florence."

"Change the pronouns."

The power the pronoun carries correlates with the masculine power or feminine absence of power in society. The use of the first person has a compelling weight of implied "truth." Suggesting that an inquiry into nonfiction "truth" requires a cultural understanding of the implicit power in words, I told the same story four times in the film using a different pronoun each time. The audience would engage in critical thinking about meaning as the point of view changed with the different pronouns.

The weight of the first person singular carries a Eurocentric or "I"-ocentric weight that separates the way peoples of the West tell stories from the community-based "we" of many other cultures. The cult of individual specificity can lead to a genetic explanation. The "I" of *Tender Fictions* becomes a strand in a community weave, supported and criticized by surrounding voices. Asking friends from the past what their favorite lesbian memory of me was, I heard multiple memories that ranged from questions of gender identity ("Was I a boy or a girl") to misplaced brassieres found in a drawer (Was sex implied?) based on questionable "truths." Multiplying voices multiplied meanings implying truths, not truth. As soon as we think we have a "true" story, the words strain, crack, and sometimes break under the burden. The fragmentary nature of their juxtaposition is to encourage the audience to wrestle with ambiguities created by disjunction.

Barbara as Charlie Chaplin, from Tender Fictions. Courtesy of Barbara Hammer.

"Eyebrow raised. The lesbian subject is a double subject. It is a homo bio graphy. 'I' is a lesbian couple. Breathe. Flirt. Breath. That doesn't feel entirely right. That means I don't have any independence if 'I' is a lesbian couple. Smile. Theory is mistaking reality. Theory is mistaking me for personality. Eyebrows raised. Stare."

"Slip from one narrative to another."

"Multiply roles."

"Mobilize for change."

Multiplicity of truths, nonhomogenous and nonlinear storytelling help us achieve a flexible position for living in this global world of complex personal and national identities. My stated goal is to empower an audience by not controlling them with a sutured and structured narrative implying truth, but rather to ask them to envision their own ideas and ways of understanding by watching a film that avoids determined answers. As a filmmaker, I see every decision to use conjunction and disjunction, layered, veiled, destroyed, and scarcely readable images as material necessary to reading the theme of histories made invisible through neglect, distortion, destruction, or the biggest killer of all—lack of interest.

If I have put a "lesbian life" on the screen in the twentieth and twenty-first centuries, it is to have put a nonfixed, transparent, morphing character as much influenced and made by the times in which she/he/we/I/you live as determined by illusory self-construction.

"Invent yourself."
"Strategize your play."
"Seduce the natural order."
"Avoid assimilation."
"Build peoples."
"Carry cultures."
"Confession = lies."

Seeing (through) Red

SU FRIEDRICH

This essay is essentially an annotated version of my recent video, Seeing Red (2005).[1] The video combines shots of myself (speaking extemporaneously about personal matters) with montages of images of red things (objects, people wearing red, etc.) accompanied by selections from the Goldberg Variations by J. S. Bach. A list of the variations used appears at the end of the essay. The script below often ends in mid-sentence to mirror the video, in which the speech fades out as the music comes up.

   The introduction is in italics; the verbatim script from the video is in regular roman type; the annotations are in a different font.

✳ ✳

After years of making auto/biographical work (about my mother, father, a breakup of a relationship, my medical problems, etc.), I thought I had fully explored the territory, as did most viewers of my work. However, I had never worked with the genre of the diary film because of a reluctance to speak directly to the camera. In fact, I tried like hell to avoid doing that, either by using voice-over actors or on-screen text even when it seemed necessary to use my own voice. Once in a while I was forced to employ my on-camera presence or voice, but only sparingly, until I made The Odds of Recovery *in 2002. In that film, I appeared on camera more than I previously thought tolerable or acceptable.*

   Early in 2005, while complaining about being mired in a (very impersonal) video about coffee, my observant and forthright partner said, "You seem to be in such pain. Why don't you make a video about that instead?" After swallowing my anger about the remark, I impulsively decided to take her up on what I saw almost as a dare, marched into my studio, turned on the camera and started talking off the top of my head.

   Almost immediately, I started crying . . . on camera . . . oh god! So, having started to shoot with little forethought, I proceeded with slightly more thought, while actually not quite knowing what it was that I wanted or needed to say. In other words, I decided to talk, once in a while, on camera, about whatever was weighing on my mind and only later would I decide to do or not do something with the material. Eight months later, voilà! *The video was finished and so also, I hoped, was my experience with being on camera.*

   For thirty years, I've worried about what it means to use private experiences — my own and those of people close to me — as subject matter. Everyone has his or her own version of every experience, so whose version is the accurate one? Can the teller ever describe experiences they've shared with others without creating huge gaps, falsities, or errors gross and small? How can one not create a false environment the moment one turns on a camera or microphone? And the most unanswerable question of all: does my account of my own life have any value to anyone but myself?

With each film or video, I've made an uneasy peace with these questions (by deciding I was fair to my subjects [including myself], or accepting that I was being unfair, or asking for outside feedback in order to avoid the gross errors and unforeseen cruelties, etc.), but I've never stopped worrying. And the films do give ample evidence of the impossibility of being entirely accurate, honest, and fair: they can't help but be flawed, and the best I can do is to try and anticipate their shortcomings.

This essay could have been based on almost any of my films. With the older work, I've been through many screenings and have been asked many questions that reveal their limitations (including ones that pertain to the concerns of this book), but Seeing Red *seemed the most germane. Since it is so recent, my ability to view it objectively is of course nonexistent, but the memory of those bothersome background noises is still fresh—which is how I refer to all the worrisome, panicky, and skeptical feelings I have while working on a new piece. So, without further ado . . .*

I walked into my studio one afternoon and set up the camera so that I was only showing my upper torso—from neck to below the breasts, with the lavaliere microphone in full view. There was no need to show my face—what mattered at the moment was what I was saying, not how I looked when speaking. But I did look rather disheveled, so that was further reason not to show too much of myself. With little forethought, I started talking.

> The fact is that I'm fifty years old and I don't seem to have any much more control over my feelings and my behavior toward other people than I did thirty years ago. I mean, I do have a little more control—sometimes I can stop and remind myself that I shouldn't be doing a certain something, or I should go out and have fun instead of driving myself crazy sitting at my desk working . . . but I just seem to be a control freak.
>
> You know, I live in this big house with her and a couple of roommates and, you know, if I walk down the hallway, I see a piece of paper and I think, "Well, I wonder if anybody's going to notice that paper and pick it up," and after three days nobody, of course, nobody has bothered to pick it up because why should people be worrying about shit like that? But I go and I pick it up and I think, "You see, nobody noticed that piece of paper!"

And I go away to school and I put a note on the door saying "Please get the mail" and sometimes people don't get the mail but most of the times they do because they also want their mail, so why do I think I'm the only one who gets the mail? And I've just worked myself up over the years into this, like, hideous, maniacal person who feels like everything has to be in its place and if things are out of their place then, you know, far better that I should go launder the napkins and pick up that piece of paper in the hall than, you know, sit. . . .

As I'm talking, I'm wondering how in god's name I can use material like this. First of all, I'm dissing my roommates, current and past, and I know that some of them will eventually see this and will probably be offended at my description of their alleged carelessness and laziness. I also suspect that they'll think I'm an ass for worrying so much about a piece of paper, and I know I am, and so begins the first circle of confusion: it's good for me to admit a weakness, but doing it involves admitting negative thoughts about others, and I shouldn't presume that my admission will compensate for the fact that I've insulted them, that they'll "admire me" for having been so open about my neuroses. No, they'll think I'm an ass and will feel offended. But they should admire me. But I've insulted them. But I'm being honest! But I've insulted them. Etc.

And boy oh boy, when I was seventeen and eighteen and nineteen I thought, "Fuck that, man, I am never gonna to do that!" And I spent a lot of years not having kids and doing . . . you know, eating out at shitty restaurants and doing my own work 'cause I thought I'll be *goddamned* if I'm going to be a fucking housewife . . . and I have turned into a fucking housewife and I can't stand it! (Cries.) . . . And then, you know, the things you can't stand, you start finding a way that they're good for you, so, you know, I bake! I bake all the fucking time and then I think, "Oh, the roommates will like it." Or I bring it to school and everybody at school is totally thrilled and meanwhile what the fuck am I doing baking all the time, why am I doing this? I just don't understand it! (Cries.)

That notation (Cries) does an inadequate job of describing the fact that, on camera, I'm bawling my eyes out. Seriously sobbing big, loud sobs. It's ludicrous. Then again, isn't it *heartbreaking*? Look how open she's being! Not only is she admitting a dirty secret about her domestic life, she's showing that it's agonizing to admit it! Isn't that a feeling shared by "millions of viewers"? Won't this searing confession be a salve, or an epiphany, for anyone watching who has suffered from the same experience?

Or am I absurd, preposterous, the worst sort of navel-gazer, one who has taken the gazing so far that doing an ordinary, pleasant activity has become a reason for the worst kind of self-laceration, not to mention self-pity?

I've probably said should about ten times already in the last three minutes, and this is a lot about should, and on the train here this morning I was talking to a friend of mine and we were both talking about how, when you get to this age, you can know what you're supposed to do . . . and never do it. And what the fuck is it that makes you get up and do the thing instead of constantly talking to your friends on the phone and to your girlfriend and to yourself and writing in your journal about, like, "I should remember not to get too tired" and "I should remember not to be too angry," and I should . . . should, should, should, should, should . . . all the time! And then it's this constant feeling of failure. And . . . I don't know . . . I don't know what to say about that. Words of wisdom don't come, don't come.

A cop-out. That ending. And I knew it when I was saying it.

When I began to talk that day, I'm quite sure I wanted to know what I thought about the problem of should, and I assumed that talking aloud would force me to reveal those thoughts, when the camera was rolling. (Though, come to think of it, videotape doesn't roll, which is probably one of the many reasons why we use these contraptions so liberally as a tool for the unchecked confession. If we had a sense of rolling, we would certainly have a better sense of a beginning, end, and all the indulgent time in between . . . But I digress.) When the camera was humming in the perpetual present, I just said what I thought and then hit the wall of no more thoughts and instead of meeting that with silence, I did a little verbal dance of departure that let me off the hook.

At this point, you might wonder why I made this video, since everything I've said so far would suggest that the experience was worthy of nothing but the garbage can or the vault. I'd like to clarify. As I said in the intro, I find the genre of the diary film to be extremely problematic and embarrassing, but in the course of making this video I discovered that the problems were interesting rather than frustrating, and that I was willing and able to embarrass myself endlessly, so I felt compelled to continue both the shooting and, later, the editing in order to learn something about this troubled and troubling genre.

It's like we keep trying to understand what it is that we do that fucks us up, and keep trying to change it, and it just seems like that is nearly impossible. And I must say there is something deeply unfair about that. There's something . . . I mean, I don't believe in god, but whoever figured this out really had a bad sense of humor, because . . . Here we all are, there are six billion of us now in the world, most of whom have jobs that don't pay enough, that make them miserable, that are boring, whatever . . . Um . . . have trouble in their families either because they have trouble with their spouses, or their kids are a wreck, or whatever, and it's like, okay, I was saying this to my roommate the other night and I said, "Probably 99 percent of the six billion are like that," and he said, "Well, maybe it's more like 90." So even if it's 90 percent, what is that? I can't do that math that fast, but that's a hell of a lot of people on this planet who, you know, invoke god every day, several times a day, that their life will be better, or play the lottery, or take drugs, or drink, or smoke, or . . . you know, cheat on their spouses. . . .

I had reached a point where I wasn't sure how to continue, wasn't sure what other subjects I could bring up that would elicit a dramatic emotional response — or even be of any interest. In other words, I wasn't sure I had anything of merit that would justify turning on the camera. But, having set the ball in motion, it was necessary to keep it rolling, so I made a somewhat desperate attempt by invoking the suffering masses. Not that I'm indifferent to the plight of the masses, but starting out with such a ridiculously minor set of concerns (My house is dirty! I bake too much!) made my discussion of the millions who toil away at exhausting, badly paid, demeaning jobs a dubious thing at best. Moreover — and this wouldn't be apparent to a viewer unacquainted with my daily life — I was saying all this while sitting in the comfortable, large office at my own place of employment, which is an Ivy League university. Hardly the stuff of human tragedy. But definitely the stuff of a confessional piece in which the maker/confessor starts to feel pangs of conscience about blabbing on and on about their aches and pains when the aches and pains of others are decidedly more to be considered.

There's an Emily Dickinson poem that I've always loved. I think it goes like this:
To make a prairie it takes a clover, a bee and revery.
The revery alone will do if bees are few.[2]

So, reverie . . . that seems to be a very hard thing to do. I don't know why . . . I guess a thought of a beautiful place leads to thinking about not being able to go there because I don't have money which leads to thinking about how I'm earning my money which leads to worrying about the students and worrying about how I'm going to grade them and worrying about whether they like me or not and then suddenly I'm worrying instead of thinking about this nice place that I could go to. And instead of using the thought of it as a restful moment, it just turns into this panic attack!

So I think I have to stop because I'm going to go see a movie and dinner as part of my plan to do things that are fun . . . and hopefully I'll enjoy myself . . . .

I didn't mind talking about this subject — my inability to be contemplative. It seemed pretty straightforward. One isn't contemplative, therefore one fails to find peace. One makes small efforts, one sometimes succeeds, and that allows for the possibility that one could succeed again in a future attempt.

What I failed to mention during my talking was that there was precious little reverie attached to the making of the video, to the process of turning on the camera and talking, and so what I failed to discover was how different the video would have been had I made some of those aforementioned small efforts.

And this is where we get into the impossibly convoluted problem at the heart of the confessional. By way of illustration, this problem is sometimes described as akin to being in a hall of mirrors. We start by attempting to look at ourselves, but we cannot do that directly, so we use indirection, reflection (sorry, no pun intended), and then that starts to seem like the thing we meant to be saying when in fact it's only a synonym or a kind of onomatopoeia. And I didn't even know I was doing that, so I couldn't backtrack and speak more directly.

Um . . . I suppose it would be great if I could think that I have a certain number of mannerisms and devices and, you know, values, uh . . . interests, whatever and I can just, you know, do variations on them, so it's not just a matter of like, you know, being a bad person and then trying to turn into a different person but instead think, well, you're a very . . . a very enthusiastic person and so sometimes that means you're manic and excessive and other times it means you're incredibly focused and appreciative and whatever. . . .

So it's just like this personality and then the different moments are variations on this personality all of which hold a certain interest or a . . . the way the *Goldberg Variations* do, um . . . but it seems instead it's like. . . .

Did I mention that all of these passages of text are excerpts from long recording sessions with myself? Reading the above makes that glaringly obvious. We are massively complicated beings. Not just those of us who have been in therapy for many years, but every one of us. We wonder, and wonder some more, and never quite know who's seeing us, how we're being seen, or how to control either of those things. We hope to be one kind of person and sometimes discover we're something else entirely. I'm sure many of us would like to have our identity be a fixed, recognizable, and likeable thing, but I'm afraid that very few have the luxury of that experience. That was one of the ironies for me in using the Goldberg Variations—I relish the fact that a piece of music can be worked and reworked until it's a flawless expression of the beauty inherent in the varieties of life (i.e., of pitch, rhythm, and dynamics), but I also envy and resent that music can do so perfectly what we can never achieve in our perception of ourselves. So as I edited, I ricocheted quite uncomfortably between the vague, confused ramblings of my speech to the precise, articulate moments provided by Bach.

(I'm on the couch holding up a copy of Leaves of Grass *by Walt Whitman)*
　　I've written on the frontispiece: "Nestled in the crook of my arm where the sweat creeps on a summer day." I guess I carried this in the crook of my arm where the sweat crept on a summer day (laughs) . . . Oh goodness . . . Oh, he's so direct. . . . Here's one, in a section called "By the Roadside," called "O Me, O Life!" . . . So much the sentiment of a twenty-year-old! I mean, I can imagine being twenty and reading this and of course, when you're twenty, you're, like, "Oh me, oh life!" I seem to be doing the same thing at fifty, but anyway . . . (Starts to read poem):

O ME, O LIFE
O me, O life! Of the questions of these recurring,
　Of the endless trains of the faithless, of cities fill'd with the foolish,
　Of myself, forever reproaching myself, (for who more foolish than I,
　　and who more faithless?)[3]

I had fun with this. I was at a point, again, when I wasn't sure what to talk about, but I had enjoyed referring to the Dickinson poem and, in thinking about my various formative experiences, I recognized that Whitman had played a significant role for me at an early age—an age when asking philosophical questions about my existence didn't seem quite as overworked or reworked as it does now. I had a little less fun with it when I started wondering whether or not I was invoking one of the great bards as a way to bolster my own musings. I mean, if Walt was writing stuff like that, why couldn't I say stuff like this? That didn't carry me very far, because of course he took his own experience and transposed it into poetry, while all I was doing was sitting on my couch reading aloud and commenting about myself. As if my version would have to be called, "O me! O me!"

It's really scary, it's really scary. . . . And what really is fucked about making a diary is that, you know, I come in here thinking, "Oh, I'm gonna do that," and then it takes me a good seven minutes or more to set up the equipment and I've gotten so preoccupied with the equipment that I've kind of forgotten my upsetness.

Then I start talking and I feel like, "Well, now I have to get back in touch with my upsetness so that this will be an interesting performance," and this is not about a performance. And then I get worked up to the point where I feel really upset, like now I'm saying it's really scary and it actually is incredibly scary and I feel like crying but then I think, "Well, now, if you cry that'll be good 'cause you'll be crying and that'll be really emotional and, you know, moving." But then I'm just doing it like a fucking *performance*!

And part of the problem . . . part of what is so fucked up is that I feel like most of life is about performing for people — it's like, being the nice teacher, being the good child, being the good parent, being the good lover, being the good neighbor, being the good citizen, you know, and probably a lot of, like, being bad is also performance, and my god, my god, I'm *sick* of it!

Well, there you have it. All the background noises finally came to the foreground and I could claim this as the moment when I was finally able to articulate the essence of the problem to which the video had been firmly pointing, and to which I have been repeatedly referring in this essay. However, I beg to differ with myself, because instead I see this as the most dishonest moment in the video. That's being very harsh, and I think that dishonest might not be the right word. It implies a moral judgment, and what bothers or interests me about this moment has nothing to do with ethics and everything to do with the nature of the camera — that intrusive, manipulative instrument which we think we use to express ourselves but which in fact uses us. I'm not getting into the paranormal here, I just mean that we're fools if we think we can use it without being used by it, which makes me want to retract my statement about the dishonest nature of the moment and assert that it was the most honest. If you think that means I'm reverting to my initial assessment, you're wrong. I still don't think I was articulating the essence of the problem, but rather that the camera created a moment that proved the impossibility of the pure confession, which means that the entire enterprise of the video would have to be called into question.

Shit . . . Somebody's here and I don't want them to overhear me . . . What am I going to do? . . . Oh . . . I think I have to wait a minute . . .

(Interval with music)

So it's, uh, ten to ten, and a little more . . . a little less than twelve hours ago I was sitting at the therapist's and I had the same feeling I had yesterday, which is that I just keep saying the same thing over and over again. And it just seems that there really must be a point that you reach where you can no longer say and do the same things again. . . .

But I don't know when that point is, and I don't know if I'm there, but it seems that the alternative is really grim, 'cause when you get to be fifty, you don't have that much time left, so if you don't do it as soon as you can, you might be fucked.

I'm playing for time here. I'm also somewhat repeating myself, although there is a place for repetition in an artwork, so that an idea, initially expressed moderately, can grow in power over time. Whether that's borne out in real life, as opposed to in a film or painting, is another matter. I think the opposite might be the case.

At least I like the fact that I'm finally saying what my fundamental concern is: that we repeat ourselves *ad nauseam* but at some point we're not allowed to do that anymore. But here's the rub: doing a confessional piece would lead the viewer to assume that there's some resultant catharsis or evolution—that in doing such a thing, the maker comes to terms with the problems being expressed, learns from that, changes, grows, whatever. . . . Not. And I was painfully aware of that even as I spoke those words to the camera. I "knew enough" to say that it was necessary, at the advanced age of fifty, to stop repeating myself, but I knew more, which was that I definitely wouldn't stop. This would suggest that I should have admitted the fact, but that wouldn't have the same dramatic appeal as this version, in which I express concern and hint at the possibility of a solution.

I wonder what it's like, you know, with parents 'cause they're always telling their kids what to do and what not do. . . . I'm sure it comes back to haunt them, um, or it comes back as a joke on them, and . . . I think when you're a teacher you get into the same position because you're constantly having to repeat what you supposedly know. . . .

My cat is, like, tearing up the couch . . .

What you supposedly know, and uh . . .

She totally, she distracted me . . .

So you're always having to tell the students what you supposedly know—I mean, that's why you got the job—because you know something like red doesn't look good on video or metaphors have to be handled carefully. . . . And I really, you know, I get to the point where I just hate saying

"Well, this is the way it's done," because I'm at the point where I think I don't *really* know how it's done.

I mean I'm not . . . I'm not saying I feel like a complete *idiot* or I'm going to jump off a bridge, but why can't I use red? You know, why can't I? Like, *red!* Blinding, mushy, hideous red, bleeding all over the screen, you don't wanna watch it, you don't get any information . . . You know, why the fuck *not?* I don't know, but chances are when I'm. . . .

Ugh. The self-referential moment: I make something with lots of red images and then talk about video's capacity to show red.

.I would have liked to avoid it, as I've always avoided it in the past, but I'd run out of steam. That's not the same thing as having said everything worth saying, but there's only so often you can say, "I don't know what I'm doing," and then you have to walk out the door. Exits can be more or less graceful; this one struck me as being on the lesser side.

On the other hand, this video wasn't just a confessional piece. It was also a visual piece, one with very neutral visual moments (varying shots of my mid torso and that microphone) alternating with montages of a great variety of images of red objects that really didn't refer to, or express all that much about, what was being spoken. To that extent, it was my pleasure to point toward that aspect of the video — to escape, for a moment, from the burden of talking about me, me, me.

(In the last segment of the video, as I peel off all the layers of red clothing I've been wearing, one hears snippets of the prior monologues. The first few moments are audible, but they quickly begin to overlap and soon the individual phrases can't be clearly discerned. Then, at the end, one phrase jumps out. What follows are the first section and the last phrase.)

The daily labor . . . and, you know, I'm a woman, and I don't overlook the fact that I think of doing all these things in light of being a woman, who . . . And we were both talking about . . . etc. . . .

. . . But then I'm just doing it like a fucking *performance!*

Which pretty much sums up my experience about making the video. For all that I wanted it to be a heartfelt, honest, probing account of my thoughts and feelings, I felt in the end that the whole video was "a fucking performance," as is the vast majority of my life. So, when it comes to doing an autobiographical piece, that either means that I failed because I didn't really get to "the real thing," or I succeeded because I came around to admitting or recognizing that my "real thing" is putting on a show. And since I started this essay by insisting that we can never know ourselves well enough to know whether we're speaking accurately about our experiences, then I'm left not even knowing whether my assessment about the video (as a performance) or my life (ditto) is correct. Which is at least knowing that I don't know, and perhaps that's better than thinking that I do.

Goldberg Variations segments in order of appearance with image notes:
Variation #1 (with opening montage)
Variation #7 (baseball catcher)
Variation #3 (pink ribbons flapping on sticks)
Variation #15 (construction site, pipes and plastic)
Variation #22 (man selling ices and counting dollars)
Variation #8 (cherry tree)
Variation #9 (robin)
Variation #29 (while poem is being read)
Variation #6 (red wall)
Variation #19 (boys, woman in park)
Variation #20 (Staples)
Variation #14 (undressing scene)

NOTES

1. *Seeing Red* script © 2005 Downstream Productions, Inc.; *Seeing Red* film (28 minutes, 2005), directed, shot, and edited by Su Friedrich, distributed by Outcast Films, www.outcast-films.com.

2. "To Make a Prairie . . ." F1779 by Emily Dickinson.
The correct version of the poem is:
> To make a prairie it takes a clover and one bee,
> One clover, and a bee.
> And revery.
> The revery alone will do,
> If bees are few.

3. "O Me, O Life!" from Leaves of Grass by Walt Whitman.

What's Wrong with This Picture?
Archival Photographs in Contemporary Narratives
MARIANNE HIRSCH AND LEO SPITZER

> Au mois de juin 1942, un officier allemand s'avance vers un jeune homme et lui dit: "Pardon monsieur, où se trouve la place de l'Etoile?" Le jeune homme désigne le côté gauche de sa poitrine. [In June 1942, a German officer approaches a young man and asks him: "Excuse me, sir, but where is the Place de l'Etoile?" The young man points to his left lapel.]
>
> — PATRICK MODIANO

✳ ✳

This is the only photograph of my parents Carl and Lotte Hirsch, taken during the war years and it is tiny, 2.5 × 3.5 cm, about the size of a 35-mm negative, with unevenly cut edges (fig. 1). I have always loved this image of a stylish young couple— newlyweds walking confidently down an active urban street. The more difficult it was to make out the details of the faded and slightly spotted black-and-white image, the more mysterious and enticing it became to me over the years. In it, my mother is wearing a flared light-colored half-length coat and attractive leather or suede shoes with heels. She is carrying a dark purse under her arm. My father wears well-cut pants and dark leather shoes, and a tweed jacket that looks slightly too small. Details of their facial expressions are difficult to read, but their strides appear animated, matching, their arms interlaced, my mother's hands in her pockets. The picture must have been taken by one of the street photographers on the "Herrengasse" (Strada Iancu Flondor) in Czernowitz/Cernăuţi (today, Chernivtsi, Ukraine) who took the photos that populated my parents' albums and those of their friends—photographs dating from the 1920s and 1930s. Equally small, they were no doubt developed and sold to clients on the spot. This picture's radical difference is marked on the back, however, where my father's handwriting reads "Cz.1942" (fig. 2).

In 1942, Czernowitz/Cernăuţi was again a Romanian city, ruled by a fascist Romanian government that collaborated with Nazi authorities. Two-thirds of the city's Jewish population—some 40,000 persons—had been deported to Transnistria in the fall of 1941, about half of those perishing from hunger and typhus during that winter, or murdered, either by Romanian gendarmes or Nazi troops. Those, like my parents, who were still in the city, had been issued special waivers by the city's mayor or the region's governor as Jews who were deemed necessary to the city's functioning. After the Jewish ghetto into which they had been forced was largely emptied and

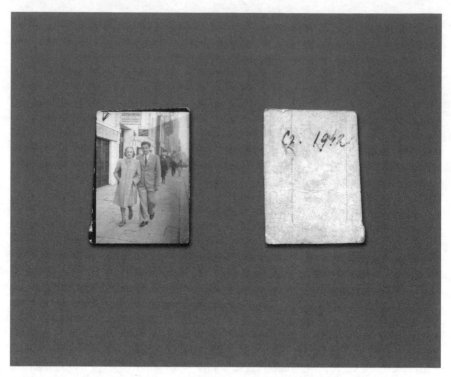

1 and 2. Carl and Lotte Hirsch, Herrengasse in Cernăuți. Verso, "CZ.1942,"
Hirsch/Spitzer family archive.

*dissolved, they were permitted to return to their own homes, but they were subject
to severe restrictions, a strict curfew, and were obliged to wear the Yellow Star. Men
were routinely taken off the street to do forced labor. Later (or earlier, depending on
exactly when the picture was taken) in the summer of 1942, they would have been
vulnerable to a second wave of deportations to Transnistria or farther east, across
the river Bug into German-administered territories and almost certain death.[1] Nothing in the picture betrays the hardship of the time. Carl and Lotte are not visibly
suffering; they do not look starved, unhealthy, or afraid. The photograph is not com-
parable to pictures of Jews in Warsaw or Lódz streets taken in 1942 — images of acute
misery and deprivation in ghettos or other restricted quarters.*

*"Here we are during the war," my parents once said to me, with what I took to
be some amount of defiance. This photograph had been a measure for me of the difference between my parents' way of telling the story about their experiences during
the war years and the much more dire and frightening narratives we read and col-*

lected from other survivors and witnesses. The photograph seemed to confirm Lotte and Carl's version of events: what they thought of as their "relatively lucky circumstances," and the "youth" and "young love" that helped them to endure and keep up their spirits. Still, I became increasingly puzzled by the little picture's incongruities: by its refusal to testify to what I knew to be true of the context in which it was taken — a time of persecution, oppression, and totalitarian constraints in which photography itself took an ominous turn from a medium of personal and familial remembrance to a threatening instrument of surveillance. Flipping the little photograph from front to back, I was unable to get its two sides to match up.

THE LITTLE PICTURE

When we began to write about the wartime in Cernăuți, this photograph was one of very few images we had on hand from there that might supplement the many written documents, memoirs, and oral testimonies on which we were basing our understanding of the place and time. However small and blurred, however seemingly incongruous, it was a valuable piece of evidence that, we hoped, would give us some greater insight into the texture of Jewish wartime life in this city. Eager for it to reveal itself even more to us, we digitally scanned and enlarged it, blowing it up several times, searching to find what might not be visible to the naked eye (fig. 3). Amazingly, as it came up to about 10 × 14 cm on the screen, the image and the story it told changed dramatically — at least on first glance. All of a sudden, it looked as if there *was* something on Carl Hirsch's left lapel that had not been noticeable before. A bright, light spot, not too large, emerged just in the place where Jews would have worn the Yellow Star in the spring or fall of 1942. Perhaps the picture was not as incongruous as we had thought: perhaps it would indeed confirm the darker version of the story we had learned and absorbed from so many other accounts. We printed the enlargement, took out magnifying glasses, went up to the window, and used the best lamps in our study to scrutinize the blowup. We played with the enlargement's resolution on the computer in Photoshop, sleuthing like detectives to determine the exact nature of the spot (figs. 4, 5, 6, and 7).

The spot's edges remained blurry. Yet did their shape not suggest points? This *must* be the Yellow Star, we concluded, what else could he be wearing on his lapel? We blew the picture up even more, then again, even a little more; yes, of course, it had the *shape* of *the* Jewish star. We began to reread the photograph's content, its message, against Lotte and Carl's facial expression and body language that were now also much more clearly visible. We remembered

3. A spot? Hirsch/Spitzer family archive.

4. Enlargement 1. Hirsch/Spitzer family archive.

some of their stories about the star, about how they sometimes went without it, daring fate, to buy groceries more easily, or simply to re-experience their former freedom and mobility. The stars in Cernăuţi were not sewn on, but affixed with safety pins: young people like Carl and Lotte sometimes wore them on the *inside* of their coats, illegally, but able to show them should they be stopped by the authorities. Yet if that, indeed, explained the seemingly missing star in Lotte's case, would the couple not have been afraid to have their picture taken by a street photographer?

The smiles with which they greeted the camera and, indeed, the fact that they had stopped to *buy* the photograph after it was developed, gave us no such impression.

We sent the enlarged photo to Lotte and Carl. "There is a small spot on my lapel," Carl wrote in an e-mail, "but it could not be *the* star. The stars were large, 6 cm in diameter. Maybe I should have written 1943 on the photo. They did away with the stars in July of 1943." "And if that is a star," Lotte wrote, "then why am I not wearing one?" In a later e-mail she said: "Yes, it

5, 6, and 7.
Enlargement 2, left.
Enlargements 3 and
4, bottom left and
bottom right.
Hirsch/Spitzer
family archive.

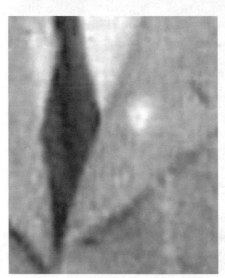

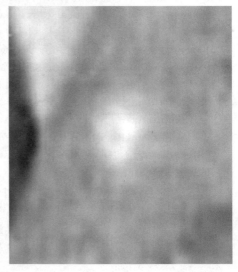

was definitely taken on the Herrengasse during the war, and to me it looks like a star, but the date is causing us problems." In fact, we later found two other photographs of Czernowitz Jews wearing the Yellow Star; these photographs are dated "around 1943" and "May 1943" (figs. 8 and 9). Their stars are larger and more distinctive than the spot on Carl Hirsch's lapel, but they also are walking through the city — seemingly on the Herrengasse — having their picture taken by a street photographer, and evidently purchasing the photograph after its development. Like Lotte's and Carl's, their stroll also seems normal, as though the temporal and political movement in which they were snapped and the otherness they were made to display were hardly relevant.

It may not be possible to determine exactly what, if anything, Carl has on his lapel. Perhaps it is *dust* — no more than a small dot of dirt on the print. Our receptions of the photograph, the questions we pose in examining it, the needs and desires that shape our viewing, inevitably exceed the image's small size and its limited ability to serve as evidence. Even after its enlargements, the results of our persistent efforts to penetrate beyond its mysterious surface are intriguing, but also inconclusive. No doubt, our determination to magnify and enhance the picture — to zoom in, blow up, sharpen — reveals more about our own projections and appropriations than about life in wartime Greater Romania. As Roland Barthes writes in *Camera Lucida*:

> If I like a photograph, if it disturbs me, I . . . look at it, I scrutinize it, as if I wanted to know more about the thing or the person it represents. . . . I want to enlarge this face in order to see it better, to understand it better, to *know* its truth. . . . I decompose, I enlarge, . . . I *retard*, in order to have time to *know* at last. . . . Alas, however hard I look, I discover nothing: if I enlarge, I see nothing but grain of the paper. . . . Such as the photograph: it cannot *say* what it lets us see. (99, 100)

So then, what can we learn about a traumatic past from photographs? Ulrich Baer recently noted that such photographs in the context of trauma constitute a kind of "spectral evidence," revealing "the striking gap between what we can see and what we can know" (Baer 2). Addressing the Second World War and the Holocaust, in particular, he argues that they mark a crisis of witnessing and "call into question the habitual reliance on vision as the principal ground for cognition" (181). Nonetheless, photography has functioned as one of the principal forms mediating the memory of this period. In recent years, a powerful memorial aesthetic has developed around archival photographs and objects from this era, inviting us to look more broadly into

8. Ilana Schmueli
and her mother.
Reproduced by
kind permission of
Ilana Schmueli.

9. City Dermer,
Berthold Geisinger,
and unidentified
person, May 1943.
Reproduced by
kind permission of
City Dermer and
Berthold Geisinger.

what knowledge they can, in fact, offer us from that past. The writings and artistic productions of, for example, Art Spiegelman, Patrick Modiano, Henri Raczymow, Anne Michaels, W. G. Sebald, Christian Boltanski, Mikael Levin, Tatana Kellner, Shimon Attie, Audrey Flack, Lorie Novak, and Muriel Hasbun, to name but a few, employ photographs — revealing them to be both limited and flawed historical documents, as well as powerful "points of memory" linking past and present, memory and postmemory, individual remembrance and cultural recall.[2] Indeed in our experience, these pervasive photographic images in the works of second- and third-generation artists, along with other material remnants of the Holocaust, do more than supplement the accounts of historians and the words of witnesses. Haunting spectres, they not only signal a visceral material connection to the past and carry its traces forward, but they also embody the very fractured process of its transmission (figs. 10 and 11).

10. Christian Boltanski, *Reliquaire*, 1989. Mixed media. In Danilo Eccher, ed., *Christian Boltanski*, Milan: 1997. Courtesy of Marian Goodman Gallery.

11. Muriel Hasbun, ¿Sólo una sombra? (Familia, Lódz), 1994. Courtesy of Muriel Hasbun.

In order to gain some insights into this postwar/post-Holocaust generational aesthetic, we turn now to *The Dark Room*, Rachel Seiffert's recent novel about German memory of the Second World War.[3] The three distinct stories around which this novel is structured are linked not by their plot, but by their exploration of the problems posed by photographic evidence and how these have evolved between the 1940s and the 1990s, connecting witnesses to their children and grandchildren (Horstkotte 275–93).

Helmut, the protagonist of the first story (which takes place in Germany during the war) is a bystander to its developments. Exempted from Wehrmacht service due to a severe physical disability, he works as a photographer's assistant and is able to witness and record on film some of the events in his native city in the early 1940s. In the section's climactic moments, Helmut watches through a camera's viewfinder and photographs a scene the narrative describes through his eyes, but that does not interpret: "There are trucks and uniformed men shouting and pushing. . . . Through the lens he sees possessions scattered: clothes, pots, boxes, sacks kicked and hurled across the muddy ground. An officer stands by screaming orders." (Seiffert 27). Helmut is agitated, frightened, but perhaps also exhilarated by what he is seeing, and he photographs furiously. "In the viewfinder his eyes meet the eyes of a shouting, pointing gypsy. Others turn to look, frightened angry faces in headscarves, hats and in uniform too" (28). However, when Helmut returns to the studio and develops his film, he is severely disappointed. The blurred, grainy photographs just refuse to show what he observed earlier in the day: the medium is simply inadequate, wrong. "The bright skirts of the gypsy women are just drab rags in his photos. . . . The dark SS uniforms blend into the soot-black walls of the buildings making them almost invisible. . . . He blows up the image, but the grain evens out the angry lines on the face of the officer who was screaming orders by the jeep, and he barely looks like he is shouting" (30). The list of the photographs' failures goes on. Ultimately, deeply disappointed, Helmut throws both the negatives and the prints into the trash can. All that remains is the enormous disjunction between the effect of the scene of witness and Helmut's encounter with his photographs: the frenzy of the moment gives way to frustration, rage, even self-hatred.

Helmut's failed photographs illustrate the belatedness of photographic looking and the temporal disjunction between the moment an image is taken and the moment it is developed and viewed—a disjunction that, paradoxically, is no less enormous within the very brief time frame of the scene in the narrative (no more than several hours) than it is for second-generation view-ers like us. Helmut's photographs are destroyed; the most important ones in his act of witnessing were never even taken. Photographs, Helmut's responses indicate, are shaped by intense emotion — in this case, by fear, nervousness, inadequacy. In this first story of *The Dark Room*, Rachel Seiffert establishes the interested nature of photographic evidence, the partial view of the photogra-pher, the contingency of the images that survive.

And yet, in the book's second story, taking place at the very end of the war amid arrests, flight, and relocation and the ensuing chaos, photographs are accorded enough evidentiary power to be burned, torn up and buried. Here a mother and daughter trying to protect the Nazi father from accusa-tion, and themselves from association with him, destroy photographs and family albums that can implicate all of them. Yet the evidentiary authority of photography is also utterly undermined, when, at the end of the section, the mysterious Tomas is found to be using an identity card and picture that clearly belongs not to him, but to a Jew who, Tomas reveals, had been killed in a camp. Why Tomas is impersonating this Jew, what he is trying to hide under this false identity, what the ID card has to do with the blue number tattooed on his arm, remains as ambiguous as the other photographs that are being used as pedagogic displays after the liberation of concentration camps in Germany. When the daughter, Lore, and her young siblings walk through various small towns on their way to Oma's house in Hamburg, they occasion-ally confront large blurry photographs tacked up in central locations. Silent crowds of onlookers surround these images.[4] Like Helmut, Lore can take in the scenes depicted in these photographs only viscerally; she is incapable of identifying their context or of interpretation:

> In front of Lore is a picture of a trash dump, or it might be a heap of ashes. She leans in closer, thinks it could be shoes. . . . She steps forward out of the group, smoothes out the damp creases with her palms. A whisper sets off behind her and makes its way around the group. The pictures are of skeletons, Lore can see that now. (76)

These pictures had been glued to a tree, but with the adhesive still wet, they have rippled upon drying. Daring to touch them, to flatten them, to step up close and then back again, Lore reveals their details to the crowd. Yet nei-ther her stroking touch nor the more distant vantage point of the onlookers help the girl understand what the pictures reveal. The images stay with her; they remain visible behind her eyelids. She is relieved when she hears adults suggest that the Americans may have staged the frightening photographs. Indistinct, unidentifiable, difficult to connect to her experience, the pictures carry a very different kind of evidence for Lore than the factual one that those posting them had most likely intended. Through their sheer emotional force, they spell out for her that crimes were committed, that those around her, even her parents, may be implicated. Yet they also remain impenetrable and inexplicable: blurry visuals of horrific scenes encountered among onlookers responding with whispers, throat-clearing, silence, or audible protests of denial and rationalization.

In these first two stories, Seiffert's point of view remains close to that of her young, uninformed, yet ultimately deeply (if indirectly) implicated German witnesses, and she records their responses in great detail. These illustrate the act of traumatic seeing, in which the image—at first felt affectively and not cognitively—acquires meaning only belatedly, in retrospect. Even later, more meaningful insights and deeper comprehension are blocked by conscious and unconscious needs—by desires and resistances, both individual and collective. Knowledge remains partial, fragmentary, with its enlightening components both partially revealed and blocked from exposure.

The Dark Room's third story then jumps ahead several decades and one generation, focusing on Micha, the grandson of a Waffen-SS officer, Askan Boell, who served in Belarus and did not return to Germany from a Soviet prison camp until 1954. The story traces the grandson's painful research into his Opa's past and his difficult realization that his grandfather was present when masses of Jewish civilians were killed in the summer and fall of 1943. Photographs are Micha's main research tools: he brings a 1938 picture of his grandfather to Belarus and shows it to witnesses who recognize Boell as one of the SS Germans who were there in 1943. However, the photographs primarily serve to bring home the disjunction between the kind grandfather Micha remembers and the Nazi killer he suspects him to have been. Micha's sister insists: "They don't show anything, the pictures. They're family shots, you know? Celebrations, always happy. You can't see anything." Yet Micha "does not want to believe her," does not give up the attempt to find "truth" in the photographs: *"He always looked away from the camera, though. Did you notice that? After the war"* (266; emphasis is from the original). Together, grandson and granddaughter, brother and sister, try to read the grandfather's postwar feelings in conventional, opaque, family snapshots. Why did Opa look away from the camera in family photographs? Did it mean he "had eyes only" for his grandchildren, standing beside him? Or did it mean he was feeling guilty about his crimes?

Micha wants and needs something from the photographs that they cannot possibly convey. However much he studies them, carries them back to Belarus and around Germany, they remain unreadable, always saying either too much or too little. At most, they can serve to identify Askan Boell to the Belorussian collaborator Kolesnik and to gain the latter's confirmation of the grandfather's presence in Belarus in 1943. Yet even here we find out more about Micha's affective response than about participation and guilt. "Micha has put the photo on the table, so that the old man won't see that his hands are shaking" (256). Kolesnik's testimony is general, vague, describing Nazi killings and the Soviet arrests of the culprits, leading Micha to ask again and again: "*Did you see my Opa do anything?*" (258; emphasis from the original). Repeatedly prodded, Kolesnik eventually admits that yes, he *knows* that Askan Boell participated *because all the Germans who were there did*, with the exception of the one who shot himself. Askan must have done it, like the others. The evidence is there, but it is not incontrovertible; the old collaborator had been present, but he was not an explicit eyewitness to Boell's participation in killings.

> There are no pictures of him holding a gun to someone's head, but I am sure he did that and pulled the trigger, too. The camera was pointing elsewhere, shutter opening and closing on the murder of another Jew, done by another man. But my Opa was no more than a few steps away. (264)

Thus, the crucial, confirming photo was *not* taken, or *did not* survive, and so the third-generation retrospective witness is left only with the ambiguous evidence carried by the photograph he inherited, and onto which he projects his own anxieties, needs, and desires—feelings disproportionate to what the pictures can, in fact, support. The truth about the past always seems to lie somewhere else, just beyond the frame. At most, the photographs can gesture toward that elsewhere, and be powerful conduits between what was then and what is now. A question thus emerges: can this type of ambiguous but affective evidence—what Ann Cvetkovich has termed "an archive of feeling"—be mined as a resource by historians seeking to grasp and transmit the past's emotional truth?

POINTS OF MEMORY

Pervasive in the personal, scholarly, and artistic work of postmemory, photographic documents bring the contradictions of the archives we have inherited into the open. Invariably, archival photographic images appear in

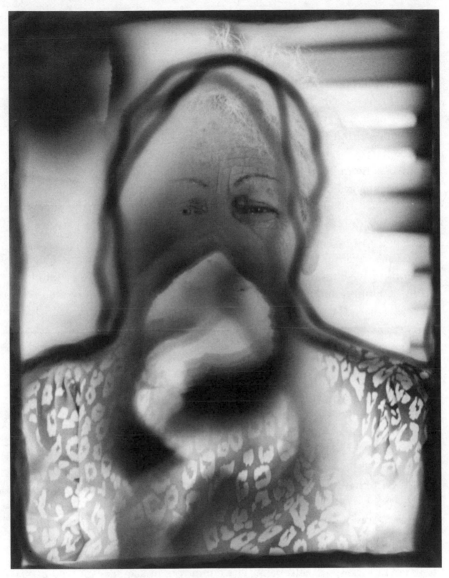

12. Muriel Hasbun, ¿Sólo una sombra? (Ester I), 1994. Courtesy of Muriel Hasbun.

postmemorial texts in altered form: they are cropped, enlarged, projected into other images; they are reframed and de- or re-contextualized; they are embedded in new narratives, new texts; they are surrounded by new frames. Muriel Hasbun's composite memorial images can sharpen our analysis of this postmemorial photographic aesthetic and the psychic structures that motivate it (fig. 12). Hasbun crops and reframes archival photographs, superimposes them on one another, reconstitutes them to alter their color, surrounds them with written text, with twigs that look like barbed wire or with old wooden frames, prints them on linens she inherited from her grandmother, and installs them amid aural recordings of music and conversations about them. The images that result are often blurry, out of focus, partial, hard to read. In spite of their obscurity—an obscurity the artist actually augments in her installations—Hasbun describes them as a "refuge against silence and forgetting" and as means to "transcend generational amnesia."[5]

Hasbun's work results from her own hybrid background as the daughter of a Polish Jewish mother who survived the war with some of her family in hiding in France, and a Palestinian Christian father who immigrated to El Salvador where Hasbun grew up. The images and objects Hasbun includes in her composite photographs and installations stem from multiple sites and archives, coming together through her own combination, synthesis, and re-creation. Even the multilingual titles of the projects that recall her mother's survival in France, with their parentheses and question marks (¿Solo una Sombra? [Only a Shadow?] and Protegida [Watched Over])—inscribe the tentative, ambiguous, and diasporic quality of Hasbun's postmemory work. In one part of the triptych Protegida: Auvergne—Hélène entitled Mes enfants—Photographe Sanitas, 1943 (fig. 13), Hasbun overlays a photo of two young children and a letter dated Paris, 3 January 1942 addressed to Mes enfants (my children). "I would love to have some photos of my two dolls," the letter says, "preferably dressed in their winter clothing and taken around the house." Did the writer, the artist's grandfather who was hiding in Paris, receive this studio picture of these two "dolls," his grandchildren hiding with his wife and daughter in le Monte Dore, or does Hasbun bring together the letter and the photograph in an act of retrospective repair? The composite image is as blurred as it is haunting, signaling loss, longing, and desire, but giving no specific insight into the circumstances of the letter or the photograph. Exhibiting the material imprint of the writer's hand, the indexical trace of the children who posed for the photograph, and of Hasbun's own postmemorial act of reframing, the image becomes a site in which present and past intersect with one

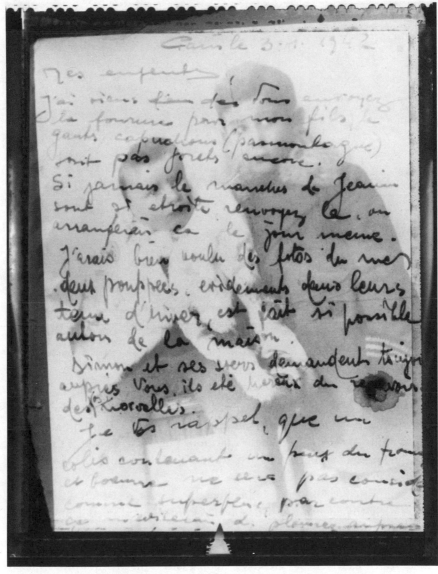

13. Muriel Hasbun, *Mes enfants — Photographe Sanitas*, 1943. Courtesy of Muriel Hasbun.

14. Muriel Hasbun, *Hélène's eye*, from the series, "Protegida: Auvergne — Hélène," 1996–2002. Courtesy of Muriel Hasbun.

another. What do we actually learn about Jewish survival in France by looking at Hasbun's images? The composite installations inscribe and highlight the inscrutability of the images and the questions they raise, as well as the artist's (and our) present needs and desires to find out more about her mother's or grandmother's past lives (fig. 14).

Hasbun's images, like those of her contemporaries, resist our desire to see more clearly, to penetrate more deeply. They are often cropped in unexpected and frustrating ways: in *Hélène's eye* we see only half of Hélène's, her great-aunt's, face, and the face is blown up, almost distorted. On the other side of the triptych, Hélène B./Hendla F. (she changed her name from Finkiel-stajn to Barthel to survive) holds the ID photograph that was attached to identity cards with the two different names (fig. 15). We see only her mouth and her hand: we cannot look into her eyes. And yet the voices playing in the background of the pictures of Ester, the sister of Hasbun's grandfather

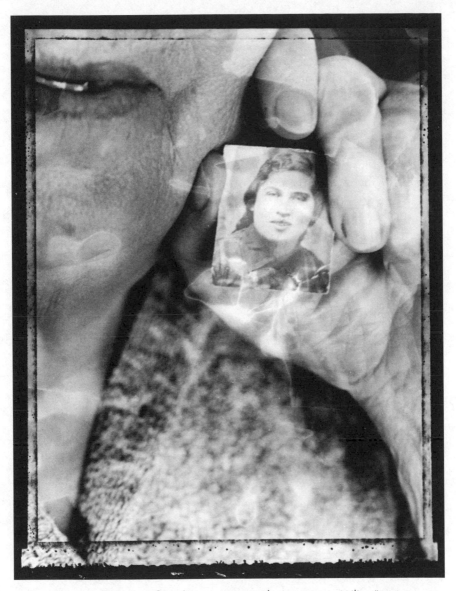

15. Muriel Hasbun, *Hélène's eye*, from the series, "Protegida: Auvergne — Hélène," 1996–2002. Courtesy of Muriel Hasbun.

whom he did not find until 1974, reveal another dimension of knowledge and transmission:

> In my darkroom, I was looking at the portrait of Ester, its image projected on the paper. Only a shadow? Impossible. The brittle leaves from an earlier autumn had already been transformed by the light. Upon finishing the portraits, I wrote to Ester: "When I make these pictures—*cuando hago estas fotografías*—it's as if I were finding what has been underneath the shadows—*es como que si encontraria lo que estaba debajo de las sombras*—or what lives inside our hearts—*o lo que vive dentro de nuestros corazones*." [Ester:] "I remember, in the camp I worked . . . Every Sunday when we don't work, we sit all the girls and look at the pictures. It was not important it was the pictures of us, but pictures from the home. . . . The first thing, when I came here, the first thing that I asked, 'Have you pictures?,' the first thing."[6]

In relation to memoir and testimony, and to historical accounts and scholarly discussions, as within new artistic texts, archival images function as supplements, both confirming and unsettling the stories that are explored and transmitted. On the one hand, they are imperfect documents, as Seiffert shows, already deeply problematic when they are taken; on the other hand, they embody an alternate discourse, create an opening in the present to something in the past that goes beyond the information they record. As Andrea Liss writes, they have the "potential to provoke historical memory and to confront the viewer's subjectivities" (86). The fantasies they call forth are deep and often inarticulable and uncontrollable, capable of provoking ethical attempts at mourning and repair, but also unwanted and illicit identifications.[7] Visual images of trauma are, as art historian Jill Bennett argues, beyond the logic of representation, possessing "the capacity to address the spectator's own bodily memory; to *touch* the viewer who *feels* rather than simply sees the event, drawn into the image through a process of affect contagion" (36; emphasis is from the original). As such, she insists, vision "has a very different relationship to affective experience—especially to experience which cannot be spoken as it is felt. The eye can often function as a mute witness by means of which events register as eidetic memory images imprinted with sensation" (35). In enlarging Hélène's eye, Hasbun calls attention to this capacity of the eye to "register" affect through vision.

We have found Roland Barthes's notion of the punctum helpful in describing this relationship of photographs and objects from the past to memory. As we have argued previously, we think of images and objects that have come down to us from the past as points of memory.[8] The term "point" is both spatial (such as a point on a map) and temporal (a moment in time), and thus it signals the intersection of spatiality and temporality that is inherent in the workings of personal and cultural memory. The sharpness of a point pierces or punctures: like the punctum, points of memory puncture through layers of oblivion, interpellating those who seek to know about the past. A point is also small, a detail, and thus it can convey the fragmentariness of the vestiges of the past—tiny images on faded cracked paper. Points of memory can produce insights that pierce and traverse temporal, spatial, and experiential divides. As points multiply, they can convey the overlay of different temporalities and interpretive frames, mitigating straightforward readings or any lure of authenticity. We think of this notion in response and as an alternative to what Pierre Nora, in a profoundly nationalist conception of cultural memory, has termed "lieux de mémoire." Points of memory, small, fragmentary, mobile, and portable, unlike Nora's stable and nationally sanctioned "lieux," are trans- or supranational, better suited to the diaspora memorial cultures that define the post-Holocaust imaginary.

As points of memory, photographs, objects, and remnants from the past interpellate the postmemorial subject powerfully. They communicate in a different register; open up an alternate memorial discourse. That is perhaps why we want and need so much from them. Following Barthes, we might say that while some images merely give information about the past, like Barthes's "studium" (25–27), others prick and wound and grab and puncture, like the "punctum"—unsettling assumptions, exposing the unexpected, suggesting what Barthes calls "a subtle beyond" or the "blind field" outside the frame. For Barthes, the punctum is first a detail in the image, one only he notices, often because of some personal connection he has with the image. This acknowledged subjectivity and positionality, this vulnerability, and this focus on the detail—the ordinary, everyday—belongs to the needs and desires of postmemory work. For Barthes, the punctum is about visibility and invisibility: once a particular detail, however off center, interpellates him, it screens out other parts of the image, however central or primary these might initially have appeared (49–51). Retrospective witnessing is torn between different details, different interpretations of the archive: in our own case, between the front and the back of the image.

In the second part of *Camera Lucida*, Barthes reconceives the punctum, bringing to it another dimension—time: the incongruity or incommensurability between the meaning of a given detail *then*, and the one it holds *now*. In staring at an image or an object from the past, we know, Barthes says, both that it "has been" and that it will die, change, be lost. The punctum carries the knowledge of inevitable loss, change, and death, and that inevitability constitutes the lens through which, as humans, we look at the past. Yet, as Michael André Bernstein warns, reading the past backward through our retrospective knowledge is a dangerous form of backshadowing, which he defines as "a kind of retroactive foreshadowing in which the shared knowledge of the outcome of a series of events by narrator and listener is used to judge the participants in those events *as though they too should have known what was to come*" (16; emphasis is from the original). The work of postmemorial reading entails juxtaposing two incommensurable temporalities, exposing and keeping open the disjunction between them.

When we blew up Carl and Lotte Hirsch's photograph to the point where all contrast was gone, but where it revealed that curious spot on Carl's lapel, we were searching for the confirmation of our own understanding of the past, one that fundamentally contradicted what the picture made visible. We very much wanted to challenge its seeming air of normality—the way it fitted like any other everyday snapshot into a page of a photograph album without proclaiming the irregularity of the place and time in which it was taken. And, like the artists who re-employ documentary images in their contemporary works, we felt we had to amend, and tweak, and modify the picture for additional reasons as well. We needed to open up the range of effects and meanings it contained, as well as those we were projecting onto it. Looking at the picture now, we realize that in it Carl and Lotte are *already* survivors, alive within a fortunate minority that had been spared a terrible fate. They are on the Herrengasse, but they are not supposed to be there; they have outstayed their welcome in this city of their birth. They are looking, shyly, smilingly, toward a future they could not, cannot foresee. This is the knowledge a retrospective witness brings to a photograph that, as Barthes says, "tells me death in the future" (96).

In wanting to restore to Carl and Lotte's photograph the hardships it seemed to be eliding, we adopted, we now see, the backshadowing glance which Eve Sedgwick has recently termed "paranoid reading"—anticipatory, eager to unveil hidden violence and to expose unseen danger (123–51). Through this reading, we wanted to find and reveal the negative lurking within and outside the frame of the image and, through our vigilance, somehow, to protect Carl and Lotte, walking down the Herrengasse, from the terrible fate that in hindsight we know could have been—and, in the summer of 1942, could still be — theirs. Yet archival photographs also challenge their viewers not to impose retrospection to the point where a photograph's own temporality and surface, however delicate and contingent, is erased. While this photograph qualifies the grand historical narrative we have of the time, it also requires (again, in Sedgwick's terms) a more generous "reparative reading" than the paranoid scrutiny we initially employed (128–129, 146–151). Such a reading would leave ambiguities unresolved, providing an expanded context for a more affective knowing. Was Lotte and Carl's photograph taken in 1942 or 1943? Were they wearing a Yellow Star, or not? If it was 1942, and they walked on the Herrengasse without it, trying to pass, why did they not fear a photographic record of their transgression? Why did they stop to buy the photo? Did their purchase accentuate an act of resistance? Alternatively, if they were both, in fact, wearing a star (Lotte, perhaps under a turned-up coat collar) were they humiliated by the photograph, yet nonetheless defiant enough to buy it as a record of an outrage Jews were forced to endure? Or, perhaps, was the inscription on the photograph's back indeed an error? Was it taken in 1943 — after the stars were discontinued in Greater Romania? The Herrengasse stroll, in that case, would attest to a moment of greater freedom, increased hope, following Carl and Lotte's fortunate evasion of mass deportations, but if so, then what is the spot on the lapel?

Muriel Hasbun's *Mes enfants* raises similar puzzling questions and incongruities. First the date: as Hasbun writes, the letter was written "in the first days of January 1943. The date on the letter is 1942, but the postmark (on the dorso) is 1943, which probably meant my grandfather made a mistake since it was the new year. They had already been hiding in Le Mont Dore since August of 1942."[9] How were her grandparents able to correspond if both were in hiding in different places? How was it possible for Jews who were passing or hiding to have their children's pictures taken in a formal photography studio such as "Photographe Sanitas"? Would they not have been afraid of detection and exposure through these two revealing media? As though to underscore the dangers that the rather benign, if blurry and haunting, image seems almost to be eliding, Hasbun includes another image on the back of the pedestal on which this picture is mounted. "*Mes enfants* has *El lobo feroz* on its dorso, which I've rephotographed from a book that came out after the war, telling the story of WWII to children, called *La Guerre chez les animaux*, and the big bad wolf is Hitler (the wolf has a swastika on the armband)" (fig. 16).[10]

By considering, rather than dismissing, these multiple and contradictory readings of Jewish existence during 1942–1943, by leaving ambiguities

16. Muriel Hasbun, El lobo feroz (*La guerre chez les Animaux, c. 1945*). Courtesy of Muriel Hasbun.

unresolved, we—like Hasbun—broaden the boundaries of our understanding and tap into a deeper register of intergenerational transmission. We gain an access to what the stories about this past do not readily reveal: the emotional fabric of daily life in extreme circumstances, its after effects in the process of survival. If our search was indeed successful in revealing the traumatic wound that seemed so strangely absent from the tiny image in the album, our scrutiny of the picture also reveals the indeterminacy of that wound and the unlocatability of its source. Yet it also reveals that as much as survival might be a struggle against the memory of trauma, structured by forgetting or denial, the mark is there, present, even if it remains submerged, disguised, invisible to the naked eye. Extracting whatever information we can from fragmentary documents, unreadable sources, and blurry, indeterminate spots in a tiny pale image, we also realize that allowing the image to fade back to its initial size, we might be able to make space for the possibility of "life" rather than "death in the future."

GÉMISSEMENTS DE DÉSESPOIR

W. G. Sebald is perhaps one of the most articulate practitioners of the photographic memorial aesthetic we have been exploring in this article. His novel *Austerlitz* not only develops a meta-photographic discourse that is certainly more layered and complex than what we find in Seiffert's novel, but he also includes a great number of archival images that both underline and complicate what he says about photography and memory. Two particular photographs relate directly to family history the protagonist is so anxiously trying to recover throughout the novel. They are given to him by Vera, the woman in Prague who knew him and his parents before the war. She found them in a volume of Balzac's *Colonel Chabert* on her shelf. Describing the photographs, Austerlitz tells the narrator what Vera said to him about them:

> I heard Vera again, speaking of the mysterious quality peculiar to such photographs when they surface from oblivion. One has the impression, she said, of something stirring in them, as if one caught small sighs of despair, *gémissements de désespoir* was her expression, said Austerlitz, as if the pictures had a memory of their own and remembered us, remembered the roles that we, the survivors, and those no longer among us had played in our former lives. (Sebald 182)

It seems to us that this may be the clearest articulation of what we fantasize and expect of archival photographs: that they have a memory of their own that they bring to us from the past; that that memory tells us something about ourselves, about what/how we and those who preceded us once were; that they carry not only information about the past, but enable us to reach an emotional register. That they require a particular kind of visual literacy, one that can decode the foreign language that they speak, for in Sebald's formulations, they do not just utter "small sighs of despair," but they do so in French, *gémissements de désespoir*. The work of postmemory consists in "learning French" (as it were) to be able to translate the *gémissements* from the past into the present and the future where they will be heard by generations not yet born.

NOTES

1. For the Holocaust in Czernowitz/Cernăuți and the deportations to Transnistria, see Carmelly; Carp; Coldewey et al.; Heymann; Ioanid; Shachan; Sella.

2. For definitions and elaborations of "postmemory," see Hirsch, *Family Frames*, "Projected Memory," "Surviving Images"; Liss.

3. We are grateful to Susan Winnett for suggesting the Seiffert novel to us. See Horstkotte for a reading of Seiffert and postmemory.

4. For a discussion of such display photos, see Brink (82–99).

5. See http://www.zonezero.com/exposiciones/fotografos/muriel2/default.html. For other examples of Muriel Hasbun's artistic work, see http://www.corcoran.org/exhibitions/Exhib_current.asp?Exhib_ID=106 and http://www.barnard.edu/sfonline/cf/hasbun.htm.

6. Transcript of soundtrack in Hasbun's installation, *Triptychon: Protegida: Auvergne—Hélène*.

7. See Radstone and Ball for discussions of such illicit structures of identification.

8. We first define the notion of "points of memory" in Hirsch and Spitzer, "Testimonial Objects." Our discussion here is adopted from that article.

9. Muriel Hasbun, e-mail communication with the authors, 19 April 2004.

10. Muriel Hasbun, e-mail communication with the authors, 19 April 2004.

REFERENCES

Baer, Ulrich. *Spectral Evidence: The Photography of Trauma*. Cambridge, MA: MIT Press, 2002.

Ball, Karyn. "Unspeakable Differences, Unseen Pleasures: The Holocaust as an Object of Desire." *Women in German Yearbook* (2003): 20–49.

Barthes, Roland. *Camera Lucida: Reflections on Photography*. New York: Hill and Wang, 1981.

Bennett, Jill. *Empathic Vision: Affect, Trauma and Contemporary Art*. Stanford, CA: Stanford University Press, 2005.

Bernstein, Michael André. *Foregone Conclusions: Against Apocalyptic History*. Berkeley, CA: University of California Press, 1994.

Brink, Cornelia. *Ikonen der Vernichtung: Öffentlicher Gebrauch von Fotografien aus nationalsozialistischen Konzentrationslagern nach 1945*. Berlin: Akademie, 1998.

Carmelly, Felicia. *Shattered! 50 Years of Silence: History and Voices of the Tragedy in Romania and Transnistria*. Scarborough, ON: Abbeyfield, 1997.

Carp, Matatias. *Holocaust in Rumania: Facts and Documents on the Annihilation of Rumania's Jews, 1940–1944*. Budapest: Primor, 1994.

Coldeway, Gaby et al. *Zwischen Pruth und Jordan: Lebenserinnerungen Czernowitzer Juden*. Köln: Böhlau Verlag, 2003.

Cvetkovich, Ann. *An Archive of Feelings: Trauma, Sexuality, and Lesbian Public Cultures*. Durham, NC: Duke University Press, 2003.

Eccher, Danilo, ed. *Christian Boltanski*. Milan: Edizoani Charta, 1997.

Heymann, Florence. *Le Crépuscule des Lieux: Identités juives de Czernowitz*. Paris: Stock, 2003.

Hirsch, Marianne. *Family Frames: Photography, Narrative, and Postmemory*. Cambridge, MA: Harvard University Press, 1997.

———. "Projected Memory: Holocaust Photographs in Personal and Public Fantasy." *Acts of Memory: Cultural Recall in the Present*, ed. Mieke Bal, Jonathan Crewe, and Leo Spitzer. Hanover, NH: University Presses of New England, 1999. 3–23.

———. "Surviving Images: Holocaust Photographs and the Work of Postmemory." *Yale Journal of Criticism* 14 (2001): 5–38.

Hirsch, Marianne and Leo Spitzer. "Erinnerungspunkte: Schoahfotografien in zeitgenössischen Erzählungen." *Fotogeschichte: Beiträge zur Geschichte und Ästhetik der Fotografie* 25 (2005): 29–44.

———. "Testimonial Objects: Memory, Gender and Transmission." *Poetics Today* 27 (2006): 355–385.

Horstkotte, Silke. "Literarische Subjektivität und die Figur des Transgenerationellen in Marcel Beyers Spione und Rachel Seiffert's *The Dark Room*." *Historisierte Subjekte — Subjektivierte Historie: Zur Verfügbarkeit und Unverfügbarkeit von Geschichte*, ed. Stefan Deines, Stephan Jaeger, and Ansgar Nünning. Berlin: Walter de Gruyter, 2003. 275–293.

Ioanid, Radu. *The Holocaust in Romania: The Destruction of Jews and Gypsies under the Antonescu Regime, 1940–1944*. Chicago, IL: Ivan Dee, 2000.

Liss, Andrea. *Trespassing through Shadows: Memory, Photography, and the Holocaust.* Minneapolis, MN: University of Minnesota Press, 1998.

Modiano, Patrick. *La Place de l'Etoile.* Paris: Éditions Gallimard, 1968.

Nora, Pierre. *Les Lieux de mémoire.* Paris: Gallimard, 1984.

Radstone, Susannah. "Social Bonds and Psychical Order: Testimonies." *Cultural Values* 5 (2001): 59–78.

Shachan, Avigdor. *Burning Ice: The Ghettos of Transnistria.* Trans. Shmuel Himelstein (East European Monographs CDXLVII). New York: Columbia University Press, 1996.

Sebald, W. G. *Austerlitz.* Trans. Anthea Bell. New York: Modern Library, 2001.

Sedgwick, Eve Kosofsky. *Touching Feeling: Affect, Pedagogy, Performativity.* Durham, NC: Duke University Press, 2003.

Seiffert, Rachel. *The Dark Room.* New York: Vintage, 2002.

Sella, Dorothea Sperber. *Der Ring des Prometheus: Denksteine im Herzen.* Jerusalem: Rubin Mass Verlag, 1996.

Contributors

✳ ✳

JOHN D'AGATA is the author of *Halls of Fame* and the editor of the anthology *The Next American Essay*. He teaches creative writing at the University of Iowa.

JUDITH ORTIZ COFER is the author of several books in various genres. Her new collection of poems is *A Love Story Beginning in Spanish*. She is the Regents' and Franklin Professor of English and Creative Writing at the University of Georgia.

MARK DOTY is the author of seven books of poems and four volumes of nonfiction prose, including *Heaven's Coast*, which won the PEN/Martha Albrand Award for First Nonfiction, *Firebird*, *Still Life with Oysters and Lemon*, and *Dog Years*. He teaches at the University of Houston and lives in Texas and in New York City.

SU FRIEDRICH has directed sixteen films and videos since 1978 which have been featured in eighteen retrospectives—including one at the Museum of Modern Art in 2007—and have been widely screened at film festivals, universities, and art centers and have won numerous awards, including Grand Prix at the Melbourne Film Festival. She teaches video production at Princeton University.

JOANNA FRUEH is an art critic, art historian, writer, actress, singer, and multidisciplinary and performance artist. Her most recent books, *Swooning Beauty: A Memoir of Pleasure* and *Clairvoyance (For Those in the Desert): Performance Pieces 1979–2004*, explore love, eros, and human relations. Frueh is Distinguished Professor in the School of Art at the University of Arizona.

RAY GONZÁLEZ's nine books of poetry include *Heat of Arrivals* (1997 PEN/Oakland Josephine Miles Book Award), *Cabato Sentora*, and *Consideration of the Guitar: New and Selected Poems*. He is also the author of a collection of essays, *The Underground Heart: A Return to a Hidden Landscape* and the editor of twelve anthologies. González is poetry editor of the *Bloomsbury Review* and founding editor of *LUNA*.

VIVIAN GORNICK is an essayist and memoirist who has taught nonfiction writing in many MFA programs. Among her books are *Fierce Attachments* (a memoir), *Approaching Eye Level* (personal essays), and *The End of the Novel of Love* (critical essays). She lives and works in New York City.

BARBARA HAMMER is considered a pioneer of queer cinema. In April 2006 she was awarded a tribute at the XI International Gay and Lesbian Film

Festival in Turin and at Cinematheque Bologna. *Optic Nerve* (1985) and *Endangered* (1988) were selected for the Whitney Museum of American Art Biennials and *Nitrate Kisses* (1992) was chosen for the 1993 Whitney Biennial. A recipient of the first Shirley Clarke Avant-Garde Filmmaker Award in October, 2006, Hammer teaches each summer at the European Graduate School in Saas-Fee, Switzerland.

KATHRYN HARRISON is the author of the novels *Thicker Than Water, Exposure, Poison, The Binding Chair, The Seal Wife,* and *Envy;* the memoirs *The Kiss, Seeking Rapture, The Road to Santiago,* and *The Mother Knot;* and a biography *Saint Therese of Lisiuex.* She is a frequent reviewer for the *New York Times Book Review,* and her work has appeared in the *New Yorker, Harper's, Vogue, O Magazine, Salon,* and other publications.

MARIANNE HIRSCH is professor of English and comparative literature and director of the Institute for Research on Women and Gender at Columbia University. Among recent publications are *Family Frames: Photography, Narrative, and Postmemory* (1997); *The Familial Gaze* (1999); the "Gender and Cultural Memory" special issue of *Signs* (2002); and *Teaching the Representation of the Holocaust* (2004). She is writing a book with Leo Spitzer, *Ghosts of Home: The Afterlife of Czernowitz in Jewish Memory and History.*

WAYNE KOESTENBAUM has published twelve books of poetry, nonfiction, and fiction, including *Hotel Theory, Best-Selling Jewish Porn Films, Moira Orfei in Aigues-Mortes, Model Homes, Andy Warhol, Cleavage, Jackie under My Skin, Rhapsodies of a Repeat Offender,* and *The Queen's Throat.* He is a distinguished professor of English at the CUNY Graduate Center.

LEONARD KRIEGEL'S essays have been widely anthologized. The author of nine books, he lives and writes in New York City. Kriegel has been a Guggenheim Fellow and his essays and stories have appeared in such magazines as *The American Scholar, Harper's, Partisan Review, Sewanee Review,* and the *Nation.*

DAVID LAZAR is the author of *The Body of Brooklyn* and *Powder Town* (forthcoming) and has edited *Conversations with M. F. K. Fisher* and *Michael Powell: Interviews.* He created the Ph.D. program in nonfiction writing at Ohio University and currently teaches at Columbia College Chicago. He is the founding editor of *Hotel Amerika.*

ALPHONSO LINGIS, a professor of philosophy at Pennsylvania State University, has published: *Excesses: Eros and Culture* (1984), *Libido: The French Existential Theories* (1985), *Phenomenological Explanations* (1986), *Deathbound Subjectivity* (1989), *The Community of Those Who Have Nothing in Common* (1994),

Abuses (1994), *Foreign Bodies* (1994), *Sensation: Intelligibility in Sensibility* (1995), *The Imperative* (1998), *Dangerous Emotions* (1999), *Trust* (2003), *Body Modifications* (2005), and *The First Person Singular* (2006).

PAUL LISICKY is the author of *Lawnboy* and *Famous Builder*. He has taught at Cornell University, NYU, Sarah Lawrence, Antioch Los Angeles, and the University of Houston, and serves on the Writing Committee of the Fine Arts Work Center in Provincetown. He recently completed *Lumina Harbor*, a novel. He lives in New York City and Fire Island Pines, New York.

NANCY MAIRS, a poet and essayist, has written ten books, among them *In All the Rooms of the Yellow House*, *Plaintext*, *Ordinary Time*, *Waist-High in the World*, and *A Dynamic God* (forthcoming). Her honors include the 1984 Western States Book Award in poetry and fellowships from the National Endowment for the Arts and the Project on Death in America of the Soros Foundation's Open Society Institute.

NANCY K. MILLER is distinguished professor of English and comparative literature at the Graduate Center, CUNY. Her most recent books are *But Enough about Me: Why We Read Other People's Lives* and the coedited collection, *Extremities: Trauma, Testimony, and Community*. She is currently coediting the journal *WSQ*.

PHYLLIS ROSE is the author of *Parallel Lives*, *Jazz Cleopatra*, and other biographical works. Her memoir, *The Year of Reading Proust*, appeared in 1997. She taught for many years at Wesleyan University in Connecticut.

OLIVER SACKS is professor of clinical neurology and psychiatry at Columbia University. He is best known for his neurological case studies, including *The Man Who Mistook His Wife for a Hat*, *Awakenings*, *An Anthropologist on Mars*, and *Musicophilia: Tales of Music and the Brain*. Dr. Sacks is a frequent contributor to the *New Yorker* and the *New York Review of Books*, as well as many medical journals.

DAVID SHIELDS is the author of eight books, including *Black Planet: Facing Race during an NBA Season*, *Remote: Reflections on Life in the Shadow of Celebrity* (winner of the PEN/Revson Award), and *Dead Languages: A Novel* (winner of a PEN/Syndicated Fiction award). Shields has published essays and stories in *New York Times Magazine*, *Harper's*, *Yale Review*, *Village Voice*, *Salon*, *Slate*, and *McSweene's*. Shields is a senior editor of *Conjunctions*. He is the recipient of a Guggenheim and two NEA fellowships.

LEO SPITZER is Vernon Professor of History at Dartmouth College and a visiting professor of history at Columbia University. His most recent book is *Hotel Bolivia: The Culture of Memory in a Refuge from Nazism*. He is also the author of *Lives in Between, The Creoles of Sierra Leone: Responses to Colonialism*, and is coeditor of *Acts of Memory: Cultural Recall in the Present*. He has received John Simon Guggenheim, Ford, SSRC, ACLS, Whiting, NEH, and the Rockefeller Bellagio and Bogliasco Foundation fellowships. With Marianne Hirsch, he is completing *Ghosts of Home: The Afterlife of Czernowitz in Jewish Memory and History*.

Permissions